Praise for *Pla*

"A true story of one man's reaching out to the enemy during a very dark time in our history. Gene Moore and his fellow sailors teach all of us that compassion and tolerance does exist, especially when the bridge builder happens to be that great American pastime: baseball. History and baseball buffs alike will revel in this episode of man's ability to reach out, even during a time of war."

— Gerald R. Molen, Academy Award–winning
producer of *Schindler's List*

"*Playing with the Enemy* is a story of the American Dream—the power, the pain, the sacrifice, the triumph, and most of all, the heart. It's about making peace with your enemies and, in Gene Moore's case, the story of a man learning to make peace with himself. A great read."

— James Riordan, author of *The New York Times* bestseller
Break on Through: The Life & Death of Jim Morrison

"Gary Moore's touching book about his father's baseball career reminds us that life is all about second chances and people inspiring each other to chase their dreams. . . . I loved *Playing with the Enemy*. You will, too."

— Baseball legend Jim Morris,
former pitcher for the Tampa Bay Devil Rays

"Being mayor of the small town of Sesser for thirty years I enjoyed this well written story about life in a simpler time. Gene Moore's desire to make it to the big leagues of baseball landed him a starring role in the big league of life. This is a heartwarming true story you don't want to miss."

— Ned Mitchell, mayor, Sesser, Illinois

"*Playing with the Enemy* SOARS! Any man who ever played catch with his dad will be reminded of the powerful bond between fathers and sons—and how sports can bring them together. A moving story of love and loss, *Playing with the Enemy* is a classic all-American sports tale that encourages us to remember where we came from—and more importantly, where we can go."　　　　— David Ranes, producer / screenwriter

"A superlative book . . . Gary Moore's epic story about his father reminds one of the importance of dreams and self-sacrifice."
　　　　　　　　　　　　　　　— Steve Canter, baseball agent

"Gene Moore was a great baseball player and a dear friend. I fondly remember watching him play behind the plate at the Sesser 'Lumberyard' while I sat in the stands picking my guitar. His son Gary has captured the people and places perfectly. I love *Playing with the Enemy*, and I know you will, too."　　　　— Billy Grammer, international recording artist, star of the Grand Ole Opry, and inventor of "The Grammer Guitar"

"Good writing is storytelling, and *Playing with the Enemy* tells a story well. Sports fans will love it for its portrait of the minor leagues and the long-forgotten days when town baseball was everything. With its tremendous plot full of twists and turns, this story touches on lost dreams and found family."　　　　　　　— Phil Angelo, senior editor, *The Daily Journal* (Kankakee, Illinois)

"A baseball passion play in everybody's wheelhouse. A small town American dream turned into a persecution only to be rescued by a woman working through heartache herself."
　　　　　　　　— Bob McNamara, veteran CBS News correspondent

PENGUIN BOOKS

PLAYING WITH THE ENEMY

Gary W. Moore is the president and CEO of Covenant Air & Water, LLC (www.aquativa.com), a motivational speaker, and an accomplished musician. He has been featured in publications such as *Entrepreneur* magazine, *Success Magazine*, *Sales & Marketing Management* magazine, and Southwest Airlines' *Spirit* magazine. Gary is a recipient of the prestigious Sam Walton Leadership Award and is a graduate of VanderCook College of Music (BMEd 1976). Gary and his wife, Arlene, have been married for more than thirty years and have three children.

Visit www.playingwiththeenemy.com

Playing with the Enemy

A Baseball Prodigy, World War II,
and the Long Journey Home

Gary W. Moore

Penguin Books

PENGUIN BOOKS

Published by the Penguin Group

Penguin Group (USA) Inc., 375 Hudson Street, New York, New York 10014, U.S.A.

Penguin Group (Canada), 90 Eglinton Avenue East, Suite 700, Toronto,
Ontario, Canada M4P 2Y3 (a division of Pearson Penguin Canada Inc.)

Penguin Books Ltd, 80 Strand, London WC2R 0RL, England

Penguin Ireland, 25 St Stephen's Green, Dublin 2, Ireland
(a division of Penguin Books Ltd)

Penguin Group (Australia), 250 Camberwell Road, Camberwell,
Victoria 3124, Australia (a division of Pearson Australia Group Pty Ltd)

Penguin Books India Pvt Ltd, 11 Community Centre,
Panchsheel Park, New Delhi – 110 017, India

Penguin Group (NZ), 67 Apollo Drive, Rosedale, North Shore 0632,
New Zealand (a division of Pearson New Zealand Ltd)

Penguin Books (South Africa) (Pty) Ltd, 24 Sturdee Avenue,
Rosebank, Johannesburg 2196, South Africa

Penguin Books Ltd, Registered Offices:
80 Strand, London WC2R 0RL, England

First published in the United States of America by Savas Beatie LLC, 2006
Published in Penguin Books 2008

10 9 8 7 6 5 4

Copyright © Gary W. Moore, 2006
Illustrations copyright © Val Laolagi, 2006
All rights reserved

ISBN 1-932714-24-3 (hc.)
ISBN 978-0-14-311388-1 (pbk.)
CIP data available

Printed in the United States of America

This book is dedicated to Gene, Ward, David and Brian Moore, Kenneth Jenkins, Harold Bright, Bill Wigant, Bob Jackson, Luther Watson, Chuck Ellens, George Langlois, Roger and Jim Roussell, Curtis Carter, Skip Swoverland, Doug Lindt, Paul Litteau, Bill Stark, Captain James Haigh, Lieutenant Colonel Stu Leach, Technical Sergeant Kyle Day, Technical Sergeant Gerald L. McIntosh, Harold Shirk, Mark Ray, Tom Billadeau, Scott Swaim, Tony Hulls, Dan Hays, Thomas M. Rounds, Janice Mickelson, Ashley Rounds, William T. Franey, Dominic Tringali, Tony Manfredi, Larry Jansick, Emil Colosimo, Edward McNamara, Clarence Chizek, Anson White, Kent White, Kevin White, Kelly DiBella, John Brasel, Michael A. Savas, James E. O'Brien, Andy Lancaster, and all the men and women who willingly served our country in the armed forces of the United States of America. Like Gene and Ward, they put their lives on hold to do their duty. Some come back and pick up their lives where they left off; some lives are forever changed by the experience; and others do not come back at all.

Thank you to all who have, are and will serve. Your willingness to defend our country is inspirational.

A Life Worth Living

Contents

Photos and illustrations have been arranged throughout
the text for the convenience of the reader.

Preface

History has little to say about Warren Eugene Moore. My father was born in Sesser, Illinois, on March 19, 1926, to John and Allie Moore. John and Allie had seven kids, five girls and two boys. Gene, as his friends and family called him, was the youngest of John and Allie's two boys and their fifth child in the birth order. He was a veteran of World War II. He earned a Purple Heart, and he returned home a much different man than the enthusiastic boy he was when he left.

A quick glance at the "facts" of his life makes Gene sound like a typical veteran. He was anything but typical.

After the outbreak of World War II interrupted his young life, duty carried him from small town Southern Illinois to the Azores, North Africa, and Louisiana. Gene later entered the Veterans' Administration Hospital in Brooklyn, New York, before returning home again. Unlike most veterans who came home and picked up their lives, Gene Moore's life—his destiny—was forever altered. Because of an unfortunate series of events, our national pastime may also have been changed. What could have been was not to be.

I have tried my very best to write the most accurate story I could about Gene Moore's life in baseball and war. But I was not there, and there are no audio or video tapes to review. Most of the research necessary to write this book came from conversations with my mom Judy Moore (Gene's wife) that spanned many years; interviews with people from my dad's hometown of Sesser, Illinois, and with others from around the country who knew my dad or knew of him; a letter dated 1949 from the Pittsburgh Pirates acknowledging that Gene had agreed to play baseball, that reporting instructions were on their way to him, and that Greenville, Mississippi, would be his destination; and finally, from Gene himself. My dad did not like to talk about his past, so his life story came out in small bites of information spread across three decades, and one hours-long conversation near the end of his life. All the typical secondary research was also performed in newspapers, books about baseball, etc.

Some names have been changed for all the usual reasons, and a few characters are composites of several people in an effort to represent the spirit of some of the men with whom my dad experienced his life. Admittedly, the scarcity of information makes it difficult to verify every account in this book, but I am confident the spirit of Gene's life has been captured within these pages.

This is Gene Moore's story.

Acknowledgements

Life is stranger than fiction. One afternoon, my wife, Arlene and I, stood in line at Los Angeles International Airport to catch our Southwest Airlines flight for Chicago and the drive home. A Southwest gate is my home away from home. In fact, the majority of this book was written during the scores of Southwest flights I have taken in the last two years as I traveled for business, or while sitting at a Southwest gate waiting for a plane to take me somewhere. The rest was written sitting alone in various hotels across the country.

As we stood in LAX waiting to board the plane, my cell phone rang. It was my oldest son Toby and his attorney on the other end. "Dad, this is Allison," Toby told me. "She's my attorney and she'll be handling the contract for the screenwriter. Do you have a few minutes before you board?"

We carried on the conversation as if it were a normal occurrence, exchanged pleasantries, and hung up. Arlene and I boarded the plane and headed for home. As the plane, painted to resemble a Killer Whale, climbed out over the Pacific Ocean before turning east, I had an earth-shattering thought. "I have written a book about my father. I am fifty years old and have never written a book before this one. My son, Toby, who is an up-and-coming Hollywood actor, might play the part of my father—his grandfather—in a movie based upon the book I have written." The fact that this was not a dream seemed almost incomprehensible to me.

The time I spent writing this book was an emotional roller coaster. My mother Judy (Gene's wife) was dying. I wanted to finish it before she left us, but God had other plans. Judy Moore passed away January 3, 2004, about nine months before I finished the first draft.

I am a pure extrovert, so I hate being alone. Writing, however, is a long and often lonely process. As I clattered at my laptop remembering and writing about my mom and dad, I shed many tears and had many moments of sheer joy. I think the experience helped me come to terms with my father's early and sudden death, and helped me better cope with the opposite—the long agonizing deterioration of my mother. I knew they were special people and wonderful parents, but this experience helped me get to know them on a different level. The Fifth Commandment is, "Honor your Father and Mother." I pray that I have done that.

There are many people to thank, and I may have inadvertently forgotten someone. If you do not find your name here, rest assured I appreciate all you have done for me and this book, and please excuse my oversight. Any errors are mine alone.

Judge Mike Kick, my friend since childhood, first suggested I write this book. During a discussion about our fathers, Mike said, "You know, that would make a great book, or even a great movie. You should write it." I took his suggestion to heart. Thanks, Mike. I'm sure you never really thought I would write this, but don't feel bad, because neither did I.

Tris Coburn, my literary agent, stepped in at a critical time and helped make it possible for this book to be published. I am looking forward to a long and successful relationship that goes far beyond this book. I am grateful.

Theodore "Ted" Savas, Sarah Stephan, Jim Zach, and everyone else associated with Savas Beatie LLC, helped make this book better. Ted read the manuscript, offered many developmental editing suggestions, and took a chance on an unknown author. Like Tris, Ted and his team have become great friends and wonderful teammates. I am grateful for his willingness to publish this book. Ted, I pray that your faith in me will be rewarded in countless ways.

Without my knowing it, and as a surprise to me, my publisher arranged with his friend, neighbor, and fellow baseball coach Val Laolagi to produce the inspiring original illustrations that accompany this book. Val is a gifted artist, whose work only served to make this a better product all the way around. This book is about destiny and a man's calling. I think I know what yours is, Val. Thank you for helping memorialize my father's life story.

The enthusiasm and creativity of my publicist, Carole Bartholomeaux and Bartholomeaux/PR, is unequalled. She always kept her head whenever I was losing mine. I am grateful to you, Carole, for all your help.

Baseball legend Jim Morris, former pitcher for the Tampa Bay Devil Rays, read a draft of the manuscript and graciously agreed to write the Foreword for *Playing with the Enemy*. His own story is inspirational and truly one of the greatest baseball sagas of all time. Jim, I am honored to have your name associated with my father's story. A special thanks is also due to Jim's friend, associate, and agent Steve Canter, for helping put all this together. Steve is the best sports agent in the business. Thank you both for your help

John C. Skipper, an example of the writer I hope to become, is the author of numerous books and provided an invaluable eye for baseball detail. John served as the book's historical editor and his input helped to make this a much better book. He also penned the Introduction, for which I am thankful.

The Pittsburgh Pirates gave my dad a second chance. It was an experience he always cherished and made this story possible. Dad always said, "The Pittsburgh Pirates, they're a class organization." Dad was right then and it's still true today. Go Pirates!

The Museum of Science and Industry in Chicago is the able custodian of *U-505*. Recently, the large German submarine has been moved underground into a hi-tech facility that is breathtaking to behold. At first glance, *U-505* appears to be floating in air. It has been completely restored and is in pristine condition. The able staff of the museum has done an incredible job of restoration and preservation. Generations to come will visit this display and imagine what it was like to be aboard a German *Unterseeboot*. I urge everyone to visit and experience *U-505*. It is well worth your time. You can learn more about this remarkable boat by visiting www.msichicago.org.

My dear friends Tim Duggan, Nicole Bonham, John Lopez, and David Thompson also deserve my thanks. It is said that a friend is someone who walks into your room when everyone else is walking out. David walked in, while Tim, John, and Nicole were the only ones who didn't walk out. Thank you for your friendship and loyalty. I am forever grateful.

Thanks are also due my youngest son and the best writer in our family, Travis. I don't think you realized it, Travis, but I felt I was always trying to write up to your expectations and in the process, it forced me to be better than I probably am. Thank you for being a wonderful son and a great inspiration. I love you, Travis.

Thank you to my beautiful daughter, Tara Beth. Like her mother, Tara Beth is a woman of great faith and tremendous leadership ability. Thank you for your continuous encouragement and for being the most wonderful daughter a father could ever have. I love you, Tara Beth.

Thank you to my oldest son, Toby. There are no words that can describe the enjoyment I have received talking back and forth with you about this story. Your creative ideas, loving criticisms, and continuous encouragement have been my catalyst to get this done. I love you, Toby.

I would also like to thank the love of my life, Arlene, who encouraged me every step of the way. Arlene, you are everything I admire that I am not. You are a woman of deep faith and incredible emotional strength. At many times in my life, I have strangely felt like a kite—soaring in the wind far above where it is safe to be. Yet, I always know you were holding the string and will never let me go or fall. I love you, Arlene, now and forever.

Thank you also Mom and Dad. This book is about you, this book is for you. This is your son's interpretation of who you were, so others may know. It is a celebration of the life and the times in which you lived. I wish you were both here to read it, but why would you need to—you lived it. I agree with Tom Brokaw, that yours was indeed the "Greatest Generation." Thank you for loving me.

Most importantly, I give thanks to my Lord and Savior, Jesus Christ, who continues to change and mold me into the man He wishes me to be, even though I sometimes fight it, every step of the way. God has blessed me with a wonderful church, dear friends, and a loving family. I am grateful beyond my ability to express it on this page.

I pray that you, the reader, will enjoy this book, and I thank you in advance for your interest in my father's story.

Dad . . . this is for you.

Foreword
by Jim Morris

Playing with the Enemy is a book about many things on many levels, but to me, it is a heartwarming story about what we do with second chances.

Gary Moore's touching book about his father serves as a reminder that life is all about second chances and people inspiring each other to chase their dreams. Long after I quit baseball, it took the belief of others (my high school baseball kids) for me to chase my dream of playing baseball again, just like it took the belief of Gene Moore's scout to get him a second chance with the Pittsburgh Pirates.

Life is full of second chances. Gene Moore never got to the big leagues, but instead of feeling sorry for himself and packing it in for good, he went out and played the game to the best of his ability until he ultimately sacrificed his own dream to help his friend and pitcher, Ray Laws, reach the majors. Gene realized that taking advantage of a second chance isn't always about your own glory: sometimes it's about making other people successful. Sometimes that is your opportunity. Any good parent will tell you that.

Gene Moore lost his dream of becoming a big league ballplayer because of the Second World War and his desire to play with the enemy. But his love for the game never died. You don't have to be a Yale graduate to know that everyone has to have hope in their life or they will eventually become your enemy. Sometimes you have to put yourself in the place of the enemy to make second chances happen. That's why

Heinrich Mueller, one of the German U-boat prisoners of war he taught the game of baseball, came back and inspired Gene to move on with life once there were no more balls for him to catch behind the plate.

Your dream doesn't have to be baseball—that isn't really important. Your second chance can be a new job after you've been fired, a chance to repair a relationship with a parent or a spouse, a second chance at marriage, or a fresh opportunity to start a new family and another business—like Gene Moore did when he finished playing baseball.

Sometimes we go through life feeling sorry for ourselves and feeling like victims. I did that, and so did Gene Moore. We've all been down on the floor, drowning in our sorrows. Second chances in life, however, are often about self-sacrifice: you always have to remember that it's not all about you.

Judy Moore knew that when she picked a drunken stranger off the floor of a dusty bar to help him stand again on his own two feet. By risking her own safety, Judy ended up with a rich and fulfilling life. Gene eventually became her husband, they had a family, and then, decades later, when confronted with "the letter," Gene sat down and bared his soul to his son about his brush with destiny and fateful odyssey through World War II and minor league baseball. That saga, in turn, became the basis for this book.

I loved *Playing with the Enemy*. You will, too.

Introduction

"For all sad words of tongue or pen,
the saddest are these: It might have been."

— John Greenleaf Whittier

A word of warning as you venture into *Playing with the Enemy*, Gary Moore's riveting story of his father's life. Don't skip any pages or peek ahead to try to figure out what's coming. Read it like you would watch a ballgame. Inning by inning. Page by page. Because you won't believe what happens in about the seventh inning of Gene Moore's life—but you must have watched the first six innings to fully appreciate it.

Gene was a farm boy living with his parents, sisters, and a brother in Sesser, Illinois, a town so small that even map makers ignored it. As a teenager, when he wasn't in school he was helping his pop on the farm, slopping the hogs and doing other chores with his older brother, Ward. Usually, though, Gene could be found down at "The Lumberyard" playing baseball with the guys on the town team, some of whom were twice his age. The older fellows didn't mind having the Moore kid on their team because he could hit a baseball farther than any of the rest of them. And, as the team's catcher, even at the age of 15, he called a pretty good ball game—and nothing got by him behind the plate.

One thing that was as true in the 1940s as it is today is that if you have talent, someone will notice—even if your team is made up of guys you know from the local bar—and they also serve as the grounds crew at the ball diamond across town. The Brooklyn Dodgers noticed Gene Moore. Word had spread halfway across the United States about the country boy who could hit the ball a country mile. The Dodgers wanted to take a look at this 15-year-old farm kid, barely old enough to shave and still awaiting his first kiss, but brash enough to call the pitches from behind the plate and motion to the infielders and outfielders as to how they should position themselves for certain hitters.

These were the Dodgers of Branch Rickey, the feisty general manager who squeezed a dollar so tightly that onlookers swore they could hear George Washington choking; of manager Leo Durocher, who many thought could fight better than he could hit and who would be forever remembered in baseball lore as the man who said, "Nice guys finish last"; and of Mickey Owen, the veteran catcher, the man who, if the fates would have it, would be succeeded behind the plate by Gene Moore one day. That same Mickey Owen would come to symbolize how the gods of baseball can sometimes turn on you. It was Owen whose dropped third strike in the ninth inning of the seventh game of the 1941 World Series turned the game around and allowed the New York Yankees to walk away with the victory.

A veteran Dodger scout ventured out to Sesser, Illinois, to take a look at Gene, and he liked what he saw. But back on the farm old "Pop" Moore was skeptical about having a son play professional baseball. It was a game, not an occupation—and what if he didn't make it? What then? These were the kinds of thoughts and questions that most any father would have in looking out for his son's best interests. But "Pop" Moore took some time away from the crops and the pigs and came to the ballpark one day and saw his son play for the first time. He saw the talent, he heard the roar of the crowd, and he sensed the potential his son had for a great future in baseball. With his parents' consent, Gene signed with the Dodgers.

On December 7, 1941, Japanese planes bombed Pearl Harbor and America was thrust into World War II. Gene Moore went into the Navy and served his country in a unique but important way as part of a traveling baseball team that went overseas and provided much-needed entertainment and times of relaxation for the fighting troops. The games kept Gene in shape for the Major League baseball career that awaited him back in the States. Later in the war he came back to America and was assigned to Camp Ruston, Louisiana, where his duty was to oversee the day-to-day activities of a select few—and very special—German prisoners of war. These U-boat (submarine) sailors were so special, in fact, that the Red Cross was not notified of their capture, and their families were left believing they were dead.

Gene's experience with these Germans was another turning point in his life, one that would turn his baseball world upside down—and it would never quite right itself again. The road to Ebbets Field in Brooklyn was a difficult one to traverse, and Gene's effort to walk it demonstrated the character of a brave and caring man far beyond any heroics he performed with a bat or catcher's mitt in his hand.

In reading the story of Gene Moore, some will think of Roy Hobbs, the slugger in "The Natural" or of Ray Kinsella, who was reunited with his father on a baseball field in "Field of Dreams"; or even Jim Morris, the Texas school teacher whose story is depicted in "The Rookie," a man who beat enormous odds to make it to the major leagues. All of these men, fictional and real, bear a resemblance to Gene Moore, the farm boy from Southern Illinois.

But when I think of Gene Moore, I think of Johnny Bench, the great catcher for the Cincinnati Reds who could do it all: hit, hit with power, control a game from behind the plate, and was the best ever at throwing out base runners, either by standing and firing the ball to second base or by making snap throws to first or third from his crouch behind the plate. Johnny Bench got his chance in the big leagues and made the most of it. He is in the Hall of Fame. Gene Moore had his chance, too, but you will never see his name there. Yet, his story is just as compelling. Read on. You'll see.

And so we end where we began . . . "It might have been."

John Skipper
Mason City, Iowa

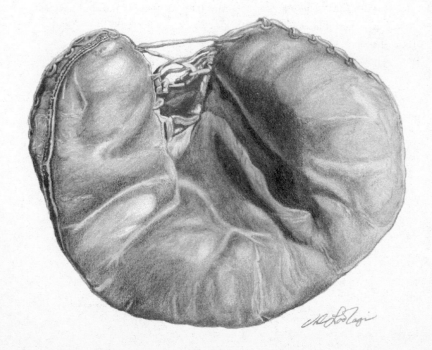

Splooie . . .

PITTSBURGH · BASE · BALL · CLUB
MINOR LEAGUE SYSTEM

Mr. Gene Moore: 1-10-49.

Dear Gene:

Your letter received and very glad to hear from you also to know you want to play ball. I will arrange to have you come to one of our training camps probably Greenville, Miss. the first part of March, and I will meet you there and assure you we will give you every chance and our ablest assistance in making a capable ball player. Am writing to and thanking him for his consideration.

Sincerely,

Ted McGrew.

The 1949 letter from Ted McGrew of the Pittsburgh Pirates.

Chapter 1

The Letter

How would I do it?

How could I ever make the leap from the chair I was in onto the speaker's platform? The thought coursed through my mind as I sat in the sales meeting, listening to the president and owner of the company. He was dynamic, charismatic, and everyone loved him.

Me? I was young then—a bit reserved, very insecure, and in total awe of the man I intently watched and listened to as he addressed us from the platform at the front of the room. He had the leadership qualities I could only dream I might one day possess. I hung on his every word, every syllable, even though I had heard it in one form or another from this man my entire life.

Gene Moore spoke with an animated, passionate style. He talked about the highest levels of achievement and made the group of thirty sales people assembled at the Chicago Heights branch of Moore Industries, Inc., want to sell and excel with passion. He brought out the best in each of us. We *wanted* to perform for him. We wanted to *be* like him. We all yearned for a pat on the back or a wink from his smiling face telling us, "good job" or "way to go." He made us believe that what we did was important, admirable, and honorable, even though what we did was sell vacuum cleaners door-to-door. Gene Moore made us believe what we did would change the world. It certainly changed our worlds. Many of those in his audience went on to achieve levels of success with Filter Queen or in other chosen professions. Most would attribute some or all of their success to the time they spent working with this man. "There is just something special about him" was a phrase heard over and over again.

As Gene was beginning to wind down his motivational talk he raised his arms in excitement—and then suddenly stopped. His eyes sought me out. "Gary take it from here," he said calmly, a small smile on his face. And then he walked out of the room. Although unusual, Gene was prone to theatrics, so I jumped up from my chair and tried to pick up where he left off, which was an insurmountable task.

Once the meeting ended a young salesman named Ed walked up to me and said something I would never forget. "What happened to Gene?" he asked.

"Nothing," I replied.

"Didn't look like nothing to me," continued Ed, his voice softer now, almost a whisper. A dark look of concern had crossed his face.

"What?" I asked. "What are you talking about?"

"When he walked out of the meeting, he stepped into the next room, doubled over, and was holding his left arm." The words sent a chill through me I still feel to this day.

I ran to the door, threw it open, and looked outside, but his gray Cadillac was gone. A glance at my watch told me the meeting had continued almost forty-five minutes after Gene had left. I stepped toward the phone to call our headquarters in Bradley, Illinois, which I assumed was Gene's destination. Before I could dial the phone number, a secretary tapped my shoulder, "Gary, your mom's on the line. She sounds real upset."

I stepped into the closest room and picked up the phone. Judy Moore was crying on the other end. "Why did you let your father drive home when he was having a heart attack?"

"A heart attack! Mom, is he okay? Where is he?"

I listened just long enough to hear her answer before dropping the phone and running to my car to speed to Riverside Hospital in Kankakee. It was normally a thirty-minute drive, but I made it in record time.

When I arrived in the emergency room the first thing I heard was laughter. Puzzled, I edged my way past bustling nurses and small knots of strangers before coming to a stop next to a curtained-off area. I slowly pulled the curtain back to find Gene sitting up on the edge of the bed. Around him were several nurses and an emergency room doctor laughing at something he had just said. As usual, Gene controlled the room and everyone in it.

My sister Debbie was there too, her eyes swollen from crying. My mother was standing next to her husband's side, rubbing his shoulder and holding back the tears. A few moments later my youngest sister Kim and her new husband Keith rushed into the emergency room.

"Calm down," Gene commanded with a sturdy laugh. "It's a false alarm. You're not getting rid of me this easy," a comment that brought more laughter from the hospital staff, but only concerned looks from his family members.

Until that moment it had never occurred to me that my mentor, my employer, and my father, all one and the same, would ever die. He was only 57, and he had always seemed indestructible.

While Gene was sharing a story with the nurses, Doctor Burnett, our family physician, arrived with what he claimed was good news. "I don't think Gene had a heart attack. He only suffered from a little overexertion. We're going to keep him overnight for observation and send him home tomorrow." The doctor also told us he would set up a round of tests with a heart specialist in Chicago. "You folks go home now and don't worry any longer about this. Gene is going to be fine."

The next day Gene took a stress test, passed, and was released. As was his nature, he walked out of the hospital and went straight to work. It was April 29, 1983.

The test with the heart specialist was eventually scheduled for Thursday, May 12, at St Luke's Presbyterian Hospital in Chicago. Our appointment was at 4:00 p.m., and my mother insisted I go along. She was afraid Gene might not tell her if the news wasn't good. I agreed, and my dad and I drove to the hospital together. The specialist agreed with Dr. Burnett: he was certain Gene did not have a heart attack. In fact, he told us Gene was in great shape and we had nothing to worry about.

As we pulled out of the parking garage, a giant weight lifted from our shoulders. I suggested we go to the George Diamond Steak House and celebrate. As we made the drive from the hospital, I thought about the feelings and anxiety I had experienced over the past few weeks worrying about my father's health. Since it would just be the two of us at dinner, I started assembling in my mind the questions I wanted my dad to answer. There were a lot of things I wanted to ask him and never had. Now was the time.

We sat down at a small corner table, he on one side and me on the other. I knew there would not be a better time, so I began:

"Dad, I have a question for you."

He just looked at me and smiled.

"You've been a wonderful father. You've always supported all of us in any and every way. We were never left wanting anything, and you never missed anything we did—drum & bugle corps, band, you were always there."

A warm smile spread across my dad's face. "I wouldn't have missed any of it for anything."

I took a deep breath, held it a second, and slowly exhaled. "But . . . you never came to any of my baseball games and you would never play catch with me." I paused and watched his smile dissipate. "Why?"

"Baseball is not important. It's just a game." His voice was low, measured, steady. He turned to find our waitress and place our order. It was obvious he didn't want to discuss it.

"I know baseball is not important in the grand scheme of things. But neither is drum & bugle corps, or band, or much of anything else I did. But you always came to see anything and everything—everything, that is, except my baseball games."

Dad held my eye but did not respond.

"Tell me about that letter, dad."

"What letter?"

"You know what letter. The letter from the Pittsburgh Pirates. The letter that said you were to report to Greenville, Mississippi, in 1949." I paused again to give him time to respond, but he just looked away into the distance as if studying something on the horizon no one else could see.

I knew I was pushing things, but I had to know. "You must have been pretty good. They don't send letters like that to everyone. Did you go?" I asked.

Dad shrugged before lifting his water glass to his lips. "Your mom is going to be relieved when we tell her what the doctor said."

"Dad! Why won't you talk to me about this?"

"Because it doesn't matter. It means nothing. And besides . . . it's just not an interesting story. I've put that part of my life behind me." He paused and thought for a moment. "It just doesn't exist anymore."

"But I want to know, dad," I insisted. "I *need* to know."

"I know you want to know more about it, but it's just not something I feel good talking about. There are some things that are better left in the past. This is one of them. Let's change the subject."

Neither of us spoke about it again until after dinner. Uncomfortable small talk filled the minutes until the waitress served us our dessert. As we ate in silence I decided to broach the subject one final time.

"Did you go to Greenville?"

Dad lifted his eyes and looked directly into mine. "Yes."

"And?"

"And what?"

I pushed aside my partially finished slice of cheesecake and leaned forward on my forearms. "If you would have died a few weeks ago, I would not have known much about your life before I was born. I am your son, and I want to know. I want to know what there is about baseball that makes you clam up."

"Why is this so important to you?"

The question made me stop and think about it. Why was it so important to me? I had never really thought about it that way. "Because," I began after collecting my thoughts, "you're my father. I love you. A few weeks ago, while I was driving to the hospital, I realized that someday you'll be gone. I want to know everything about your life, and I really don't know anything about it."

My dad placed his elbow on the tabletop and rested his head in his hand, rubbing his furrowed forehead and nodding in slow resignation.

And then he began to speak.

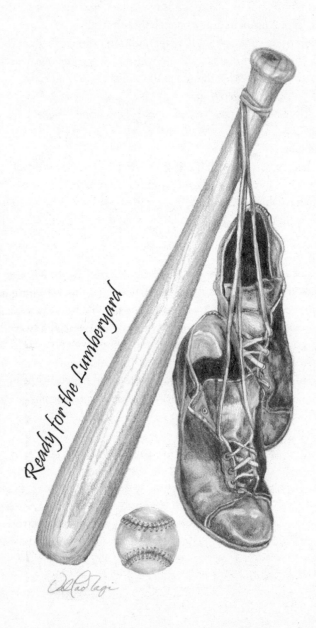

Ready for the Lumberyard

Chapter 2

July 21, 1941

Summers in Southern Illinois are hot, and July 1941 was hotter and more humid than most. Sesser is a small country town in "downstate" Illinois, ninety miles southeast of St. Louis. Although the entire country had suffered from the ravages of the Great Depression, this small coal mining town was particularly hard hit. Ten years into the economic misery and not a sign of recovery was anywhere to be seen. Once a thriving little mining town, Sesser and its coal mine, Old Ben #9, were now all but spent. Only a skeleton crew remained to work the mine.

Dirt poor and seemingly dying, Sesser had its interesting quirks. The town's single strand of Christmas lights spanned Main Street between the old decaying Sesser Opera House and the now-closed Miners Building and Loan. The lights stayed up year-round, but were only switched on between Thanksgiving and New Year's Day.

Although most of Sesser's once-bustling downtown area was now empty, Bruno's Mine Shaft Inn, the local tap, was always busy. The town's men gathered there every evening to drown their sorrows in St. Louis' finest: Busch Beer. Bruno's atmosphere was dark and dingy. The elegant cherry woodwork had once reflected the craftsmanship of years past. Now the wood was chipped and dusty. Although clean, the hardwood floor creaked with every step and was in desperate need of refinishing.

Hanging on the wall, opposite the bar that stretched from the front window to the back of the long narrow room, was a reprint of the painting

"Last Stand at The Alamo." The art had been commissioned by the now defunct Radeke Brewing Company of Kankakee and distributed to local beer joints in 1919. The old and dusty print featured Davy Crockett in his coonskin cap, swinging his trusted musket 'Ole Betsy' as a club to knock attacking Mexicans off the wall. The beautifully framed print was the focal point at Bruno's, and never failed to elicit animated discussion. The Alamo was one of America's defining moments, and it was not hard for the patrons to see similarities between the storm that engulfed the small mission and the tidal wave of despair and bad luck that had swept across Sesser. The town was now as dead as Crockett himself.

The talk in Bruno's usually focused on the misery of its patrons. Farms were little more than dust bowls. Little coal was coming from the mine. Few had enough to eat, and many had nothing at all except what others were willing to share. There were many things to argue and disagree about, but one thing nearly everyone in Sesser agreed upon: President Hoover had sold their lives down the river. "You vote Republican, you'll pick shit with the chickens," Bruno Pilate often proclaimed from behind the bar. The pronouncement was always answered by raised glasses and salutes to President Franklin D. Roosevelt.

There was also a popular topic of conversation of a more positive variety: "the kid." Sesser's townsfolk didn't have much, but they loved their baseball. "The kid" who was causing all the talk was a young local named Gene Moore, a teenager from a dirt-poor family living on the east side of the tracks. Gene had been tearing up the Sesser ball diamond, or what the locals called "The Lumberyard," in a loose reference to the faded sign hanging on the centerfield fence advertising "Huie Lumber."

The Cardinals were the favorite Major League team in these parts, but a trip to St. Louis and a ticket to the game were just a dream. So Sesser folk loved their Egyptians. The Southern Illinois team was a semi-pro organization made up of has-been players and young up-and-comers. On paper, the average age of the Egyptians was 27. Gene pulled the average down and skewed the true make-up of the team, however, because he was just 15. The Egyptians were the pride and joy of not just Sesser, but all of Southern Illinois. For reasons long since forgotten, this region of the state was known as "Little Egypt." Gene was the team's starting catcher, and was quickly becoming well known across the state—and beyond.

Author

The only known picture of Gene Moore playing with the Sesser Egyptians, circa 1941. Back row: Gene Moore, "The Pride of the Egyptians," is standing fourth from the left. Standing next to Gene, with his arm on another man's shoulder, is Barney Daniels. On the far right is Harry Boyd. Front row: kneeling in the center is Walter Klein, and on the far right is Hobart Sammons. Unfortunately, the names of the rest of the players are unknown.

In baseball, a good catcher controls the game. He calms or fires up the pitcher, and calls for various pitches to be thrown. With a full view of the field, the catcher can move the defense around to better match his view of where the ball might be hit. At barely 15, Gene controlled the game—not just from behind the plate but also with his bat. He led the team in home runs, walks, and, of course, strikeouts. Gene Moore was a boy playing like a man, in a game played by men who act like boys.

The Egyptians' catcher was a big farm kid, six feet tall with his wide shoulders and a large frame set upon a pair of spindly legs. His hair was shiny, thick, and as black as the coal Sesser workers used to pull from Old Ben #9. When he slipped on his catcher's mask and squatted behind the plate, Gene looked like an all-star catcher in his mid-to-late twenties. It was not until he peeled off the mask that fans in the stands realized he was but a boy, too young to shave.

On July 21, 1941, Gene was warming up Davy Thompson in the bullpen a few minutes before the game. Davy was a tall, red-headed 23-year-old flame-thrower. He was playing with the Egyptians during his recovery from a spring training injury he suffered with the Class C minor league team of the Detroit Tigers in Evansville. Almost fully healed, Davy was looking forward to returning to Evansville the following week.

"Come on Davy . . . your slider's not sliding! Get your release up over your shoulder or they're gonna knock you off the mound today," spat Gene through his mask. The 15-year-old was coaching the pro pitcher with the confidence of a veteran. The odd thing was that Davy, eight years older than Gene, listened and responded with enthusiasm.

After a few more pitches, Davy was ready. He walked out of the bullpen, slipped his jacket over his arm, nodded and smiled to Gene, and headed for the bench.

The umpire was old Joe "Vino" Caveglia. Joe lived for baseball, and he had played the game passionately until his body no longer permitted it. Unable to stay away from the ball park, he began calling games. Old Joe was the preferred umpire for any game played in and around Sesser.

"Vino" watched as the young catcher ambled onto the field and stood behind the plate. With his mask in hand, Gene looked over the Lumberyard. It was barely suitable for a game of baseball at any level. There were more weeds in the field than grass, and the weathered green bleachers were in desperate need of a fresh coat of paint. Despite its ramshackle condition, The Lumberyard was home and all Gene could think of when he slipped his mask over his head was how much he loved to play the game. His thoughts were interrupted by a stranger's voice coming from behind the chicken-wire backstop.

"You catch one heck of a game, son." Gene twisted his head to see an older man standing behind the backstop. He was dressed in a long sleeved, starched, and pressed white shirt, accented with a bright blue tie. His tan face, rugged and weathered, was framed by short light brown hair highlighted with a touch of gray on both temples.

Gene flipped up his mask. "Thanks."

"You hit that ball last night four-hundred feet," the stranger continued. "I know. I walked it off this morning. That's one heck of a wallop for a kid!"

"I am not a kid!" Gene snapped.

"How old are you, son?"

"I'll be 16," Gene answered, looking over the field before turning his gaze back to the stranger, adding in a barely audible voice, "next year."

The stranger laughed, "Well, I didn't mean anything by that, other than to compliment you on your skill on the field for such a young man."

"Thank you," replied Gene, who trotted off toward the dugout wondering who the stranger was and why he was sitting behind a chicken-wire backstop in Sesser, Illinois.

Frank Boudreau knew baseball, and he had an eye for talent. A veteran scout for the Brooklyn Dodgers, Frank knew a future Major Leaguer when he saw one, and Gene Moore was exactly that. The kid swung a big bat fast and hard and controlled the game like a field marshal. What really impressed Frank was that older ballplayers listened to this kid about how to play ball. Gene was not just an equal, but a team leader. Frank knew from experience that the only thing that mattered when you stepped onto a baseball field was what you know and what you could do. And Gene seemed to be able to do it all and everyone respected him for it, fans and teammates alike.

"I gotta sign this kid before anyone else sees him," Frank mumbled to himself as he walked back to the bleachers. "Yeah, I gotta sign this kid."

Frank had been around the game for a long, long time. He knocked around the Dodgers' farm system as a mediocre utility infielder, then as a pretty good coach. But his abilities were best employed as a scout. Frank knew and loved baseball, but never had the tools to make it to the big leagues. The Dodgers organization liked his sharp eye for talent. He was a trusted scout, but like every other job in baseball, on or off the field, he had to keep producing. Frank needed a big signing. The last three players he had inked deals with fizzled, so his standing in the organization and his future with the Dodgers depended on his bringing in a big fish.

Frank took a seat in the bleachers near the plate, on the first base side. It was there he began questioning his instincts. His current prospect was a 15-year-old boy? Sure he hit the ball a mile last night, but the shot could have been nothing more than a lucky fast swing at exactly the right place. Did he want to risk his reputation on one long ball? What are the odds a young kid could consistently do that? Frank's anxiety grew as he waited to see how Gene did that day against a quality team. And the Paducah Wildcats were recognized as the league's best. They swept last year's championship series and looked unstoppable again this year.

Frank watched as Gene walked out of the dugout and took his place behind the plate as if he owned it. Davy Thompson ambled up to the mound and took his last few warm-up pitches. Davy threw hard. Frank didn't know how fast Davy's fastball was, but he could hear the ball pop into Gene's mitt. It was a sound every ballplayer loved to hear.

From the first pitch Frank was drawn deeply into the game, mesmerized by what he saw the boy behind the plate do on the field. The game was tight for a few innings. Gene homered in the first, struck out in the third, smacked a double in the fifth, struck out again in the seventh, and hit a long line drive double in the ninth. Through it all Frank saw exactly what he knew to be true: a boy who knew the game of baseball inside and out and could control the game from behind the plate. The Egyptians won 12-2.

As the teams cleared the field, Gene paused to talk with his teammates and dissect the game. Frank made his move, sliding his way between players and fans to reach the knot of elated Egyptians.

"Gene, can I speak with you for a minute?" asked Frank, guiding the catcher over to one side. When they were out of earshot of the rest of the players he made his own pitch. "My name is Frank Boudreau. I'm a scout with the Dodgers."

"Dodgers? Where do they play?" Gene asked.

"Brooklyn, of course! You've never heard of the Brooklyn Dodgers?" Frank's eyebrows arched up in a look of genuine surprise.

Gene stared at Frank for a moment and rubbed his eyebrows in disbelief. "You're a scout for the Brooklyn Dodgers Major League baseball team?"

Frank nodded and reached inside his shirt pocket. "Here's my card, Gene."

The catcher gazed at the crisp white card he suddenly found in his dusty hand. He ran his finger over the raised "Dodger blue" letters as though holding something of great value. He looked up at the scout. Unsure what to say, he said nothing.

"I don't know if you know this, but there is a Gene Moore playing for the Dodgers right now," said Frank.

A small smile broke across Gene's face. "I know. An outfielder. He came up through the Reds organization."

Frank laughed. "You know more about him than I do. But, today, you are the Gene Moore I'm interested in. Let me tell you what I saw. I saw a young man with tremendous bat speed who hits harder than anyone I know, and certainly harder than anyone I have ever seen at your age. There are a lot of hard hitters around, but the fact is, you catch one hell of a game and shoot the ball down to second base as fast and as accurately as I have ever seen. Good catchers are common, Gene. Great catchers, now that's something altogether different. They are few and far between." Frank paused for a few seconds to let his words sink in. "Gene, you are a great catcher."

"I love to catch," Gene answered truthfully. "More than anything."

"I know and it shows every time you take the field," Frank continued. "Mechanically, you're excellent, but what makes you so much fun to watch is how you control the game. You're mature beyond your years and you play each game like it's the seventh game of the World Series. I love passionate ballplayers, and, above everything I've seen while watching, you play with heartfelt passion. I think the Dodgers would rather have you in their organization than have you playing for the opposition."

"What do you mean?" Gene asked innocently.

"Gene," Frank continued, "I'd like to meet your parents."

"Why? What do they have to do with the Brooklyn Dodgers?"

"I need to discuss this with your mom and dad. If you'd like to play professional baseball, I'd like to offer you a contract with the Brooklyn Dodgers. But you're only 15, son, and I need to talk this over with your parents."

Gene stared down at his worn catcher's mitt, not believing what he was hearing. He tried to swallow but his mouth was so dry he could barely open it to speak. He looked up one more time at the stranger with the pressed white shirt and sharp business card and managed to stammer out, "You mean Leo Durocher's Brooklyn Dodgers?"

Frank laughed, "Well, Gene, I think my boss, Branch Rickey, the General Manager of the Dodgers, might take issue with you about exactly whose Brooklyn Dodgers they are, but, yes, one and the same." A brief but uncomfortable silence followed before Frank decided to take control of the situation. "Come on, Gene." He put his hand on Gene's shoulder and squeezed it gently. "Let's go meet your mom and dad. We can take my car."

As they walked off the field, Frank noticed for the first time the awkwardness of this young boy. Gene was like a Great Dane puppy that had reached adult size, but didn't know exactly what to do with his long legs and giant paws. Off the field, Gene seemed to be a kid in a grown-up body. It was easy to forget while watching him play that he was really only a small-town boy.

Gene's eyes widened when Frank stopped next to a shiny blue 1938 Buick. The catcher had never seen a fancy car like that before. Frank opened the passenger door and leaned forward, resting his elbows on the top. "Why do you love to catch so much, Gene?"

Gene didn't even hesitate in his answer. "Because I love baseball, and I'm the only guy on the field who can watch the whole game." His voice grew louder and more passionate as the words tumbled from his lips. "Mr. Boudreau, squatting behind the plate, I have the best seat in the house! I hope I can do it forever."

Gene turned to look back at The Lumberyard, as if suddenly mindful that once he climbed into the stranger's car, his life would change forever.

"I love to catch."

Chapter 3

The Corner of Matthew and Mulberry

Frank's car stood out in Sesser like a Roman chariot at a rodeo. There weren't many new things in town, so the Buick Century Coupe, with its bright chrome air vents and wide whitewall tires, quickly caught everyone's eye on Main Street. Everyone stopped whatever they were doing, young and old alike, to stare at the freshly-waxed automobile. They also stopped to talk. Like every small town, anything out of the ordinary is a fresh topic of conversation.

"Is it someone from the Mine Workers Union?" asked Billy Kirkpatrick.

"No," another onlooker answered. "Probably a man from the Federal Government."

"You think? Then why is Gene Moore riding in that fancy new car?" asked Raymond Lowe, shading his eyes against the sun as he watched the Buick slowly cruise its way down Main.

"He's probably in some kind of trouble," replied Puny Eubanks.

"Gene Moore in trouble? I can't see that boy doing anything serious enough to land him in a car like that!" chimed in Billy. "But you never know. The driver looks like he could be a Hoover man, you know, FBI."

The one-car parade turned off Main and onto Mulberry before pulling up to the corner. Gene's house was a small single-story three room house with a slight tilt to it. Obviously old, it was covered in a tar wrap that simulated brick. Next to the house was a small barn desperate for a coat of paint. Several pigs behind a four-board flaking white fence rooted in the dirt or lay on their sides, twitching their large ears to keep the flies away. A dozen chickens and a strutting rooster milled about on the formless dirt path between the barn and the house. A pair of goats in another small pen nearby brayed softly as they scratched themselves against the rough boards that barely kept them enclosed.

John Moore was sitting in his rocking chair on the front porch when the Buick carrying his son and a stranger rolled to a stop in front of the house.

Gene snapped open the car door and jumped out of the Buick. "Hi Pop!" he shouted, bounding up the walkway and onto the porch. "Just listen before you say no!"

Frank eased his way more slowly out of the car, shut the door firmly, and nodded in the direction of the elder Moore, who slowly stood up from his chair. John was a big man, about six-foot-one and close to 250 pounds. The resemblance between Gene and his father was easy to see, even at a distance. It was no mystery where the boy got his height. As Frank approached he saw the father was dressed in denim bib overalls that proudly displayed the tag "Osh Kosh B'Gosh." Under his bibs was a burgundy and white plaid shirt. A silver watch chain ran from one of his brass buttons to his pocket. Hidden from view was the old pocket watch John used to keep track of his day.

John took a long draw from a Lucky Strike and exhaled without glancing in the direction of his son, all the while wondering just what it was Gene had done to warrant a visit from an important looking stranger in a fancy new car.

"Mr. Moore?" Frank inquired as he neared the porch. "My name is Frank Boudreau. I'm with the Brooklyn Dodgers professional baseball club. If you don't mind, I would like to talk to you about your son Gene."

John looked down at Frank for a moment before turning his eyes to stare at Gene. A puzzled look crossed his face. "Talk about what? What has he done?"

Frank smiled and glanced over at Gene, who was beginning to squirm under the scrutiny of his father's withering stare. "He hasn't done anything wrong, Mr. Moore," Frank chuckled softly. "In fact, he does everything right—on a ball diamond. Your son is quite an athlete." Frank waited, expecting to see a smile and hear a laugh. Instead, John shifted his eyes back to the man in front of him and said nothing. Frank shot a glance toward Gene, cleared his throat, and continued. "As I said, Mr. Moore, I represent the Brooklyn Dodgers, and I want to talk to you about making Gene part of our organization."

A small scowl lined the older man's face. "Gene is only 15," John answered firmly. "He left school to help me on the farm. Playing games is for kids. I need Gene to be a man and help his family here at home."

Frank could see the effect of John's response on Gene, whose shoulders began to sag under the weight of disappointment. "Mr. Moore, I completely understand," answered the baseball scout. "May I please come up and sit down?"

A Scout Visits Sesser

John shrugged and tilted his head toward the small wooden stool sitting against the wall. "Gene, go see your mom. She needs help inside."

Gene winced at the order. "But Pop! Can I please stay and . . ."

Frank interrupted before Gene could finish his sentence. "Gene, I need to speak with your father alone." Outnumbered, Gene mumbled his understanding, opened the screen door, and stepped into the little house. He let the door slam shut behind him.

Frank waited until John sat back in his rocking chair before leaning on the railing of the porch next to him. "Mr. Moore, your son has a gift. I'm sure you know how well he plays baseball. At 15, the way he plays against these men . . . well, he's an amazing young athlete. I don't see raw talent like his very often. In fact, I rarely see it."

"I'm sorry, what did you say your name was? Baker?"

"No sir, Boudreau, Frank Boudreau." The scout dug into his shirt pocket and handed John his business card. The elder Moore did not even glance at what was printed on it. "Please call me Frank. May I call you John?"

John shrugged again. "Mr. Boudreau, I don't play games. I don't watch games. I got laid off from the mine seven years ago back in '33. Since then, I've raised pigs, hauled garbage, and shoveled manure at the Livestock Auction Barn. I don't have time to do anything but provide for my family. I hear things, sure. People 'round town tell me Gene can play ball pretty good, but I don't know if he's good, and I don't know anything about baseball. I do know Gene is a good boy—he could work a little harder around here instead of throwing a ball around a field with other men who should be out providing for their families—but he's still learning to be a man."

"John," Frank interrupted. "What if I told you Gene could make good money playing ball?"

"Who would pay him to play a game?" John asked with a skeptical look on his face.

"Well, some people might well do just that. Your son, if he keeps progressing, could be one of the most exciting young ballplayers in the Major Leagues. A few very rich men around the country own these baseball franchises, and they pay players more than you can imagine to play this game."

John looked off toward the pig pen when one of the sows let out a long low squeal and shook his head in disbelief. "I find that hard to believe, Mr. Boudreau. But, I can imagine a lot."

Gene was inside the house, pressing himself flat against the fading yellow wallpaper near the screen door in an effort to remain hidden from the men outside discussing his future. He wanted to hear every word, but the men spoke in low tones and only snippets of their conversation were audible. His shirt was soaking wet from sweat, a combination of the anxiety of the moment and the sticky hot summer day. After fifteen agonizingly long minutes laughter suddenly erupted from the porch. Gene flinched at the unexpected outburst, and then flinched a second time when John yelled through the screen door just a foot away, "Mom! Frank and I are going downtown for a bit."

Allie Moore knew "going downtown" meant a trip to Bruno's for a cold beer. A God-fearing woman of Irish descent, she did not approve of drinking alcohol, but after years of protesting she had given up that battle. There were too many others to fight, and she was too tired to wage them all. Wiping her hands on a towel she walked toward the door and nodded her understanding. Gene eased himself away from the wall and exchanged glances with his father. Without offering so much as a word John turned and walked away, the porch creaking under the weight of his footsteps.

Frank handed John the keys. "Would you like to drive?" he asked as they walked toward the Buick, slapping John on the back as if they had been friends for years.

John reached for the keys as a smile broke across his face. "Well, sure. I'd love to!"

Gene ran to the window and watched the shiny blue Buick drive off with his Pop behind the wheel. He was pushing the door open when Allie brought his plans to a halt. "Not so fast!" Gene stopped dead in his tracks and turned to look at his mother. He slowly let the door shut behind him. "Who was that man?" she asked.

"He says he's with the Brooklyn Dodgers," Gene answered.

"Who?" Allie asked.

"You know, mom. The Dodgers. The baseball team."

"Where's Brooklyn?" she asked.

"It's near New York City . . . I think."

"Hmm. He's a long way from home," replied Allie as she lifted her towel to wipe the dust from a small table near the door. "Why is he talking to your father?"

"He says he wants me to play ball for the Dodgers."

"Oh," was Allie's only response.

Gene headed for the door a second time but Allie stopped him again. "Wait!" Gene groaned aloud and stopped with the door open and his body half outside. "If they wanted you in their conversation, they would have asked you to come, don't you think? Besides, Bruno's is no place for a young man, and I need your help in the kitchen. Go wash your hands."

"Yes, mam." Gene never argued with his mom.

An hour passed quickly as Gene finished his chores in the kitchen. Another hour was consumed with work in the barn and feeding the animals. "Where was Pop and what was he talking to Frank about for this long?" wondered Gene as he wrestled with the idea of disobeying his mother and striking out for Bruno's. Instead, he settled himself on the porch swing and promptly fell fast asleep. He awoke with a start thirty minutes later when he heard a pair of car doors slam shut, one after the other. The big blue Buick and the two men had finally returned to Mulberry Street.

Gene jumped up off the swing and bounded down the steps, but by the time he reached the street the Buick was already pulling away from the curb. He turned to ask his father a question, but the elder Moore was already halfway up the porch stairs.

Gene trotted after him. "Well?" he asked as he reached his side.

The two men—one young, enthusiastic, and strong, the other older, subdued, and tired—stood facing one another on the porch. It was the first time the father realized his son could look him directly in the eye.

"Well what?" John asked. "You should be in bed. Tomorrow's your morning to feed the hogs."

The smell of beer lingered in the air between them. "Pop! What did you talk about? Where did Mr. Boudreau go?" Gene asked as a sinking feeling of despair washed over him. His father had turned the scout down. His dream of playing in the Major Leagues was over.

"Where did he go? I don't know. I didn't ask him."

Gene felt his heart skip a beat as his father reached for the screen door handle and pulled the rickety affair open. He stopped at the threshold and turned back to look at his son. "Oh, Frank said to tell you he'd see you at the game tomorrow afternoon." A small smile broke across John's face.

"Tomorrow? Tomorrow! At the game?" Gene closed his eyes and let out a shout of joy. "He's coming back to watch me play again!"

John nibbled at his upper lip, his front teeth scratching the two-day stubble that had taken root there. "Gene," he said softly, looking his boy squarely in the eye. "I may come see this baseball game tomorrow. Frank said he couldn't believe I've never seen you play. Made me feel like a bad father. I think I'll come see what this baseball's all about. I just don't understand why someone would pay anyone, anywhere, to play a damn game!"

Gene felt a lump in his throat and tried to swallow it away. "Pop, it would be great if you could come and watch. I'd really like that."

"Get to bed, boy. You have a long day tomorrow and it starts before sunup." He stepped into the house and let the door clatter shut behind him.

Gene sat down on his father's rocking chair and began pumping his legs. His chest swelled with excitement and it took him a few moments to realize he was holding his breath. He exhaled noisily and said aloud, "The Brooklyn Dodgers know who I am!"

Gene lay on his bed that night well past midnight, unable to fall asleep. Although the room was hot and mosquitoes buzzed around his ears in the darkness, all he could think about was Ebbets Field, the Dodgers' ballpark in Brooklyn. It might as well have been in Rome or Paris—it seemed that far away from Sesser, Illinois, and the Egyptians. And now, without any advance warning, it was within the reach of a young farm boy's dream. The Brooklyn Dodgers—with Mickey Owen behind the plate, big Dolph Camilli at first, Billy Herman at second, Cookie Lavagetto at third, and Pee Wee Reese at short. Gene whispered each name aloud. With his eyes squeezed shut he pictured himself walking onto the field for the first time. He thought of Dixie Walker and Pete Reiser and Joe Medwick roaming the outfield, and Kirby Higbe and Whitlow Wyatt leading the pitching staff.

The last thing he remembered was drifting off to sleep looking out his window at the stars in the night sky, with Wyatt's fastball snapping into his catcher's mitt.

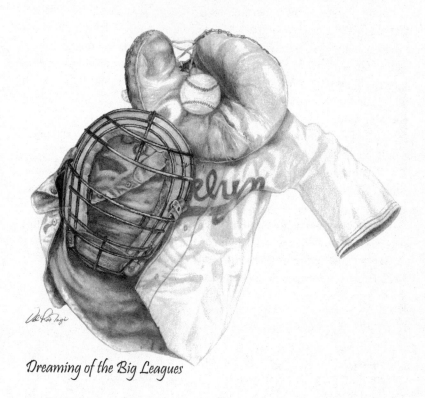

Dreaming of the Big Leagues

Chapter 4

Sunday, July 22, 1941

Nothing said at Bruno's ever stayed at Bruno's. Within hours word that a baseball scout with the Brooklyn Dodgers was in town to sign Sesser's Gene Moore was on everyone's lips.

The Egyptians always drew a respectable crowd on Sundays. Sometimes more than 100 people would turn out to see a game at The Lumberyard. It was a good way to forget the common problems everyone faced each day. This particular Sunday was different. The atmosphere felt more like a carnival—festive and alive with excitement. Old man Basso was there, selling beer out of an iced bucket for a nickel a bottle, and today he had plenty of takers.

By the time the game was ready to begin more than 500 people were crowded around the dusty little diamond to see Gene Moore and the Egyptians play ball. The majority of the fans were from Sesser, but people from neighboring Valier, Pinckneyville, and Christopher were also there, determined not to miss the birth of a new Major League star. Cars full of people arrived from as far away as Mount Vernon and Marion, more than thirty miles as the crow flies. Some carried wooden buckets or boxes to sit on, while others brought wooden chairs, blankets, and stools. Those who were able climbed trees to catch a bird's eye view of the spectacle about to unfold. Small children smiled with excitement while perched high on their fathers' shoulders, watching with breathless anticipation.

An hour before the game, Gene left his house as usual for his walk to the field. He had barely reached the street when Puny Eubanks screeched his aging red Dodge pickup truck to a halt next to Gene. "Get in Gene! This truck's headed for The Lumberyard! Can't have you late for your big day!"

"Thanks, Puny!" Gene laughed, tossing his gear in the bed and jumping in after it.

Two minutes later Puny reached the field and yelled out his window to the gathering crowd, "Hey, everyone! I got Gene Moore in the back of my truck! The next starting catcher for the Brooklyn Dodgers!"

Gene was used to attention, but nothing like this. Dozens of people, friends and strangers alike, surged toward him as he climbed out of the truck. Someone began shouting something Gene could not make out, and within seconds everyone was yelling words of encouragement. Even those who had never bothered to acknowledge him wanted to offer their best wishes, a pat on the back, or simply catch his eye. A dozen hands stretched toward him in an effort to shake his own. Gene was speechless.

"Come on, Gene. Show them Sesser's best!"

"We love you, Gene!"

"Send us a post card from Brooklyn!"

Gene pasted a smile on his face, nodded in reply, and made his way to the bench. He dropped his gear on the ground and was reaching for his mitt when Frank walked up to greet him.

When Gene saw the scout he could feel the blood rush into his face from embarrassment. "I'm so sorry, Mr. Boudreau. I didn't tell anyone. I don't know why they're all here."

Frank laughed and shook hands with the young catcher. "I know why they're here, Gene. This town seems to have endured more than its share of sorrow over the last ten years. They need something good to happen to Sesser, and they are here to root you on. They need this. I think they need you, Gene. This is what baseball is all about."

Frank watched as Gene shifted his gaze and locked his eyes somewhere in the distance. "I don't think I feel well, Mr. Boudreau."

"Son, you can forget all these people and even forget I'm a scout. I've already made up my mind to sign you—no matter how you play today. Just go out there and play like you have nothing to lose and give these good people of Sesser a game they won't soon forget."

"Mr. Boudreau, it's not the people. I've played in front of lots of people before."

"Then what's the problem?" Frank followed Gene's gaze, which had settled on someone standing near the street. It was John Moore.

"Your father is very proud of you, son. He doesn't understand your love of this game, but he loves you. He tells me he has never seen you play before. Go show him what his son is made of."

Gene knelt down by his gear and looked up at Frank. A smile had replaced his look of concern. The catcher pulled the bill of his cap down over his eyes and took off for the bench. The crowd exploded with enthusiastic applause when their Egyptians took the field a few minutes later. Their opponent was the Mississippi Mudcats, another semi-pro team out of Cairo, Illinois.

Despite Gene's best effort, pitcher Tim Duggan's warm-up was a disaster. His pitches came in too high, too low, and way too slow—everywhere but across the plate. Like nearly everyone else on the field that afternoon, the tall and lanky left-hander with the jet black hair had never played in front of such a large and rowdy crowd. And Gene had never seen such a bad case of nerves.

"Coming down!" shouted Gene. He took Duggan's last warm-up pitch—a high hanging duck anyone could have knocked over the fence—and shot the ball down to second base. The umpire called for the ball, took his place behind the plate, and yelled out two words every baseball player and fan loves to hear: "PLAY BALL!"

The entire crowd stood as one and cheered.

Todd Blake, the Mudcats' first batter, looked down to the third base coach, took the sign, and stepped up to the plate. Duggan looked at Gene for the sign. He was usually a very methodical pitcher with a great slider and a knack for hitting the outside corner, but he rarely threw with much speed. Gene dropped two fingers for a slider, but Duggan shrugged off the first sign. Gene repeated the sign. Another shake of the head. Gene changed the call and Duggan shrugged a third time. With a sigh, Gene gave in and called for the fastball.

Duggan wound up and threw the ball with everything he had . . . right between the shoulder blades of the batter, who was unable to avoid the pitch. Blake winced in pain and threw his bat down in disgust and anger, straightening up a few seconds later to glare at Duggan.

"Take your base!" yelled the umpire. Blake took a few steps toward the mound before thinking better of it and trotted down to first.

The next Mudcat batter, Bobby Robbins, was twenty-five and bitter about his Major League career, which had never quite materialized. Bobby was on a nine-game hitting streak. After watching Duggan's slow pitches during warm-up, he was anxious to rip one into the outfield. Bobby took the call, took a pair of practice swings, and stepped into the batter's box. He eyed Duggan and inched his way forward, crowding the plate.

Gene dropped his fingers and called for a slider. Tim shrugged him off. Gene shook his head. "Time!" he called out, jogging to the mound.

"Don't like my pitch selection today, Tim?"

"Gotta lot of nervous energy, Gene. I wanna throw hard," answered the pitcher through clenched teeth as he looked down at the mound, moving dirt around with his spikes.

"Well, we'll check number seven's back after the game, and see how hard you're actually throwing," Gene chuckled, "but if I were nervous, I'd want to throw my best stuff. Tim, this guy can't hit your slider. Throw it for me."

"Okay, Gene, whatever you want."

Gene gave him a wink and trotted back behind the plate. As he squatted he looked up at Bobby and said, "I don't think I'd get that close to the plate. He's wild today."

"Yeah, right," Bobby shot back. He stepped out and took another swing before crowding the plate once more. When his eyes caught sight of Blake at first base, reaching behind himself to rub his aching back, Bobby thought better of Gene's warning and eased a few inches away from the plate.

"Smart move," Gene said through his mask. Bobby ignored him.

Duggan was about halfway through his wind up when Blake took off for second base. Bobby swung hard at the slider that came in straight across the plate, but missed. Gene caught the ball and, without getting up out of his crouch, whipped it toward second—straight across the mound to the shortstop moving to cover the steal. Duggan fell to the ground as the ball hissed its way through the hot and heavy July air, missing his right ear by inches. The throw was just about textbook perfect, six inches off the ground and about two feet in front of second base. Blake slid into the tag.

"You're out!" yelled the umpire, pumping his right arm along his side, his hand clenched in a fist. The fans jumped to their feet and roared themselves hoarse with enthusiasm.

Frank, who was seated directly behind the Egyptians' bench next to John Moore, stood with his mouth open but did not make a sound. He had never seen an arm like that on a kid that young. "He never got up," the scout shouted as he turned toward John. Frank had to look down to see the father, who was still seated on the bleacher. "Gene is a complete ballplayer. He can do it all!" Frank thought to himself. John, meanwhile, stood slowly and clapped with the rest of the crowd, amazed at their admiration for his son.

The first inning ended quickly when Bobby grounded out to third and the last batter popped up to left field. The game was tight for several innings, but the Egyptians came to play, and play they did. Gene had one of his best days at and behind the plate. No one else tried to steal a base for the balance of the game. Gene just wouldn't allow it.

Although he struck out once, he smacked a hard single into left and sailed a long sacrifice fly to score a run. In the bottom of the ninth with one out he took his turn at bat for a fourth time that Sunday afternoon. The count was two and two and the pitch was a high fast ball. Gene swung with everything he had and connected, driving the ball deep into center field. Five hundred people stood as one and watched the ball sail over the Huie Lumber sign and disappear into the grove of Locust trees. The noise was deafening. Gene raised his arms in triumph as he trotted toward second base. His home run sealed the win 5-4.

The win was important, but the only thing that truly mattered to Gene was that his Pop saw him play baseball for the first time.

Through it all John Moore sat next to Frank, watching the scout with one eye and the crowd with the other. Now he understood why everyone in town was talking about his son. He wasn't just another ballplayer. He was special.

John didn't remember the walk home that afternoon, but he remembered to the day he died the pride he felt knowing his son had a gift few others were blessed with.

Chapter 5

Monday, August 6, 1941

Gene walked outside and stood on the porch.

Two weeks had passed since Frank Boudreau left Sesser, and no one had heard a word. He was beginning to think the scout had second thoughts about signing a 15-year-old kid. "Maybe I'm not as good as everyone thinks I am," thought Gene. "Maybe Frank knows that now."

Who was he kidding? The Dodgers—the Brooklyn Dodgers—were seriously interested in having him play in their organization? He sighed with disappointment and shook his head as he walked toward the barn. How could he have been so naïve? How would he explain it to his friends?

It was noon in Sesser and, as usual, it was hot. Ward, Gene's older brother, was in the barn unloading coal from Pop's wagon with a shovel.

"What's in your hand?" Ward asked when Gene entered the barn, stopping to lean on his shovel. He had been unloading the coal for nearly thirty minutes and he needed a break.

"A bucket," answered Gene.

Ward twisted his face in disgust. "Not that hand," he said nodding toward the bucket. "The *other* hand."

"Baseball cards," Gene answered with enthusiasm. He dropped the bucket and spread the cards out on the top of a barrel. "Look! Enos Slaughter, Joe DiMaggio, Ted Williams, Dizzy Dean . . . and look at this one, the rookie, Pee Wee Reese!"

"Why do they call him Pee Wee?" asked Ward.

"I don't know," Gene said with a shrug. "He's small I guess. But he sure plays big . . . and that's what I love about baseball. When you step onto that field, the size of the man is determined by his heart, not his height."

Ward furrowed his brow and shook his head. He had never gotten into baseball like his brother. "Why are you so crazy about that baseball? You're 15. You're almost a man, Gene. I don't understand why you are so taken by that stupid game."

"Ward, baseball is America's game," Gene shot back defensively. "All true Americans love baseball. It's a game that only belongs to us. No one else in the world plays it."

"So what? Maybe there's a reason no one else plays it. Ever think about that?" Ward replied with equal vigor, edging closer and tensing up as he glared at his little brother.

Gene sighed. The last thing he wanted was a fight. "Baseball is more than a game, Ward—at least to me it is. I don't know how to explain it. You either get it or you don't. I think it brings out the best in us." He paused and watched Ward relax a bit. "Do you know what I mean?

"No."

Gene slipped the baseball cards into his back pocket, lifted off the Egyptians baseball cap he wore each day, and ran his fingers through his thick mane of hair. "You want to know something about a man, just play ball with him. You'll learn everything you need to know about him. Who he is, what he believes . . . it's all revealed as the game unfolds. You just have to be open and watch what he does—*feel* what he does. You'll see if he reacts or responds to the challenges." When he saw the perplexed look on Ward's face, Gene continued in an effort to explain it to him. "There's a difference, you know. If he reacts, you have him beat. If he responds, you have a formidable opponent. Besides, baseball defines us as a country. It's a game that is purely American. That's why I said all Americans love baseball, Ward. I'm no different."

There was no doubting Ward and Gene were brothers—the coal black hair and dark eyes were a dead giveaway. But that is where the similarities ended. Almost four years older than Gene, Ward rarely complimented his little brother and paid even less attention to him. Although he did not verbalize it, Ward knew Gene was different somehow. When Gene was in the barn or around the house, he was just Ward's kid brother. But when Gene picked up a bat or put a catcher's mitt on his hand, he had no equal in Sesser. And since the Brooklyn Dodgers' scout had come to town, the men in town had talked about nothing else except Gene and the Major Leagues. Now everyone referred to Ward as "Gene's older brother" and Ward didn't like it one bit. The fact that Gene was also a couple inches taller than Ward didn't help matters.

Ward was the oldest Moore boy, and he took life far more seriously than any of his siblings. Pop's expectations for him were high, and at times he seemed to stumble under the weight. His sense of responsibility and the additional pressures of being the oldest during the worst depression the country had ever witnessed made him feel that Gene was wasting his time and getting off easy when he could have been working more to put food on the table.

Ward listened to his brother try to explain the game he so loved, but when Gene stopped talking he just shook his head and sighed. "When are you gonna grow up, Gene? You're not gonna be a big league baseball player. Where is this Brooklyn big shot? He drives up in his fancy car and fills your head with a bunch of lies, gets your hopes up, and then drives out of our world and back into his own. Rich and famous people are all alike, Gene. They don't care about you and I one whit."

The words stung Gene deeply because he was already half convinced Ward was right. He leaned back against the barrel, folded his arms across his chest, and lowered his eyes so his brother would not see the tears aching to run down his cheeks.

"You know what you're gonna be?" continued Ward. "A coal miner or a pig farmer. That's what we do here in Franklin County. That's what all Sesser men do. We mine or we farm. What else is there? What else can we do? You might as well just get used to the idea." Ward leaned his shovel against the wagon and wiped the coal dust on his pants. "You know, it's not just baseball that comes outta that radio. If you'd listen to the news reports or read a newspaper, you might find out that you and I— heck, probably most of the boys here in Sesser—are gonna be soldiers soon. The Germans are all over Europe, Gene! Do you think they're gonna stop there? When our country calls, we have to answer!"

Gene lifted his eyes and looked at his brother. "Soldiers?" He shook his head. "I'm not going to be a soldier. I couldn't shoot anybody." In control of his emotions once again, Gene straightened himself up and shifted the cap on his head. "I am going to play baseball, and I am going to get better than I am today, and someday I'm going to play in the Major

Leagues. You, big brother, will be listening to me play on the radio."
Gene picked up a corncob and pretended it was a microphone. He cleared
his throat and deepened his voice. "Batting clean-up and catching for the
St. Louis Cardinals, Gene Moore!"

Ward shook his head but could not hold back a small chuckle.
Without thinking he reached over and tried to pluck the corncob out of
Gene's hand, but his brother's reflexes were too quick and he pulled it
back out of reach.

"Oh, yeah?" laughed Ward. "Try this." He jumped to one side,
picked up another cob, and threw it at his sibling. Gene's right hand shot
up and caught it. Ward stared openmouthed for a few seconds before both
brothers erupted in laughter.

"Can't get anything past me, Ward," chuckled Gene. "I don't let balls
get past me just as a matter of principle. If it's thrown to me, I'll catch it.
If I have a bat in my hand, I'll hit it."

"Gene? Gene! I need that coal!"

Gene gritted his teeth. "Oh, no! I forgot about mom!" He picked up
his shovel and began filling a bucket with the coal his mother needed for
the cook stove. "Everything in this world has a purpose, Ward,"
continued Gene as he dumped another shovelful of the black rocks into
the bucket. "A ball is meant to be hit or caught. It demands it of us. I was
made to do both. That's my purpose. It's what I was built to do."

Ward could not believe what he was hearing. "The ball demands it?
You've lost it, little brother. Every kid likes baseball . . . but then they
grow up. But not you. Now you're talking to the ball? The ball makes
demands? You think about the ball as though it has a life. You hear the
ball giving you orders. 'Catch me Gene! Hit me Gene!' If you're not
careful, they're gonna reserve a room for you at the Anna-Jonesboro
Hospital!"

"Think what you want, Ward," Gene said with a wide grin.
"Someone has to feed the pigs and mine the coal while I'm playing
baseball all over the country and you are trying to catch me on the radio!"

"Maybe you'll be on the radio, maybe you won't," Ward conceded
somewhat, "but one thing's for sure. Pop will be out soon, and if we don't
get this coal unloaded and help him feed these pigs, we ain't gonna live
long enough to know for sure whether you could make it or not."

"Gene!"

"Coming, mom!"

Gene turned to face Ward. "Okay, but give me your best shot," he said as he stepped back a few yards and dropped into his catcher's squat.

Ward looked at Gene and slowly smiled. "Okay little brother, but I'm warning you. It's gonna hurt!" Ward picked up another corncob, but this time he broke it in half to make it easier to throw and harder to catch. He did his best to stare Gene down, began a slow and awkward wind-up, and was ready to let the cob fly when John Moore walked into the barn.

"What's going on in here?" he demanded.

"Nothing, Pop," Ward laughed. "Gene was just telling me how he has conversations with a baseball."

Pop looked from one son to another as if both had lost their minds. "Well, let's go have a conversation with these pigs. They told me on my way into the barn they were hungry."

Pop, Ward, and Gene were out slopping the pigs when a familiar blue Buick turned once again onto Mulberry Street. John saw it first.

"Tell me, Gene, did you really believe that scout would come back?" Pop asked.

Both sons shot a glance at their father. It was the first time he had mentioned the matter since Frank Boudreau left town. "No, I guess not," answered Gene slowly, doing his best to hide his disappointment.

John nudged Ward and tilted his head toward the street, lifting a finger to his lips. Ward turned and spotted the Buick. His face failed to betray any emotion at the sight of the returned scout.

"Looks like someone's here to see you," John calmly announced.

"See who? Ward?" Gene asked without looking up.

"No, not Ward. You." John motioned to the street, where Frank Boudreau was climbing out of his car. Gene felt Ward give him a light punch on the shoulder, but he felt as if someone had socked him in the chest. For a moment, he found it difficult to catch his breath.

"It's hard to believe that something that produces a smell so bad can taste so good," Frank called out as he walked toward the pigpen.

"Smells like a living to me," John answered. This time he greeted the scout's arrival with a smile instead of cold silence. He eased open the gate to step out and grab a bucket of slop. "Not all of us can get paid to play a game."

"Well, I'm glad to say that at least one person here can." A big smile spread across Frank's face as he took a step through the open gate and came to a halt on a fresh pile of pig manure. "Oh, no!" Frank spat as he jumped backward out of the pen. He quickly saw the humor in the situation and broke into a laugh. John joined in. Gene was so excited to see the scout he just stood there, mouth open and unable to say a word.

Frank wiped the bottom of his leather shoe on a fence board. "Gene, I have good news for you. The Dodgers agree with me and want you as part of their organization. But you'll have to step out of the pen if you want to hear more. I just can't take any future Major Leaguer seriously when he's standing knee-deep in pig shit."

Gene looked at his dad, unable to believe his ears or say a word. John merely nodded his approval. "Come on, let's go up to the house and talk there with your mom and dad. John, do you have a few minutes?" Frank waited a moment, but neither Gene nor John moved a muscle or said a word. Gene was stunned, and his young age and innocence was clearly on display for both men to see. John was torn between helping his son realize his dream and losing him from the farm.

"Sure, let's go have some lemonade," John finally said as he put down the galvanized steel bucket he was carrying and slapped Gene on the back. "Ward, can you finish up here?"

"Sure Pop. No problem."

As Gene, Pop, and Frank walked away Ward shook his head, picked up the bucket, and continued feeding the hogs. He was secretly proud of his brother, but he found it hard to hide the jealously that coursed through him.

"John and Allie, your son has a gift," Frank began as they all sat on the porch sipping ice cold lemonade from different colored glasses. None of them matched. "I know it, and the Dodgers know it. We don't want Gene to be taken by one of the other teams, but he's too young to take into our farm system. What we would like to do is have you, John, sign for Gene, and we will place him with the St. Louis Granary Team. The Grain Elevator has a team that plays in the Industrial League. We'll pay The Granary to have Gene play on the team, and they'll pay Gene as though he works at the Granary. His only job will be to play baseball. That's it. He will play there the balance of this season, and all of next season. If he plays well there, in 1942 we'll move him up to our Minor League system. I think by mid-season '43, maybe '44 at the latest, he could be playing in Brooklyn, catching in the big show."

John had grown to like Frank Boudreau, but he was naturally skeptical. "And how much would he earn?" he asked.

"Gene can earn almost a dollar an hour with his production bonus with the Granary team, but that's just a fraction of what he can earn if he performs well and moves up. He just has to play there the way he played a couple of weeks ago."

"And what if he don't?" asked John.

Frank paused a moment before answering. "Well, John, then you can have your farm helper back. It's important that you all understand this is business—big business. Those who play and help the team win will move up. Those who don't, move out. It's as simple as that."

For the first time Allie joined into the conversation. "Gene, do you want to move to St. Louis and play baseball?"

Gene, who had been hanging on every syllable, was bursting with excitement. "It's all I wanna do, mom!"

A long stretch of silence followed. Gene looked back and forth at each of the adults. John stared directly at his son. Allie stared at John. Frank just sat back and smiled at all three.

"Frank," John finally answered, putting down his lemonade glass and standing up tall and proud. "You take good care of my boy." Seven words. A young man's future in the balance. John stepped off the porch and headed for the barn.

Gene Moore left the next day for St. Louis and the beginning of his baseball career. Although the season was nearly over, he was able to play in 22 games. He made quite an impression on the league, hitting six home runs and making plays behind the plate that amazed even the old-timers who were sure they had seen it all. In 22 games, 27 men tried to steal on Gene. Only six succeeded.

Gene just wouldn't allow it.

Chapter 6

A Day of Infamy

December 7, 1941, dawned blue, clear, crisp in Southern Illinois. Although it was unusually warm for a Sesser December, Gene could still see traces of his breath lingering in the air. Home from his first season with the Granary team in St. Louis, he felt invigorated by the cool temperature and beautiful sky. With Gene's help and outstanding catching abilities, the Granary team won the League Championship and Gene was named Rookie of the Year, even though he had only played in twenty-two games.

The Granary and the league were delighted with Gene's performance; Frank and the Dodgers were ecstatic.

Gene returned home from St. Louis to help Pop on the farm. He received quite a welcome from the town. Mayor Noble Vaughn stopped by Gene's house to present him with a certificate for a free breakfast at Lena Van Horn's Café and a letter from the town council recognizing Gene for his accomplishments. Dr. Ward stopped by the house and encouraged Gene to take his dream and abilities as far as they would carry him, saying, "I just would like to know that I delivered a Major Leaguer before I retire." He looked at John and continued, "Not every doctor can say that, you know."

Sesser had never had a hero, and Gene Moore was the closest they had ever come to putting one of their own on a pedestal. It gave the townsfolk a sense of pride beyond anything they had ever experienced.

The people of Sesser had taken notice of Gene long before the Dodgers caught up with him. It started when he was only eight. The old men downtown would stop him on the street to talk baseball because Gene knew every player on the Cardinals' roster and could recite their stats without fail. Frankie Frisch was the manager and the second baseman of the team everyone called "The Gasshouse Gang." He hit .305. Gene knew the other batting averages, too. Rip Collins, the first baseman, hit .333 with 35 home runs. Pepper Martin played third and hit .289. Joe Medwick played left field and hit .318. Dizzy Dean won 30 games and his brother Paul won 19. Gene was only a kid but, when talking baseball, he could keep up with any adult.

Gene was up early, shoveling coal from Pop's wagon into the barn and thinking back to the time when he was a little kid impressing the graybeards with his knowledge. Maybe someday another little kid yet unborn would impress others by reciting Gene Moore's statistics. The thought brought a smile to his face.

Gene was leaning into another shovel full of coal when Billy Grammer stopped by. Billy was his best friend, and had been from a very early age. Billy didn't play baseball and knew nothing, and cared less, about the game. What he loved was the guitar, and he was the best picker in Sesser. People said Billy was as good a musician as Gene was a ballplayer. Billy would sit, hour after hour, on the old porch of the Grammer home playing his guitar.

The fact that Billy couldn't read music didn't slow him down. He listened to the country and western station out of St. Louis, KMOX AM, during the week and especially enjoyed listening to the Grand Ole Opry on Saturday nights on WSM out of Nashville. Billy would listen, hear the music in his head, and then play it on his guitar from memory—usually without making a single mistake. Billy could play anything he heard on the radio. Gene loved country and western music and would sit and listen to Billy play for hours.

"Gene, what are you doing later today?" Billy asked. "They're showing a movie at the Old Opera House and I thought you might wanna go."

"What's showing?"

"I don't know, but it'll be more fun than shoveling coal," Billy replied.

"No kidding," Gene responded. "Sure . . . what time?"

"I think they open the doors at one o'clock."

"Okay, let me finish up here and I'll meet you there," answered Gene.

The morning passed quickly. Gene finished up his chores and washed up at the pump outside the barn before hurrying to meet Billy in front of the Opera House.

"Hey, Gene, look," said Billy, pointing down the street as they were about to enter the theater. "It's Ward's girlfriend, Jamie Reid."

"Yeah, I see her. Too bad Ward's not here."

Jamie was a beautiful 18-year-old woman with a glowing smile and long, silky, blonde hair. Her sparkling sapphire blue eyes had captivated Ward at first glance. In fact, she attracted the attention of all the young men in town, but she only had eyes for Ward.

Jamie noticed them and walked over to say hello. "Hey Gene. Hey Billy." Jamie looked around, "Where's your big brother, Gene? Is he coming to the movie today?"

"No," Gene laughed, "But if he knew you were here, he'd be here. You going in, Jamie?"

"Sure, I'll join you," she answered, slipping her arm into Gene's. "Maybe it will make Ward jealous," she joked. All three laughed at the thought.

When the movie, "Citizen Kane," ended about 3:30 p.m., Billy and Gene stood up to leave. "He named his sled Rosebud?" Billy laughed. "I don't get it."

"I don't get it either, Billy," admitted Gene.

"Don't you have a name for your guitar, Billy?" Jamie asked.

"No, but if I did, I wouldn't name it after some silly flower. What about you, Gene? Do you have a name for your bat?" Billy asked as they walked outside into the blinding sunshine. Gene was about to answer when the sound of loud footsteps running up behind him interrupted his thoughts. It was Ward, and he was coming at them as fast as he could move.

"Gene! Gene!" he announced breathlessly, nearly doubled over and out of breath. "The Japs have bombed Pearl Harbor!"

It took a moment for Ward's words to sink in. "Why would they do that?" asked Billy. "And where's Pearl Harbor?"

"Who cares why? They did!" Ward screamed. "Pearl Harbor is in Hawaii, somewhere in the Pacific Ocean. Gene, we are at war! Or at least, we will be officially soon. I'm joining the Army tomorrow. You'll turn 17 in March and as soon as you do, I want you to join me as fast as you can. We'll teach these bums a lesson!"

"Hey, don't forget me!" Billy shouted. "I'm gonna join the Navy. If they bombed Pearl Harbor, the Navy's gonna be where the fighting is. What about you, Gene?"

Gene had no idea what to say. He shrugged. "I gotta go with Ward, Billy. I can't swim!"

"Wait a second," Jamie interrupted. "You can't go running off to war. You're all too young and none of you really know what is going on yet. There might not even be a war. Billy, you're a musician. What are you gonna do in the Navy?"

"There's time for music later, Jamie. Besides, I'm a pretty good boxer, too, and I ain't gonna take no crap from someone who would attack us, especially on a Sunday! I bet some of our men were in church or sleeping when the bombs fell!"

Realizing she wasn't getting anywhere with Billy, Jamie shifted her focus to Ward. "Your brother Gene isn't a soldier, he's a baseball player. He's waiting to hear where to report for spring training. He's been talking about it all winter! He can't go join the Army, Ward. My dad says everyone in Sesser is counting on him to play baseball in the Major Leagues."

"Come on, Jamie! That's a game. Gene, she's talking about a stupid game! This is war! The Japs have attacked us and we're gonna make 'em pay," Ward shouted.

"Don't you yell at me, Ward Moore!" Jamie shot back. "You're all riled up and you just better settle down!"

Gene stepped between them. "Jamie, there'll be time for baseball, music, and everything else. If our country needs us, we'll pitch in and do our part."

"I know Gene, but you didn't start this war—if there really is one— the Japs did. Besides, you could get hurt or even killed." Jamie lifted a hand to her mouth and stifled a sob.

By this time Ward was visibly agitated. Gene's nonchalant shrugs only made him more incensed. "Wait a minute, little brother. You're not listening to this crap, are you?"

"Of course I'll join, Ward. I mean if there is a war, we're needed, it can't take that long to beat the Japs."

"If you all wanna run off to war, go ahead," Jamie said. "But I don't understand why. Gene and Billy, you weren't mad at the Japs when we walked into the theater. I don't know who they're mad at, but I'm pretty certain it ain't me, you, or anyone else in Sesser!"

"And you Ward Moore! Can't you think of one very important reason why you shouldn't go away?"

"Jamie," Ward answered in a softer tone. "That's exactly why I have to go . . . why we all have to go. If they'll attack us at Pearl Harbor, they'll attack us anywhere . . . even here."

"Ward, the Japs aren't coming here. I bet they couldn't find Sesser with a map!" Jamie snickered.

"Go ahead and laugh, Jamie, but this is serious business." Ward shook his head in disbelief and angrily walked away.

"Why is he so upset, Gene?" she finally asked when Ward disappeared around the corner.

"Maybe he's mad because he wants to protect you," Gene replied.

Jamie smiled. "Does he ever talk about me?"

"Oh, not much . . . only all the time," chuckled Gene.

"Gene, I don't want anything bad to happen to him. I just don't know what I'd do if the Japs killed him."

"Don't worry, Jamie," Billy spoke up. "Nothing will happen to Ward. Those Japs don't stand a chance when all of us Sesser men get there!"

"Besides, once they see Ward's temper, they'll run back to Japan as fast as they can," Gene said with a smile. They all laughed together.

"I better get home," Billy said. "My mom's gonna be real upset when she gets this news. I need to be there."

"Sure, Billy. I'll talk to you soon."

The three were parting company when Billy turned back. "Hey, Gene. I bet this is a day we won't soon forget."

Gene nodded in agreement.

"Gene, Ward, Helen, Margaret, Beth, Erma, Hilda . . . everyone get in here! The president's wife, Mrs. Roosevelt, is going to speak!" Allie called out as she gathered her children into the living room of the old house on the corner of Matthew and Mulberry. Gene walked out of the kitchen eating a piece of his mom's homemade bread with last year's blueberry jam smeared all over one side. Pop tuned in their old RCA radio to KMOX in St. Louis.

"I want all you kids to hear this," John said. "This is the First Lady and she's going to talk to us about what happened today at Pearl Harbor." The radio crackled and snapped as a woman's voice began speaking:

> Good evening, ladies and gentlemen. I am speaking to you tonight, at a very serious moment in our history. The Cabinet is convening and our leaders in Congress are meeting with the President. The State Department and Army and Navy officials have been with the President all afternoon. In fact, the Japanese ambassador was talking to the President at the very time Japan's airships were bombing our citizens in Hawaii and. the Philippines, and sinking one of our transports loaded with lumber on its way to Hawaii.

Mrs. Roosevelt's calm and reassuring voice helped settle the nation's fear and anxiety. She expressed the necessity of being prepared and facing the challenges at hand. Most importantly, she spoke to the mothers and wives of those who would be soon going off to war.

"I have a boy at sea on a destroyer. For all I know, he may be on his way to the Pacific," continued the First Lady. She had more to say on the subject:

> "Two of my children live in coastal cities on the Pacific. Many of you, all over the country, have boys in the services who will now be called upon to go into action. You cannot escape anxiety. You cannot escape a clutch of fear at your heart, and yet, I hope the certainty of what we have to meet will make you rise above these fears. We must go about our daily business, more determined than ever, to do the ordinary things as well as we can.

The Moore family was captivated by the voice of the woman they had come to love. She was the wife of their leader, the president of the United States of America, but she, too, was a mother and would have a son in harm's way. She reached out to all mothers to let them know she understood what they were feeling. But she also talked directly to the sons and daughters of a nation that suddenly found itself at war.

Gene felt as though she was talking directly to him, and the First Lady's words inspired him to a new feeling of valor.

"To the young people of the nation, I must speak a final word tonight," concluded the voice on the radio. "You are going to have a great opportunity. There will be high moments in which your strength and your ability will be tested. I have faith in you. I feel as though I was standing upon a rock and that rock is my faith in you, my fellow citizens."

When Mrs. Roosevelt finished speaking, John reached over and turned off the radio. Ward turned to face his dad. "Pop, I'm joining up first thing in the morning. I have to, Pop. Our country needs me, and it'll need Gene, too. As soon as he turns 17. You heard what she said!"

Mom got up out of her chair, wrapped her arms around Ward, and began to cry. "No, you don't have to go so soon, Ward. Let's wait and see. It may be over in a few days or a few weeks. Let's not . . . jump right into this war . . . Yet." Allie pulled out a handkerchief and blew her nose.

"Mom, I have to go. You raised me this way. They've attacked us and we can't let 'em get away with it. I'm sorry, mom . . . I'll be okay, but I have to go. I wanna be that rock Mrs. Roosevelt can stand on, that all of you can stand on."

Pop put his hand on her shoulder. "Mom, Ward's right. I'm sure if he doesn't join, they'll just call him up anyway."

"Gene, you can join me in March, on your birthday," announced his older brother. "By then, I'll have the Army all figured out and you'll have it made."

"Don't be putting those ideas in your brother's head," Allie stuttered as she wiped her eyes with the apron she still had tied around her waist. "He's too young for the Army, and besides, it will all be over by then." The doubting look on the faces of her husband and eldest son only stiffened her resolve. "Besides, he's a ballplayer, not a soldier. He's waiting to find out where he's going to report for spring training."

"Wait a minute, mom!" Ward interrupted. "Where have you been all day? We've been attacked! Hundreds, maybe thousands of Americans were murdered today! I don't give a damn about all this baseball crap!" Ward stepped away from his mom and started to walk out.

"Russell Ward Moore! Don't you *ever* talk to your mother that way!" John thundered. It was one of few times they had heard him yell. The news of Pearl Harbor had gotten to John, too.

Ward stopped in mid-stride and turned around to face his father, a look of angry frustration plainly written across his face. "I'm sick and tired of hearing about Gene and baseball. That's all everyone in this stinking town cares about. There's a war going on and what are we talking about? Gene the baseball player! I walk down Main Street and people say, 'Hey, isn't that Gene's brother?' It's as if I don't even have a name anymore! Now, my own mother's telling me he's a ballplayer. Jamie Reid, today at the Opera House, telling us that Gene shouldn't join up. Well, what about me? I guess it's okay if I go risk my life for our country, but not Gene? He's too valuable? Not Gene, your little baby ballplayer?"

Ward was crossing a line and everyone knew it. Gene reached out in an effort to calm Ward down, but the move prompted the older brother to take a swing that hit Gene squarely on his nose, knocking him to the floor.

"Guess you weren't fast enough to duck that!" spat Ward as he stood over his sibling.

John jumped between the two boys, pushing Ward backward and away from the prostrate Gene. Allie knelt down beside her son.

"Enough Russell Ward Moore! Take a walk and simmer down," John demanded, grabbing Ward by both shoulders and forcing him toward the front door. Clenching and unclenching his sore hand, Ward stormed out of the house, slamming the door behind him for good measure.

"Gene, are you alright?" Allie asked her son as he got up from the floor. She was crying again.

"Yeah, I'm fine." A tiny trickle of blood dripped from his nose, but Gene felt more embarrassment than pain.

"Gene, come help me get a bucket of coal," commanded John. "The stove's getting low and it's going to be cold tonight." The two Moores walked to the barn together.

"Don't be angry at your brother, Gene. This war has him all worked up. It has us all worked up, I guess. He's not mad at you."

"I know, Pop. I'm not sore at him, either. But I didn't know my playing baseball bothered him so much."

"He'll be fine. You're brothers. No argument will ever change that. He's much more proud of you than he lets on."

Gene remained silent, rubbing his nose before checking to see if any teeth were loose.

"What are you going to do, Gene?"

"What should I do?"

"Ward's over eighteen. If he wants to join the Army, he can do as he pleases. I wouldn't stop him even if I wanted to, which I don't. I'm proud of your brother. You're only sixteen, though. You can't join until March, but even then only if I sign for you."

Gene nodded his understanding but remained silent, knowing his father was not yet done speaking.

"You don't have to make any decisions tonight, but let me tell you something. I know it doesn't seem like we have much. This little farm doesn't produce enough to take care of all our needs. I do odd jobs. We get by." He shrugged. "Lots of people have it a lot worse than we do. We aren't starving and things . . . well, they'll get better. Even though we struggle, we're free. This country has been good to us, and we have to do what we can to protect what's ours. I did. I served in Europe before you were born." That news surprised Gene, who suddenly looked upon his father in a different light.

"I've seen things I've never been able to talk about," the elder Moore continued. "But we did what we had to do. Because of that war, we're still free." He paused briefly, narrowing his eyes as Gene imagined him reliving some of the horrors of war.

"The thought of my sons going off to war, well, it makes me plain sick. I thought I did it so you wouldn't have to. They told us that the last war would end all wars." John was growing more angry as he spoke, his voice getting louder with each word. He caught himself, as he always did, took a breath, and began again. "I guess what I'm saying . . ."

"I know what you're saying, Pop," interrupted Gene. "You can count on me. Ward can count on me. I'll do my part. I've never said otherwise. Jamie, mom, everyone's trying to speak for me. It's everyone else who keeps talking like I should play ball instead of defending my country. If it's not over by March 19, I intend to sign up. I'll do my part."

John nodded in reply and began filling his bucket with coal.

President Roosevelt addressed a joint session of Congress the next day. The entire nation listened.

"Yesterday, December 7, 1941, a date which will live in infamy, the United States of America was suddenly and deliberately attacked by naval and air forces of the Empire of Japan."

For most Americans it was the first time they ever heard the word infamy, but they didn't need a dictionary to understand its meaning. America had been attacked, and the Japanese had awakened a sleeping giant.

True to his word, Russell Ward Moore enlisted in the United States Army the morning of December 8, 1941. He shipped out for basic training by rail from Carbondale, Illinois, on the morning of December 12. Ward kissed Jamie goodbye, but didn't say much to Gene before he left. His abrupt departure hurt Gene even though he was used to not getting much attention from his older brother. Gene loved Ward, and was proud of his brother's patriotic stance. As he watched Ward's train pull away from the station, Gene confirmed again in his own mind that he would join him as soon as he turned 17.

World War II touched everyone and every institution, including baseball. Gene received a letter from Frank Boudreau and the Dodgers on the afternoon of December 21. The day Gene turned 18, explained the letter, he'd be drafted into the military. In an effort to continue his baseball career, the Dodgers made arrangements for Gene to join the Navy and play ball with a Navy exhibition team. Gene would have to go into the service one year early, at age 17. The news was not overly disappointing. The immediate future of professional baseball was in doubt, anyway.

Frank's letter instructed him to take the accompanying documents to the Navy recruiter and they would make all the arrangements. Gene did as instructed and shipped off to the Great Lakes Naval Air Station near Chicago, one day after he turned 17.

Chapter 7

In the Navy

From the window of the northbound Illinois Central train, Chicago looked like something out of a motion picture. To Gene, the city appeared big, bustling, and most of all, intimidating.

From the time he left Carbondale, Gene's train carried him on a tour of one small town after another—Effingham, Rantoul, Ashkum, Bradley, Manteno, and Monee. Chicago arose from the landscape like some miraculous growth from the flat earth. As the train drew closer, Chicago appeared to Gene like The Emerald City from "The Wizard of Oz," shining gloriously on the horizon. Gene had spent time in St. Louis playing with the Granary team. The city by the Mississippi River was bigger than any he had ever imagined could be. Chicago dwarfed St. Louis in every way.

Gene and the other new recruits and passengers disembarked at Union Station. The catcher from Sesser marveled at the lively atmosphere and stunning architecture. Union Station looked like it had been lifted from a history book. The beautiful marble interior, complete with Greek statues looking down from Mt. Olympus, was unlike anything he had ever seen.

Tens of hundreds of people were there, each one going about his or her business. Some were dressed in business suits, though most were in uniform. Entire families were gathered together to send a loved one off to

Gene Moore's basic training photograph,
taken at the Great Lakes Naval Air Station, early 1942.

war. Everyone was in a hurry. The looks, the smells, and the sounds of the big city train station were simultaneously exciting and threatening.

Gene stepped out onto Madison Street, unable to reconcile the contrast in sights and sounds between Sesser and Chicago. In Sesser, sounds flowed through the trees, fields, and rolling hills. In Chicago, the noise bounced back and forth from building to building. The sounds echoing in front of Union Station reminded Gene of being in a gymnasium in rural Illinois. He was outside, and yet he felt closed in.

The recruits milled about in front of the station for a few minutes before boarding a bus that would carry them to Navy Pier. The ride took less than fifteen minutes. The half-mile long pier stretched from Chicago's lakeshore into Lake Michigan. Gene walked out onto the pier and marveled at the size of the second largest of the five Great Lakes. "This is a lake?" Gene uttered to no one in particular. As far as the eye could see was water. Lakes were small, and you could see across to the other side. This one looked too much like what he imagined an ocean would be. Besides the old Keller Mine Pond, the Mississippi River was the largest body of water he had ever seen.

Gene was processed into the Navy with several hundred other recruits. He was issued a seabag, two sets of uniforms, and a blanket. His first meal in the Navy followed, a hearty helping of chipped beef in milk and flour gravy, served on toast. As he quickly learned, the meal was referred to by Navy vets as SOS.

"SOS?" he repeated to a guy a couple years older sitting next to him. "What does that mean?"

"It means 'shit on a shingle.' You never heard that before?"

Gene laughed and shook his head. "Nope. Never heard that one." That was one menu item he wasn't going to mention back home, either, because he knew if his mom heard him say it, she would wash his mouth out with Ivory soap—even if he was a grown man discharged from the Navy with a medal. The others around him complained about the food, but Gene thought it was rather good. If nothing else, it was hot and filling.

After dinner, Gene sat on his cot in a cavernous room with hundreds of other young men. He was surrounded by a sea of strangers. It was the first time he began to feel homesick. Playing ball in St. Louis felt nothing like this because he knew he was only a little more than an hour away from Sesser. If he didn't like it, he could quit and hitchhike home. Now he was in Chicago, and had been told in no uncertain terms when he was sworn in that quitting the Navy would be desertion, and deserters were shot.

Bored and homesick, Gene stretched out on his cot and decided to get some sleep. Five short minutes later, just as he was beginning to drift off, he heard a loud voice shouting his name.

"Sailor Warren Eugene Moore! Identify yourself!"

Gene leaped to his feet. "Here!"

A tall officer in dress uniform was moving in his direction. "You Moore?" he inquired.

"Yes. I'm Moore. They call me Gene—."

"You mean 'yes sir,' don't you, sailor? You're addressing an ensign in the United States Navy!" The officer glared at the new recruit, his face just six inches from Gene's nose.

Gene swallowed and held his temper. "Yes, I'm sorry," he stammered, not knowing the exact protocol for addressing an ensign. "Sir, I mean, yes sir."

The ensign glared at him for a few more seconds before bursting into laughter and taking a step backward. "Stop it, I'm just kidding," he chuckled, reaching out to shake Gene's hand. "I'm Buck Nelson, your new baseball coach, but in front of the real sailors, you have to call me 'sir.' The rest of the time, call me coach or just plain Buck."

Gene let out a long sigh and shook his new coach's hand. "Hi Buck, it's good to—."

"You will address me as sir!" Buck shot back, adding under his breath, "when others are around."

Gene offered a vigorous nod of understanding. "Sir . . . yes sir!"

"That's better." Buck looked around and moved closer to Gene, whispering, "You know, I'm not really sure about that. To tell you the truth, today is my first day in the Navy, too, but I think it's 'Aye, aye, sir,' but don't quote me, though." Buck cracked a grin and backed up a second time. "Let's take a walk, and talk a bit."

Buck Nelson was nothing like Gene. He was twenty-nine years old and a graduate of Columbia, where he attended school on a baseball scholarship. Standing tall in his perfectly pressed dress blue Navy uniform, there was something quite proper about Buck. He looked like he just stepped out of a Navy recruiting poster—an All-American boy. He had short blond hair, penetrating green eyes, and the whitest and straightest teeth Gene had ever seen. He pitched well in college and signed with the Dodgers after graduation. He threw hard, too hard, as it turned out. Buck blew out his arm during his first year in the minors. He never pitched again.

Buck's education and knowledge of the game motivated the Dodgers to keep him on as a pitching coach. He earned quite a reputation in the minors developing good young pitchers. When war broke out and it was apparent baseball was in trouble, the Dodgers put Buck in the Navy. His Columbia degree made him eligible to become an officer, which in turned allowed him to coach the Dodgers' new kids. Buck and Gene stepped out of the building and onto the pier.

"Sure is a lotta water," Gene said, staring east across the lake.

"Yes, it is," Buck answered. "A testament to the power of nature. Did you know this lake was carved by a glacier?" Buck paused, but Gene didn't respond. "So Gene, I am told you are quite the catcher."

The Sesser boy shrugged. "I love to catch, and I love the game. It's my life." Buck laughed. "What's so funny?" asked Gene.

"That's exactly what Frank Boudreau said you would say."

"You know Frank?" Gene asked, excited at the mention of Frank's name. It was another link to his home on Mulberry Street.

"Everyone knows Frank in the Dodgers organization. He signed me from Columbia University, and has a reputation for being the very best at spotting talent. I shouldn't tell you this," continued the ensign, "but Frank says you are the best young catcher he has ever seen. But, you need to know something. The guys you will be playing with over the next few months are also the best from wherever they come from. You'll have to play hard to compete, Gene. Harder than you ever imagined. If you think playing with the Sesser Egyptians was competition, you haven't seen anything yet. Are you up to the challenge?"

Gene stuck out his chin. "I'll do my best. I think I can hold my own."

Buck looked him over and nodded. "Frank seems to think so, too. Don't be too modest, and don't let Frank down. He hasn't stopped talking about you, so give it your best. There will be two other catchers you will meet in a few days." He stopped and watched Gene's face. The boy from Sesser didn't seem to get it. "No one is guaranteed a spot on the team, Gene," Buck added. "You will have to earn it."

"This team will have three catchers?"

Buck held his gaze. "No, Gene. It will have just two."

Gene frowned. "What happens to the third guy?"

"He'll be cut from the team, and will serve at the pleasure of Uncle Sam in the United States Navy."

Buck watched Gene nod slowly as the news sunk in. He reached out and grabbed the catcher's hand, gripping it tightly. "Remember, in front of the regular Navy guys, watch the Buck stuff. Call me sir. Got it?"

"Aye, aye, sir!" Gene responded with a big smile.

Buck laughed, gave Gene a little push, and said, "Go to bed. You're going to need your rest." He turned and began walking down the pier, but stopped after a few steps. "Hey, Gene? Have you ever caught a forkball?"

"No, but I know how the ball acts. It comes in hard and fast, then drops like a rock over the plate. Do we have someone who can throw it?" he asked.

"Oh, yeah. Ray Laws. He says when he's hot, catchers have as much trouble with his pitching as the batters do. Says he has never known a catcher who could catch him."

"That sounds like a challenge," Gene responded with a smirk. "He's never met me!"

"You'll get your chance. We'll see if you can catch him in a few days. The other catchers say they can do it, too. Now, go get some sleep." Buck turned and began walking away again. This time he did not stop.

Lost in his thoughts, Gene looked over the vast lake. For the first time in his life he was faced with the prospect of not being the best. Everywhere, even in St. Louis, Gene had been the best overall player on the field, and always a starter. Now the odds were one in three he would not make the team. It was a strange and unsettling feeling.

"I can catch this Laws guy," Gene mumbled to himself. "I can catch anyone." He took one last look across the water. "A glacier?" he thought. "What's a glacier?"

The next morning, Gene and the other recruits were moved to Great Lakes Naval Air Station, just outside of Chicago. They were processed there and reported for swim testing on the first day of basic training.

On the second day of basic, Gene was separated from the rest, taken to a barracks apart from the others, and met his teammates for the first time—his shipmates of the United States Navy Touring Baseball Team.

Chapter 8

Team Navy!

Gene walked out of the barracks and pulled his collar around his neck. It was cold in Chicago. The Great Lakes Naval Air Station was bigger than the entire town of Sesser. There were more people within a mile or two of where he stood than there were in all of Franklin County.

"Moore! Gene Moore! Over here!" Gene saw Buck waving him over from across the road.

"Hey, Buck. What are we doing today?" Gene asked.

"We're going to see what our pitchers have, and see how our catchers catch. Are you ready to play ball?"

Gene smiled. "I was born to play ball. It's the last thing I think about before I fall asleep. It's the first thing I think about when I wake up. So, yes," he laughed, "I'm ready to play ball and have been dying to get a mitt on again."

"Well, let's grab a pitcher, and see how you catch." Buck searched the group with his eyes until he found who he was looking for. "Hey, Wigant! Grab your glove and get over here."

Bill Wigant nodded an acknowledgment and hustled over to Buck. Wigant was a short, stocky kid from Waterloo, Iowa. He was in high school when the war broke out and was being courted by the Dodgers. Like Gene, he was offered a spot on the Navy team and enlisted right away.

"Bill Wigant, this is Gene Moore." Bill and Gene shook hands. "You all warmed up?" asked Buck.

"Yeah, I'm ready."

"Good. Let's play ball." Buck ordered Bill out to the makeshift mound. "Let's see what you can do." With that, he turned and walked away to begin matching other pitchers with the two remaining catchers. Gene squatted behind the plate and Wigant planted a hard fastball into his mitt. Over and over. He also had a curve that Gene really had to keep an eye on.

In between pitches Gene noticed Buck standing behind him and off to one side, watching the duo perform. He had been so focused on Wigant he failed to take note of the coach's arrival. "Bill, hold it," ordered Buck. "I'm going to switch catchers with you."

Gene stood up, looked at Buck, and asked, "Am I doing something wrong?"

"Nope. Just switching catchers," answered Buck, who motioned for another player to join them. "Gene, this is Greg Pacer. Greg is a catcher from here in Chicago." Greg and Gene exchanged greetings and a handshake. Buck motioned for Gene to walk to where another player was standing. "Ray Laws, this is Gene Moore. Ray is from New Jersey." Ray and Gene shook hands.

"Ray, Gene feels confident he can catch your forkball."

Ray gave a half-laugh before answering, "I hope someone can. He sure had trouble," tilting his head toward Greg, who was now catching for Wigant.

"If you can throw it, I can catch it," Gene said with a smile.

"Think so, huh?" Ray asked in a skeptical voice.

"If I can't catch it, I'll stop it. I don't let balls get past me. As long as I keep the ball in front of me and within reach, no one will advance on me."

"You ever catch a forkball before?" Ray asked.

"No," Gene responded. "I've never even seen one. But I know what it does."

Ray looked over at Buck and shook his head. "Hell, I can tell my baby sister what it does, but it doesn't mean she can catch it. Buck, isn't there a real catcher in the entire Navy?"

Gene was taken aback by Ray's attitude. "I can catch you Ray, just pitch me a few and let's see," Gene shot back.

"I'm through trying out catchers," Ray said, turning his head and spitting to the side.

Gene had heard enough. He glanced at Buck and stepped closer to Ray, who turned back to look deeply into his dark eyes. "Are you as good at throwing that thing as you are at trying to make people feel incompetent?"

No one had ever talked to Ray Laws that way before, something that was obvious from the look that crossed his face. "Yeah, I am that good at throwing it." Neither player blinked.

Gene held the pitcher's steely gaze. "Then get your cocky-ass sixty feet, six inches away from me, and let's see if you are half as good at baseball as you are at talking. I'm hoping the further you get away, the more I'll like you."

"Hey, Buck—I don't need this crap," Ray replied.

Buck was about to jump in when Gene stuck out his arm and cut him off. "This is between me and Ray."

"Fair enough," answered the coach.

Gene lowered his arm but had never taken his eyes off Ray's face. "Sorry, pal, but you do need this crap. You can dish it out. Let's see how good you are."

Ray's eyes narrowed as he tried to size up this new kid from Southern Illinois. Clearly he had underestimated his fortitude. The kid continued speaking before he could formulate a clever comeback. Buck lifted his hand to cover the grin spreading across his face.

"Here's how I see it, Ray. If you want to pitch, you have to have someone catch. You tell me no one can catch you? Well, maybe you end up in a boat with Japs shooting at you if no one can catch you—have you ever thought of that? While you're target practice for Tojo, I'll be catching for someone else. I think it's really that simple. I can catch your pitch, Ray. If you want to throw it, well, that's your choice. If not, I'll find a pitcher who can do something besides whine."

Ray smiled, an ice cold sneer that Gene found slightly unnerving. "Alright, hot shot. Let's see if you can catch what I can bring."

"You guys going to talk or play ball?" Buck finally asked.

"I'm already warmed up, Buck. I'm ready if he is," shot back Ray.

"Go to the mound, then, and let's see this magic pitch of yours," Gene laughed.

Ray swaggered his way to the mound, where he began rearranging some of the dirt with the toe of his right shoe. Buck winked at Gene,

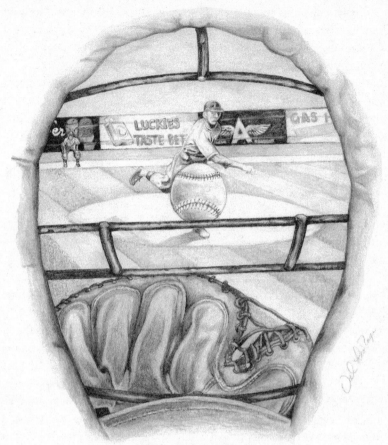

Catching the Forkball

folded his arms, and waited for the fireworks to begin. Frank was right, he thought. This kid has a lot of heart.

Once he was settled in, Ray looked at Gene, wound up, and let it fly. The ball didn't have a lot of spin and came in fast—really fast—right down the middle. As the ball crossed the plate, it dropped as if something had hit it. The ball hit the dirt, but Gene scooped it up without missing a beat. He held the baseball up and looked at it as if he had never seen one before. "Well, I've never seen a ball do that! Nice pitch."

Ray caught the throw back to him and offered a grudging smile. "Nice catch, too. Let's see if that was beginner's luck."

It wasn't. Ray threw another dozen pitches, and Gene, true to his word, caught, scooped up, or blocked every one. By this time the two players were chattering back and forth like old friends who had been playing together since grammar school. Buck and several other players and coaches stood off to one side, watching the chemistry develop between Gene Moore and Ray Laws.

"I think I like what I see," Buck said to another coach standing next to him. "Ray can make that ball dance, and Gene is handling it, no problem. I think this is going to be fun."

Over the next few weeks, the team worked on physical training and practice games, while Buck assessed their talent and coached them on basic skills. In the evening, they received training in military protocol and procedures. After all, they were in the Navy.

The pitchers and catchers were separated from the rest of the team for a few days. It was apparent from the beginning that Gene was different. He was fundamentally sound and as good, if not better technically, than the other two catchers. But it was his understanding of the fundamentals of pitching and of pitchers as people that separated him from the rest of the pack.

Gene was a player's player. He knew when to be funny, and he knew when to be serious. The pitchers gravitated to him. This team of up-and-coming raw talent was beginning to bond, and Gene was rapidly becoming their leader, both on and off the field.

The Navy team continued to progress. Rarely was any mention of war discussed. While the country mobilized its vast resources to fight a global conflict, producing equipment and supplies, training men to fight and women to work on the home front, Gene, Ray, and the rest of the team played baseball. They were lost in their love for the game and obsession to play well. Most of the time they had to remind themselves they were in the Navy—and their country was fighting a world war.

Chapter 9

North Africa

Gene's life experiences were expanding faster than he ever dreamed possible. In the space of two years he had gone from small town catcher to the Brooklyn Dodgers organization, and played ball with some of the best young prospects in the country. Now he was in the Navy in North Africa—a far cry from a one-hour hitchhiking trip home from St. Louis to Sesser. He knew nothing of Africa except there were lions and elephants there—or at least he thought so. It had been several weeks since he set foot on the continent, and he still had not seen a single lion or elephant. There was, however, an enormous amount of military activity, plenty of sand, hordes of flies, and the occasional camel.

The young Dodgers' prospect landed in Africa in November 1942 as part of Operation Torch, a massive three-prong naval invasion designed to open a second front against Nazi Germany. By the summer of 1942, Germany seemed unstoppable. Most of Europe had been overrun, German submarines (U-boats) were terrorizing the high seas, and England had barely survived a massive air assault. In June of 1941, Adolf Hitler launched a massive invasion of the Soviet Union nicknamed Operation Barbarossa. The Germans drove within sight of Moscow, where the early onset of winter and a heroic defensive stand by the Red Army stopped the advance, saved the capital city, and kept Russia in the war.

Another powerful German-Italian army under Field Marshal Erwin Rommel (the "Desert Fox") operated in North Africa. One of Germany's finest field commanders, Rommel and his Afrika Corps drove British forces hundreds of miles east across the desert into Egypt. Rommel intended not only to defeat the enemy there, but to capture the precious oil fields that lay beyond. In an effort to dilute Nazi power and reverse the course of the war, the Allies decided to land in North Africa, defeat Rommel, and regain control of the Mediterranean Sea. General Dwight D. Eisenhower was appointed Allied commander of Operation Torch— one of the largest amphibious operations in world history.

More than 100,000 French (Vichy) troops were stationed in Algeria, Morocco, and Tunisia. It was widely believed that these troops, which had cast their lot with Hitler's Germany, would not put up much, if any, fight against the Allies. The Allied landings began on November 8 in Casablanca, Oran, and Algiers. To the surprise of many, the French troops in Oran offered more than token resistance, but control of the landing areas was quickly gained and the beachheads firmly established.

The United States landed 134,000 men on the beaches of North Africa, together with tons of equipment, trucks, tanks, and gasoline—as well as baseballs, gloves, caps, and bats.

The trip from the States to North Africa was anything but exciting. Gene had never seen the ocean before, but once he climbed aboard the transport ship it was all he saw for two weeks. Endless tracks of empty sea stretched from horizon to horizon, with nothing in between except other Allied ships cutting through the same blue-green swells. Like most of the men on board, it took Gene several days to find his "sea legs" and settle his stomach. The heaving sea and constant motion made it impossible to keep food or drink down for long. The hours spent hanging over the railing retching into the sea seemed to last forever. Once adapted to the endless ups and downs of a sea voyage, Gene and his teammates found walkways long enough to play catch, which broke the monotony and lifted their spirits. But there was no hitting and of course, no games.

Before arriving in North Africa, the convoy made a stop in the Azores, a Portuguese island chain 1,000 miles west of Africa, to drop off supplies and the baseball team. Gene and his teammates stayed there for about a month, practicing and preparing to play ball. For the rest of his

If you can't take PART in SPORTS, *BE ONE*

Gene Moore (back row, middle) with the United States Navy North African Exhibition Baseball Team in the Azores Islands of Portugal, 1942. The team practiced here before moving on to Africa. Twenty years after the war, a local recalled that he was digging around one of the quonset huts in the background when he discovered a cache of American beer someone had hidden during the war.

life he remembered how good it felt to feel solid ground under his feet and stretch his legs as he ran the bases. The team was picked up by another convoy and landed in North Africa in Casablanca, Morocco, as part of the Western arm of the naval task force. The beachhead was already well established by the time Gene arrived. It was now time for he and his teammates to complete their mission: playing ball for the troops.

Gene discovered that sand does strange things to a baseball. There were no short hops in the infield. Once the ball hit the ground, it stopped. Dead. Playing in the sand changed the entire nature of the game. But Americans loved baseball enough that entire crews of soldiers were assigned the task of doing whatever was necessary to construct ball diamonds at area military encampments. There was a war raging, and the United States had mobilized like never before in its history. But live without baseball? Not a chance. Where there were Americans, there was baseball. War or not, the game lived on—even in North Africa.

The United States Navy's Exhibition Baseball Team needed about three weeks before it was ready to play its first game. The fields were playable, the players were used to the sand, and they were back in shape after their debilitating sea journey. Buck assembled the team for a status report and addressed them.

"Okay, men," he began. "The opposition—the US Army Exhibition Team—should arrive tonight." The name of the "opposition" brought forth a stream of good-natured boos and hissing. Buck twisted a smile on his tanned face and raised his hands to calm the crowd. "Okay, okay. We really don't know how many times we'll be playing the same Army team. I don't know much about these guys, but we'll get to know them well, I'm sure."

"Are they any good?" Ray Laws asked.

"I'm sure they are," answered the coach. "They're a team assembled just as we are. These are ballplayers who have tried out and made it into Major League organizations, or were placed by a professional club on the team. So, yes, I'm sure they're good."

"Where are we going to play, Buck? Always here or will we be moving around?" asked Gene.

Buck shook his head. "I don't know. They want us close enough to the front to be able to bring troops out for a day of baseball, and return them the same day. But we have to be far enough away not to put the troops or ourselves in the line of fire. War is new to me too. The front, I hear, is pretty fluid and so shifting up and back. I guess our field will, too. We'll travel with the portable backstop we built, but we must remain flexible and cooperative. Above all, remember we are the sideshow, gentlemen. We are not—I repeat, *not*–the main event. The war is why we're here, not baseball."

"If they are the Army team, and we are entertaining army troops . . . then does that mean we are always the visiting team?" Tim Milner asked.

"Good question. It would seem so, but no." He laughed as he reached down and lifted a wooden sign. He turned it around so everyone could read what was painted on the other side: "Ebbets Field." The players cheered when they read the words. "We will alternate everyday. The Army team is made up mostly of Yankee prospects, so they have a sign reading "Yankee Stadium." Buck waited for the booing to subside. "Each day we will alternate by hanging our signs on the back stop. That will identify which team is home."

Ron Callais, a 17-year-old center fielder from Houma, Louisiana, asked, "Ah we en ahne donger here, Buck?" Ron's Cajun-Southern accent was so thick it was hard for most of the team to understand him when he spoke.

"I'm sorry, Ron . . . can you repeat the question?"

"Are we in any danger here?" Ron said slowly and more deliberately. It was still difficult to understand.

"Well, yeah, I guess so. There is a war on. I have no idea how great our risk is, but sure. We're close to an enemy who is hell-bent on winning, commanded by one of the best the Krauts have," Buck replied.

Buck was calling on another player when a siren sounded. It started low and grew progressively louder and higher in pitch. He looked out the door and saw everyone outside running. A young soldier ducked his head into the barracks and yelled, "Air Raid! Air Raid! Follow me!"

"I guess that answers your question!" Buck shouted to Ron as the men headed for the door.

The entire team ran through the door and followed the nameless soldier down a sandy path to a cave dug into the sand. Sandbags piled ten high surrounded the doorway and were stacked on top of the makeshift bunker. They were squeezing their way into the hole in the ground when the seriousness of what was happening began to set in.

The most visibly disturbed was Callais, who was sitting on Gene's left. His hands were shaking almost as bad as his voice when he suddenly asked to no one in particular, "Are we gonna be okay?" Gene sensed the fear building, especially since they were all crammed underground waiting to see what would happen next. A distant memory flooded into his mind from a time when he was a small child. His father had herded the family into the cellar when it was reported that a tornado was spotted outside Sesser heading for the town. His father's calm voice had kept the family distracted and thinking about something else, and the danger passed them by.

"Hey, everyone! I have a question," announced Gene. "Nine batters came to bat in the first half of an inning, and not a man scored." Gene paused for a few seconds, taking in the looks of confusion on his teammates' faces. "How's that possible?"

Silence greeted his question. Buck, who was seated across from Gene, squinted and leaned forward a few inches, as if he had not heard his star catcher correctly. "What in the hell are you talking about, Gene? We are being attacked by the Luftwaffe!"

"I know, Buck, but this question is specifically for Ron." Gene repeated the question. "Think about it. Do you know the answer?"

"Well, lemme think about it." Ron rubbed his forehead with nervous fingers as he tried to focus his mind on Gene's riddle. "If the first three batters get on base. Then the next batter gets a base hit, but the man on third is thrown out at home . . . no . . . wait, that's not it."

Ray jumped in. "I got it. The bases are loaded, and the batter gets a hit, but the man scoring is thrown out at the plate. And that happens three times."

"That would only be six batters," someone else chimed in.

The debate—sometimes lively, and always interesting—continued for ten minutes as everyone tried to figure out how nine batters can come to the plate in the first half of one inning, and yet not score a single run. Gene's trick worked exactly as he hoped it would. Everyone on the team forgot they were crammed into a hole in the ground in a desert in North Africa, waiting for the German Luftwaffe to drop a bomb or two on their heads and bury them alive.

The riddle remained unsolved when the eerie siren sounded again. Everyone stopped talking. A soldier stuck his head into the bomb shelter and announced, "All clear!"

"You heard the man," Buck said with a big smile. "Let's get out of this rat hole!"

As the team emptied out into the bright sunshine of another clear desert day, Buck put his hand on Gene's shoulder. "Good job, Gene. But next time, do me a favor and pick a riddle that can be solved. That one is impossible."

Gene smiled slyly and replied, "No, it's very possible, Buck. Don't let that Columbia education of yours get in the way of logic."

Buck stopped walking and shot Gene a perplexed look. "Okay, professor, tell me how it's possible."

Gene nodded and began speaking, very slowly and deliberately. "Nine batters came to bat in the first half of the inning, but not a man scored." Gene smiled again, broadly this time. He was as amused as Buck was mystified.

"That's impossible!" he protested.

The catcher erupted in laughter. "It was a girl's softball game, Buck!" Gene turned and walked away, laughing hysterically as if he had just told the funniest joke on earth.

Buck tilted his head and stood quiet for a moment until he finally figured it out. When he realized the joke, he could not help laughing himself. Gene Moore, he thought, had the presence of mind and natural instincts to know exactly what to do to relax his team while in danger—even though he was also experiencing an air raid for the first time. "Impressive," Buck said aloud. "Very impressive."

By the time Buck arrived in the barracks Gene had already shared the answer to the riddle with most of his teammates, who had gathered around demanding he let them in on the secret. Some were laughing, some were shaking their heads, and others were protesting, claiming they had been misled. By this time everyone had forgotten about the air raid—except Ron Callais.

Buck reassembled the team and finished delivering the information about upcoming games when a lone hand shot up into the air. It was Ron's. "When we're playing ball," he began, "will there be anyone shooting at us?"

Some of his teammates chuckled. For a few moments Buck looked unsure how to answer. He finally looked out over the team and replied, "Hey, everyone, this isn't funny. I guess it's possible, Ron, yes. Again, I don't want to keep reminding you that there's a war going on. Let's not forget that the war is the reason we're here. But, I kind of doubt anyone will be shooting directly at us. We are not playing at the front, only near the front. These base camps are well guarded by trained soldiers. We'll play ball—that's our job. They'll protect us and the base—that's their job."

Buck nodded with satisfaction at his own answer. "Men, let's hit the field."

Chapter 10

Casablanca

"Gather round," Buck ordered as the team assembled in the tent next to the makeshift field just outside of Casablanca. "The US Army's North Africa Exhibition Baseball Team arrived last night, and today begins what I hope will be a long series of games all over North Africa, and beyond. I think we are ready, don't you?" Buck asked as he looked around at each of his players in turn. Everyone was nodding in agreement.

"How many men are we playing for today?" Ray asked.

"Not many," Buck replied, "but it doesn't matter. This is our first of many games, and I can't think of a better way to begin than with a win. Ray is pitching today, so let's show them how we play ball in the Navy." Buck assumed his best game face and then spat out one of his favorite lines: "Let's hit the field!"

The team trotted out of the tent about fifty yards to the makeshift diamond, where Buck was met by the coach of the Army team, Lieutenant Darren Berline. Darren was a graduate of the University of Connecticut. Like Buck, he had played ball in college on a scholarship and spent a short time in the minors. Before the war broke out, he was planning to go back for his second year as a class C minor league coach with the New York Yankees, but the opportunity to lead an Army team appealed to Darren, and he jumped at the chance.

"Buck, it's good to meet you. I guess we'll be spending quite a bit of time together."

Buck and Darren exchanged pleasantries and small talk. "How's your team handling the danger?" Darren asked.

"Danger?" Buck asked. "What danger?"

"You didn't hear? Last night, they were transporting us here as part of a supply convoy. We came under attack about twenty miles out. We were strafed from the air by German fighter planes. Unfortunately, several of our men were killed, but no one from the team was hurt." Darren was still shaken by the event. "I knew there was a war on," he continued. "I just didn't expect to be this close to the shooting."

"Holy cow. I had no idea," Buck replied. "We had an air alert yesterday, but nothing happened. I didn't even hear a plane."

"I guess we just have to keep our eyes open and trust that God and the real soldiers will keep the Nazis away. What else can we do? Do any of your men have the shakes, Buck?"

"Not really. Well, one does for sure. My center fielder is only 17, and has never been out of Louisiana. He seems a bit rattled by all this, but none of us has come under fire like you. Can your guys play today?"

"What choice do we have, Buck? That's why they sent us over here, right? We have to do our part."

"Okay, then let's try playing ball," answered Buck, reaching out to shake Darren's hand.

"Yeah, let's play ball. As long as we're moving, we're a harder target to hit!" Buck and Darren wished one another good luck without meaning it and walked to their respective benches.

Gene was still warming up Ray when Buck called them over. "How's the arm, Ray?" he asked.

"Feels really good," answered the pitcher. "But have you seen that mound? It's awful! It's too high, and it's a few inches off on the right side."

"We are in the middle of a world war and are playing baseball," Buck replied. "Somehow we will deal with a screwed up mound. I think we're lucky to have a mound to pitch from." Buck looked at Gene. "You ready?"

"I'm always ready."

"Then let's get moving. We're the visitors, so we're up first."

Ron Callais was the lead-off batter. He walked a few feet over from the bench, picked up his bat, took a couple of swings, looked back at Buck for the sign, and headed for the plate. As he stepped into the batter's box, he turned to the Army catcher. "Think we're in any danger here?"

The catcher took the time to lift his mask before answering. "We were attacked last night coming in," he replied. "So, yeah, I'd call that danger."

"What? You were attacked? By Germans? They shot at you?"

"What do you think?" the catcher answered sarcastically. "Where do you think we are? This ain't Wrigley Field—or maybe you haven't noticed."

Ron stepped out of the box.

"Time!" The umpire yelled, looking over at the Navy bench.

Buck came running over. "What's the problem, Ron?" he asked, looking back and forth from Ron to the ump.

"Holy Moly, coach! These guys were attacked last night! I can't stay here! They have to move us away from the fighting! I didn't sign up for this!" Ron was pacing back and forth around the box, waving his bat in the air.

"Ron!" Buck shot out forcefully. "Stop pacing and look at me."

"Sorry, coach," the umpire interjected. "We need a batter in here. The troops are getting restless and we're the entertainment. Can we please play some baseball?"

"Sure, ump. Sorry." Buck turned to the bench. "Tim Milner! You're up! Grab a bat, and get over here." Milner, a lanky kid from Fort Lauderdale, Florida, jumped up, grabbed his bat, and headed for the plate. Buck turned to Ron, who now had tears in his eyes. The kid was obviously unsuited to play ball. "Ron, it's no problem. Go grab a seat and calm down. We'll get you back in the next game." Buck turned to the umpire. "Sorry again ump. We're ready."

If Buck thought sending Ron back to the bench would solve the problem, he was wrong. Ron was now more animated than ever, and had already told the guys about the Army team being attacked. Everyone was gathered around the Louisianan listening to his every word.

"Hey, hey . . . hey!" Buck shot out when he realized what was going on. "Ron, you sit your butt down and shut your mouth. That's an order. The rest of you, we have a game to play!"

Ray looked over at Buck. "Is it true? Were they attacked last night?"

"Damn it, Ray, this is a war! What did you expect happens during a war?"

"If the Army thinks that was bad, wait until they see what we do to them," Gene announced. "They'll rather face the Luftwaffe than us after today!" Everyone relaxed a bit and several chuckled as they moved back to take their seats.

"We're gonna give them a shelling today to put the Germans to shame!" yelled out another player.

A loud crack of the bat interrupted the boasting. Everyone instinctively turned to watch the ball hit sharply to leftfield. As one, the team leapt to its feet and screamed, encouraging Milner as he rounded first base and headed hard toward second. The left-fielder scooped the ball on one hop and fired it to second, but Tim slid beneath the tag for a double.

Tim Milner fired the opening salvo of the first baseball exhibition game of the war. Although all the players on both teams were nervous, the idea of German planes flying overhead was quickly forgotten by the natural rush they all experienced playing the game they loved more than anything in the entire world. By the end of the first inning, everyone had forgotten where they were.

Everyone but Ron.

Chapter 11

War Games

The American army had a much tougher time in North Africa than many expected it might. On November 4, four days before the Operation Torch landings began, the British under General Bernard Montgomery, soundly defeated Field Marshal Rommel and his vaunted *Afrika Korps* at El Alamein, 65 miles west of Alexandria, Egypt. The Germans were on the run across North Africa, moving west as quickly as possible. The news deceived the overly-optimistic green American troops into thinking Rommel and his men no longer posed a serious threat.

As the Americans soon discovered, Rommel fully intended to keep fighting. He was consolidating his command and shortening his supply line, which had been grossly overextended by his lightening westward drive. The British continued pursuing the Germans across North Africa and captured Tripoli before January 1943 expired. The Americans, however, now in force on Rommel's western flank, moved slowly, "violating every recognized principle of war," General Eisenhower later wrote.

The Desert Fox planned his inaugural welcome for the Americans carefully and delivered it through the Faïd Pass on February 14, driving the Americans rearward and setting up one of the major engagements of the war five days later at Kasserine Pass, in the Tunisian Dorsal Mountains. Rommel led the attack through the pass, broke open the American lines, and destroyed every illusion his enemy had previously held about fighting Germans. American tanks proved utterly ineffective against veteran and well-handled German armor. No one was ready for the rapid attack and concentrated firepower of the Germans. More than 1,000 young boys from New York to San Diego, from North Dakota, to Alabama, were killed, many more were wounded, and hundreds were taken prisoner.

But the Americans learned quickly from their mistakes, bringing in new equipment and learning to concentrate their firepower. Three days later air strikes forced Rommel to retreat to a 22-mile string of defenses known as the Mareth Line. Once again the Americans moved slowly in pursuit. British probing attacks confused and weakened the Germans and Italians, and the fighting, for a while at least, fell into a large-scale but bloody stalemate.

Gene knew they were lucky. His Navy team had been playing the same Army team nearly every day for four weeks. Twenty-eight days with only one day off during the entire run, a stretch that included a pair of double-headers. After playing twenty-nine games, it was Navy 16 and Army 13. If either team was dramatically better than the other, the routine could have gotten old fast. But as it was, the two teams were pretty evenly matched.

For the first three weeks, every game was played just outside Casablanca. Without any advance notice, they packed up one morning and moved to Tebourba, a place no one had ever heard of. They were now close enough to the fighting that they could hear the bombing in the distance. But they were playing baseball and still having fun, though now the potential danger was very real to them.

The nights he spent sitting outside his tent reminded Gene of summers in Sesser, where the hot days were often followed by evenings of heat lightning. The distant flashes in the skies above North Africa mimicked what he had seen as a boy back home—with one major difference. The flashes in the sky were not lightning, but exploding bombs and massive artillery bombardments many miles to the southeast, reflecting against the African night skies. Occasionally he could hear the dull rumbling, which was always fascinating but disconcerting.

The entire experience was surreal. It brought to mind a hymn his mom used to sing in the kitchen. "I see the stars, I hear the rolling thunder," were the only words he remembered, but it described perfectly what he was experiencing. The sporadic lights were beautiful, almost hypnotic at times. It was the aftermath that brought Gene back to reality—the trucks rushing the wounded and the dead back to the hospital tents or makeshift morgues. Each beautiful flash reflecting in the night sky snuffed out lives in any number of hideous ways.

After four weeks, the ballplayers had adjusted pretty well to their surroundings. Even Ron Callais stopped asking if they were in danger. The poor guy was still rattled, however, and had not played much ball.

War and baseball seemed to carry on as if in parallel theaters. Baseball played out on one stage, while the war raged next door on the other. Baseball and war coexisted in North Africa. The terrifying nights passed, as they always did; the next day there was always a baseball game to play.

After one particularly unnerving night of enemy shelling and flyovers by American aircraft, Buck walked into the team tent. Gene was the only one dressed and ready to play.

"You want to play today?" Buck asked.

Gene shrugged, "Why not?"

Buck motioned with his head and Gene followed him out of the tent. "I was going to cancel the game," answered the coach. "We weren't going to have an audience because no soldiers are going to be leaving the front. Something big seems to be taking place—or has already. The casualties started arriving heavy a few hours ago. The docs over at the hospital asked if they could bring over some of the less seriously wounded. They think it might do them some good to get a little sun and see a little ball."

"Then playing is the least we can do for those guys," answered Gene. "I'm up for it."

Buck nodded his approval. "Good, then let's do it. Milner's shoulder was still sore last night, so I'm going to start Ron in his place."

Gene licked his dry lips before answering. "You think you can get Ron to actually go out into centerfield? If he isn't with a group, he still gets rattled. Frankly, I'm surprised by how poorly he has taken to being here."

"Well, I guess we'll find out," replied Buck. "If we can't get him to play today, there is no reason to keep him on the team. Tim has played great, and his positive influence on everyone is impressive, but he needs the day off. Ron will go out into centerfield, or I'll draw up papers to release him from the team. I have no idea what the Navy will do with him. Given that choice, I think he'll go out and play."

With that, Gene and Buck walked back into the tent and began getting the team ready for another day of baseball.

An hour later, Gene found himself walking toward the diamond with Ron by his side. "I'm starting today," announced the Cajun teenager. "You know, I was a little scared when Buck told me."

"Really?" Gene replied, unable to hide his sarcasm. "I don't think anyone noticed, Ron. I mean you almost forfeited our first game before the first pitch was thrown. Since then, Tim has had to play more than his share in centerfield, and you haven't done much of anything."

Ron looked hurt by Gene's sharp response. "I've never been this close to a war before."

Gene stopped walking and the two players faced off. "Do you think the rest of us have?" asked the catcher.

Ron hung his head and toed the sand. "No, of course not." He paused, but Gene did not speak up. "I guess what I am trying to tell you is that I am fine now. I have a . . . I have a bad feeling about things, but for some reason I'm okay with it. Besides, if I don't get out on the field and play today, Buck told me he will cut me from the team."

"A bad feeling?" Gene inquired. "What do you mean?"

"Just a bad feeling. But I'm alright."

Puzzled but unsure where to take the conversation, Gene sighed deeply and put his hand on Ron's shoulder, squeezing it gently. "Buck told me he would have to do something today if you did not play. And I'm sorry I snapped at you. We're all nervous. I still am, at times. I think we would feel better if we had rifles or even pistols tucked beneath our bench, but we don't. I'll be glad when this is all over and we're heading back home to play ball in the States again. And to think I used to get worked up about someone throwing a wad of gum at me!" Both players laughed. "You get out there today and play well. That will satisfy Buck and everything will be fine."

Once the day's game began, Army jumped out to a 3-0 lead. The bottom of the sixth inning was underway when a low rumbling thunder to the southeast, first heard during the early minutes of the third inning, intensified. By the time the inning finished the din had moved closer—or at least that was how it sounded to the players. The end of the eighth inning brought an entirely new sound to the ballplayers' ears. Between the muffled rolling distant kettle drums was a smattering of higher pitched popping and snapping: small arms fire. Behind the diamond was a series of rising sand dunes and ravines clawing up to higher, more rugged terrain a few hundred yards distant.

Gene stood and shot a glance at Ron in the outfield, lifted his mask, and looked over to find Buck. At that moment a jeep braked to a cloudy stop and an officer jumped out. The coach trotted over to meet him. The Sesser native tilted his head slightly and listened to the popping sounds, which reminded him of the Fourth of July firecrackers he and his friends enjoyed setting off. Within thirty seconds the snapping and popping petered away into a fitful silence—except for the rumbling artillery fire, which continued unabated.

"Time out!" yelled Buck as he trotted onto the field. The plate umpire waved his arms and the coaches from both teams gathered to discuss the situation well away from the players.

"Buck, we better call this one now," urged the umpire.

"I don't know, we're behind." Buck smiled. "The lieutenant just told me someone else radioed in that there is heavy shelling—as if we don't know that—and that a small Kraut patrol has slipped through the front on a reconnaissance, and that accounted for the small arms fire we heard for a while. Our boys have trapped the patrol and are mopping up now."

Buck glanced back at the plate, where Gene was now standing with his mask up on his head. Every player on the field had turned to gaze into the distance from which the rolling artillery fire emanated. Everyone— even Ron, who was jawing in the outfield with another player—seemed remarkably calm. The fifty or so wounded men watching the game seemed utterly unfazed by the commotion.

Buck turned back to the opposing coach and umpire. "The lieutenant said he would immediately let us know if we were in any danger, but he doubts we are. We're nearly finished with the game, Darren, and the rifle fire has ended. Let's play out the last inning."

Darren looked unconvinced until the shouts of the wounded army guys lining the sidelines prompted his agreement. "Let's get this one wrapped up."

"Fine," confirmed the umpire, who lifted his head and faced the players. "Let's play ball!"

Neither coach had yet reached their respective bench when a faint thumping sound, followed by a whistle, was heard. None of the ballplayers had a clue what it was, but the wounded on the sidelines knew immediately. "Incoming!" screamed one of the soldiers standing along first base line on a pair of crutches. "Drop to the ground!" he shouted, before doing exactly that himself.

Those army veterans able to comply were already hugging the sand, but the ball players froze in place, as if unsure what to do or how to do it.

Halfway between second base and the makeshift outfield wall the entire world went dark. The blast knocked Gene and many others to the ground, which shook beneath them as if Goliath had returned to stomp the earth. Gene pulled his knees up and hugged them, unable to do anything but listen and feel as the air exploded and the ground shook from multiple explosions, one every few seconds. And then it was all over.

Gene opened his eyes and sat up as bits of sand and grit rained down on his head. He could hear shouts, cries, curses, though from whom and from where, he was unsure. A cloud of dust hung in the air in the outfield, the heavier sand particles falling back to the ground. A tightness gripped his gut as the realization of what had just occurred struck him. The catcher picked himself up, threw the mask from his head, and started walking, slowly at first, toward centerfield. Before he reached the pitcher's mound he was running for all he was worth.

"Ron!" Gene yelled. "Ron . . . where are you? Are you okay?" Beyond second base the dust was choking and thick. Gene yanked his jersey from his pants and covered his nose to filter out the fine grit. The blood pounded in his ears like a drum. He was aware that other players were running behind and alongside him in his quest to find the Louisiana teenager, but he didn't turn his head to try and figure out who was following him. "Ron!" There was no answer.

They found the teenager lying on his stomach about ten yards from the edge of a shallow smoking crater. The round had landed in the middle of centerfield. Another had hit twenty yards beyond, while a third struck the makeshift home run wall. Gene knelt next to Ron and softly spoke his name.

"Here's his glove," Ray said quietly as he reached down to pick it up off the sand. "I don't believe this is happening. Is he okay? Can he hear us?" The pitcher was about to tuck the glove under his arm and kneel next to Gene when Tim Milner, who had been standing beside him, began to scream. He motioned wildly toward the glove with one hand while the other caught the vomit gushing from his mouth.

 Ron's hand and wrist were still inside.

"Oh my God!" Ray screamed, dropping the glove onto the sand. "Oh my God!"

Gene gently turned Ron onto his side before reeling back in disgust. He, too, turned and began retching into the hot African sand. Blood was running from Ron's ears, nose, mouth, and eyes, and his chest was a mass of unrecognizable gore. His left arm was entirely gone, severed at the shoulder. Where the rest was, was anyone's guess.

Someone was screaming for a medic. Buck knelt beside Gene and gripped his shoulder to support him. Within a few seconds nearly every player from both teams arrived. Few were thinking clearly. Some were obviously in shock.

"Medic!" someone screamed again.

"He doesn't need a medic!" yelled out Darren, the coach for the Army team.

Buck stood and looked around. "Is anyone else hurt?" he asked in as loud a voice as he could muster. The players began looking at their own arms and legs and eyeing the men standing next to them. Everyone was shaking their head, stunned that Ron had been killed.

"We gotta help him," stammered Ray, who began crying.

"He's gone, Ray," said Gene, who had finished throwing up and was now standing next to Ray.

"Gone where, Gene? His glove is here!" He pointed to the glove near his feet.

Buck tried to embrace and console Ray, but the pitcher struggled loose. "What in the hell is wrong with all of you?" he screamed. "We have to help . . . " Ray stopped in mid-sentence, looked again at the glove with Ron's hand still inside, and closed his eyes tightly. When he spoke again his voice was softer, steadier. "We told him he would be safe. I told him he would be safe."

Buck suddenly realized the teams were still vulnerable. He turned to Darren and suggested, "We need to get our men into the ditches." Darren nodded and yelled out for everyone to follow him.

A soldier no one had seen before suddenly appeared at Buck's side. "What the hell happened?" Buck demanded. "A lieutenant told me not five minutes ago my team was safe out here!"

The soldier spotted Ron's corpse and winced at the sight. "I'm sorry, sir. A Nazi mortar team snuck in through one of the draws and opened up. We got em quick, though."

"Not quick enough!" spat Tim, glaring over his shoulder at the soldier as he trotted with the rest of his teammates off the field.

The soldier could only nod in agreement. "Anyone else hurt, sir?"

Buck just shook his head. Gene was still standing above Ron's body. "Moore, get moving with the rest of the team. Get off this field now. That's an order." Gene complied, trotting off after the rest of his comrades.

Once that terrible day ended and the next began, the players never spoke of Ron's horrific death again. They spoke of the player, of his smile, shyness, and innocence, and even his fear, but never about the specifics of his passing. That day changed them all. There was never any question raised again about safety. They were in a war zone, and death arrived in a wide variety of packages from unexpected quarters.

They never forgot Ron Callais. Someone cleaned up his baseball glove, and it went with the team everywhere they played.

Chapter 12

Rumors

After weeks of bloody fighting, British and American forces broke the Mareth Line on March 20, 1943. The Allies joined forces on April 8, sealing the doom of Erwin Rommel's dying *Afrika Korps*.

Rommel was no longer in North Africa. Hitler had ordered he be flown out. The months of hard fighting under extreme conditions had exhausted the field marshal to the edge of a breakdown. In addition to being very ill, however, the last thing Hitler wanted was one of his most prominent field commanders captured by the Allies. Africa was lost, but Rommel could be saved. He had other parts to play in the world drama playing out across the globe.

Winston Churchill, the prime minister of England and one of Hitler's most dogged opponents, had uttered one of his most famous observations when news of the American invasion of North Africa had reached him the previous November. The invasion, explained Churchill on the tenth of that month, "is not the end. It is not even the beginning of the end. But it is, perhaps, the end of the beginning."

The prime minister was correct. The fighting ended in Africa on May 13, when 250,000 German and Italian soldiers surrendered. Although a few were predicting the quick fall of Hitler's Third Reich, nearly three years of the war's most difficult fighting was still ahead of the Allies and the Axis soldiers. America's contribution to the victory had been critical, and the proving ground that was North Africa forged an army of veterans prepared for the next stage of their journey, wherever destiny carried them.

There were always rumors in the military. Some were true, some were not. Often, however, the scuttlebutt that reached the men in the ranks turned out to have at least some basis in fact. The team had been hearing through the grapevine that the war was about to move into Europe. If it did, went the rumor, there would be no room for baseball and they would be sent home. Could the rumor be true? No one knew for sure, but the scuttlebutt was never far from everyone's lips.

Gene and Ray were hearing the buzz all over, so they decided to ask Buck if he knew anything about it. It was cooler that night than usual, and things around the base were quiet.

"Buck? Can we come in?" Gene asked as they approached his tent. Buck was sitting on his cot reading a letter.

"Sure. Come on in," he said, setting the letter down and standing up. "Love to offer you a seat," he laughed, "but I don't have one." Buck looked first at Gene, then Ray, then back at Gene. "What's on your mind, guys?"

"We've been talking to Lieutenant Haigh, the supply officer over at the quartermaster's tent," began Ray. "I need a new pair of cleats," he explained.

"And?" Buck asked with his eyebrows arched high.

"Well," Gene continued, "The quartermaster told Ray there wouldn't be any new equipment for the team."

"Yes, I know," Buck answered casually.

Now Gene raised his own eyebrows as if to ask a question. When Buck remained silent he decided to take a gamble and press ahead. "Buck, the word is they're sending us home. Can you confirm or deny that for us?"

The coach shook his head. "I don't know a thing about it, Gene. They haven't told me any more than you already know. I do know we are not moving any farther forward, the enemy has surrendered, and we are here to play baseball. The lieutenant is right about the equipment. Nothing else is heading our way."

"So we could be going home?" asked Ray expectantly.

Gene Moore (standing, third from right) visiting a friend in a military hospital in North Africa.

"I suppose so," Buck slowly answered. "It could mean that. Or, it could mean our equipment is just not on anyone's priority list. Now that wouldn't surprise anyone, would it?"

"Nothing surprises me any more," replied Gene.

"But if you knew what was gonna happen, Buck . . . you wouldn't keep it from us, would you?" Ray inquired.

"Well, if you ask it that way, Ray, yes," Buck responded honestly. "If I was ordered not to say anything, then you guys would be the last to know. Don't forget, they expect me to act like an officer now and then. I am a higher pay grade." All three men laughed at Buck's joke.

"Okay, you've acted like an officer," Gene chuckled. "So, are we going home or not?"

Buck tilted his head toward the flap. "Ray, pull the flap down on the tent door."

"Aye, aye, sir!" Ray laughed as he reached back and pulled the olive drab canvas down.

Buck cleared his throat and then began speaking. "I really don't know much more than you, but the quartermaster is not ordering and will not be getting any more equipment. I heard a week ago they may be sending us to the Pacific Theater, but I've since heard they are not. Honestly, guys, I just don't know what is going on, but I think we will find out in days or maybe a few weeks, and not months."

"If they send us home, will we be discharged?" Ray asked hopefully.

"I doubt it, Ray. In order to play on this team, you signed up for the duration of the war. I'm not sure what they'll do with us, but I am certain they aren't going to discharge us. And I don't think this war is even close to being over."

"They wouldn't break us up, would they Buck?" Gene asked, having considered for the first time that the team could be splintered and its members deployed as common sailors.

Buck turned his hands palm up as he pulled his elbows back to his sides. "I truly have no idea. If they need you on a ship, I'm sure they will not hesitate taking you, me, Ray, or anyone. I'm not too worried about that, frankly. Now, Darren and his guys are very worried. I suspect if the United States needs bodies to carry weapons, they'll go before we do."

Gene sighed. "If they need me somewhere else, I'll go. The more we all dig in to get this thing over with, the better off we'll all be. But I would sure hate to see this team broken up. If they want us to fight, they should let us fight together." Ray nodded in agreement.

"I know, Gene," replied Buck. "We'll just have to wait and see. I don't make those decisions and they don't consult me."

The men exchanged some small talk and called it a night. They were scheduled to play a late morning game the following day in front of some men from an armored division. None of them knew the Americans were about to be called up with their Sherman tanks to confront the larger and more deadly Nazi Tiger tanks in a bloody campaign in Italy that would open on the island of Sicily.

Chapter 13

Reunion

The Allied victory in North Africa left the American Seventh Army and the British Eighth Army unemployed. The issue facing the high command was what to do with those resources. Some, like Winston Churchill, were in favor of an invasion of France before the end of 1943. Russian dictator Josef Stalin was crying loud and hard for a second front anywhere to relieve the pressure that was threatening to crack open the Russian Front. General Dwight D. Eisenhower knew that a large-scale invasion of France would require a significant amount of time and massive preparation. The next Allied step was anything but clear in the spring of 1943.

It was Churchill who broke the logjam when he argued for an invasion of what he described as "the soft underbelly of Europe," which included Italy, Greece, and the Balkans. The description was anything but accurate, for there was no "soft" spot anywhere in the German lines. An invasion, regardless of where it was launched, would be a long and bloody slog to an unknown end.

At a conference in Washington in May of 1943, President Roosevelt and Prime Minister Churchill agreed to coordinate their efforts and invade Italy. Both men believed the move would knock that country out of the war, elevate Allied morale, and threaten Germany with an invasion into the heart of Europe. Almost certainly Hitler would be forced to send reinforcements from the Russian Front. Control of the Italian peninsula would also solidify Allied domination of the Mediterranean Sea and provide airfields for strikes deep into the Balkans and other parts of Europe, Germany included.

The first objective was to capture the largest island in the Mediterranean basin: Sicily. Eisenhower was once again tapped to serve as the supreme commander of the operation. Lieutenant General George S. Patton would lead the American Seventh Army, while General Bernard L. Montgomery would lead the British Eighth Army. The enemy numbered more than 400,000 men, and included some of the Axis' best generals, easily defensive terrain, and outstanding new Tiger tanks.

The Sicily Campaign began on July 10, when Allied paratroopers— including the newly-formed American 82nd Airborne Division—jumped onto the island. The paratroopers were highly trained fighters, but most did not yet have combat experience. Their job was to cover the landings, which they did well.

It took nearly forty days to secure the large island. General George Patton solidified the sterling reputation he had earned in North Africa, while General Montgomery tended to confirm some of the suspicions about him that he was too deliberate and slow in his movements. Through a combination of hard fighting, difficult terrain, and Allied mistakes, the Axis forces managed to evacuate 41,000 men, 10,000 vehicles, dozens of heavy tanks, and thousands of tons of precious ammunition and supplies they would need to stop the Allied advance up the Italian peninsula everyone knew was coming.

The capture of Sicily toppled the fascist Mussolini regime in Italy, and the new government immediately opened negotiations with the Allies to withdraw from the war. The fighting in Italy, however, was a terrible mile-by-mile grind against some of the best German field commanders. The narrow front, coupled with the mountainous terrain, chewed up units and killed and wounded tens of thousands of men.

It was a hot day, and the baseball field was in terrible shape. Gene was amazed at the color of the soil. It was hard packed and red. Being a farm boy from the Midwest, he was used to the rich black dirt of corn country.

He walked across the diamond on the way to the team tent. Hot winds blew the sand in drifts that nearly obscured the neatly drawn base lines and the pitcher's mound. Third base was completely buried. There was lots of work to do to prepare the field for play. Lots of men from an American tank division were already gathering, even though the game was not scheduled to begin for two hours. One guy in particular had been standing on a tank that had rolled into the area thirty minutes earlier. He was standing now on the back of the monster machine, his hands on his hips watching while Gene walked along the diamond and examined the ground behind home plate. Gene lifted a hand and waved at the soldier. The soldier only nodded in return.

"Gene?" The catcher turned to discover who was shouting his name. It was Buck. "There's a tank crew looking for you!"

Ray was standing next to Buck. "Some guy says they are gonna roll into Berlin, and he has an extra seat. He wanted to know if you'd like to ride along!"

Gene began walking toward the two men. "What in the world are you talking about?" he asked.

"You heard them right, little brother."

Gene whipped around and dropped his mouth wide open in surprise. The soldier who had been watching him from the top of a tank was now halfway onto the field and striding purposefully toward him. "Wanna ride in to Berlin with us? I am personally going to kick Hitler in the ass!"

"Ward Moore! What are you doing here?" Gene yelled out as he trotted to meet his brother halfway. The two looked awkward in their reunion, unsure whether to shake hands or hug. They decided on both. It was the first time they had been together in more than two years.

"Well," Ward laughed, "we're gonna take that tank right into Germany, if I get my way. But I'm here to watch a baseball game first. Army pride is very high in our division. Word is the Navy has some hotshot catcher from some hick town in 'Little Egypt.' We hear he's been giving our Army team a bad time, so they asked for reinforcements. In fact, they called us and said to bring a tank! So, I volunteered. It took a lot of scraping to let me drive this thing here, and a whole lot of gas, too!"

"I can't believe you are here!" answered Gene. "Mom wrote in her letter that you transferred into a division here in North Africa, but I never thought I would actually see you, let alone play a game of baseball in front of you!"

Ward nodded and swallowed. For a long minute the brothers just looked at each other. "I'm sorry, Gene," he finally stammered. "I was pretty hard on you before I left and I didn't tell you goodbye before I caught the train. I've been afraid that something would happen to you before I could tell you what a horse's behind I was. I'm sorry."

Gene nearly fell over. It was the first time he had ever heard Ward sincerely apologize for anything. "No sweat," he lied. "I'm just glad we are both safe and sound. We need to stay that way. I think we'll be back in Sesser before we know it."

"And I'll buy the first round at Bruno's when we get home! You get ready for the game, and I'll see you afterward. I hear we're leaving right away, but we should have a few moments. This time I aim to actually tell you goodbye." The older brother smiled widely, his dimples set deep in his ruddy cheeks.

"Okay. Damn, it's good to see you, Ward."

"Good to see you, too, little brother. Just take it easy on Army today. Remember, you are outnumbered!" Ward laughed as he walked off the field to return to his tank and watch the game.

The sign blowing in the hot breeze on the backstop read "Yankee Stadium," so Navy was first up to bat. The tank crews were loud and rowdy, which made the game that much more fun to play. Naturally, they were all rooting for Army—all that is except one tank crew. Ward and his comrades were the proud recipients of a wide chorus of boos and Brooklyn cheers from the rest of the men of their division on hand to see the game, but everyone took the razzing in good form.

Gene was batting clean-up and stepped up to the plate in the top of the first inning. There was one out, with men on first and second. Army knew Gene's brother was in the stands, so the catcher stood up and pointed his hand out to the right, signaling an intentional walk. Gene jumped out of the box, mad as could be.

"Come on! This is baloney!" he yelled. "I want you to pitch to me!" The catcher burst out laughing and Gene turned to look at him. "What the hell is the matter with you?" he demanded. When he heard laughter erupt

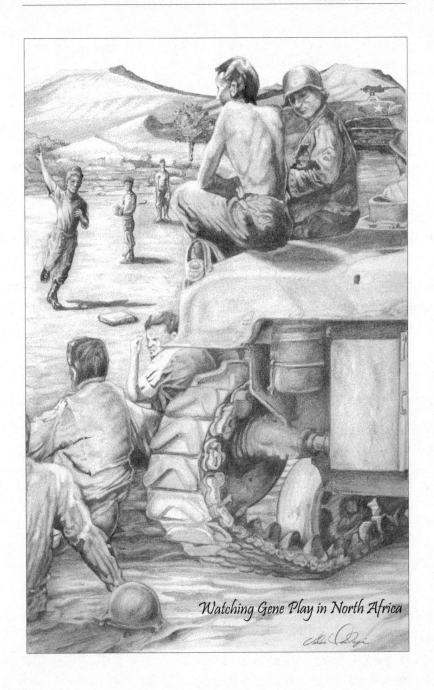

Watching Gene Play in North Africa

from the audience, he turned back around to find the pitcher on his knees, grabbing his sides to keep from busting a rib.

"Moore, it's just a joke," the Army righthander finally responded after catching his breath. "Courtesy of your brother Ward. I'll pitch to you, because you'll only strike out anyway. In about two minutes you'll wish you had taken a walk!"

Gene felt his face turn red in embarrassment, but had to admit it was a funny prank. He turned around and pointed his bat at Ward, who was standing on the tank while clapping his hands above his head. The joke could not have come off any better. Gene stepped back into the box. The pitcher was no longer smiling. Now it was for real.

The first pitch came in high for a ball. The second was low and away. Ball two. Gene stepped out and took a practice swing. He glanced down third line to the coach standing there. The signal was as he expected: hit away. He stepped back up to the plate. The third pitch was low and just caught the outside corner.

"Strike!" yelled out the umpire, making a fist and pumping his right hand to thunderous applause from the Army-heavy audience.

Gene glared at the pitcher, who smirked at him before checking the runners and going into his windup. Gene cocked back, ready for a high fast ball. The pitch came in slightly inside. He turned hard and fast on the ball and connected, sending it sailing deep over the left field fence. Gene raised both arms in the air and slowly trotted the bases. The booing from the Army team was loud and hard. As he turned toward third on his trot toward home plate, he made out one face that was beaming from ear to ear. Ward Moore finally got to see his little brother hit a home run. The feeling was almost as good as the day Gene turned to see his Pop sitting in the stands back at "The Lumberyard."

Navy won the game 9-8. Although the Army spectators were disappointed with the final result, everyone knew they had seen one heck of a ball game. The brothers from Sesser spent a few moments chatting about small things and ignoring the bigger issues before Ward finally stuck out his hand and said goodbye. Gene grasped it firmly, gave his brother a hug, and watched as he jumped onto the back of his tank and waved goodbye. It was a day neither brother would ever forget.

Later that evening in the mess tent, Buck approached Gene and said softly, "Help me quietly gather the men for a meeting in the team tent."

"What's up, Buck?"

"See you at the tent," was all Buck would say.

Gene gathered the men. Some were eating; others were in their own tents reading or writing letters home. Everyone knew a gathering after dinner was unusual.

"Sorry to disrupt your dinner," Buck began once everyone arrived, "but I knew you would want to hear the news directly from the horse's mouth." Buck screwed a big smile on his face and announced, "Pack your seabags, gentlemen! You're headed back to the States!"

Before he had even finished speaking, every man was on his feet screaming with enthusiasm, shaking hands, embracing, and patting one another on the back.

Buck raised his arms and tried to quiet them down. "Unfortunately, there's more news." That dropped the yelling down several notches.

"The reason I didn't want to say anything out there is that it's not all good news for both teams. Our partners and friends on the Army team, they're not going home." A few of the men groaned aloud. "They'll continue their deployment as we advance into Europe." The tent was deathly quiet. "I didn't want anyone celebrating out there, which is why I called all of you in here." Buck sighed. "They're getting the news now."

"Who will we play in the States, Buck?" Jim Riordan asked.

"I don't know who you'll play, if anyone. All I know is that you are shipping out late tomorrow afternoon."

"What do you mean 'you'll' be shipping out?" Ray asked. "Don't you mean 'we' will be shipping out?"

Buck looked at the floor, his hands on his hips. No one said a word. When he looked up, he had tears in his eyes. "Gentlemen. Being your manager, your friend, and your superior officer over these last twenty or so months has truly been one of the highlights of my life. It has been my honor and privilege to be on your team. You guys have played some of the best baseball I have ever seen. But that's over now—it's over for the rest of the war for us. So, I've requested duty at sea. Most of you have a Major League career waiting for you when you return. I don't. I just think it best that I stay over here and see this thing through."

"But Buck, we're a team!" Gene exclaimed. "We're not leaving here without you!" Everyone joined in to protest his decision.

Buck shook his head vigorously. "I've requested sea duty. It's what I want. You guys need to get home and out of harm's way. I truly believe each and every one of you can have an outstanding career in baseball. Quite frankly, I think we have future Hall-of-Famers sitting in this room. I'll be home soon. This thing's moving in our direction, and I want to help get it done. Who knows? When I return, maybe I'll be your manager someday, somewhere. Regardless of what the future holds, I'm grateful for all you have done. You played hard, and gave your all. Be proud of your contribution to the war effort. You made a lot of soldiers happy men, if even for just a couple hours at a time. I think you—we—made a difference."

With that, Buck walked over to a large piece of canvas and pulled it away to reveal a very tall stack of beer. It was sitting on ice. "I'm buying the first round!"

The United States Navy North Africa Exhibition Baseball Team celebrated throughout the night and left North Africa late the next day. The team stopped for one final week in the Azores Islands before heading by ship to Norfolk, Virginia.

Chapter 14

U-505

On March 16, 1944, a gray submarine with streaks of rust and cracked top decking threw off her lines and motored slowly away from her berth in Brest, France. Although constructed as work order 295, she was better known as *U-505*, a large Type IXC designed for long lone patrols to distant waters. Her hull had first felt water on Saturday, May 24, 1941, when she slid laterally off the ways into the muddy Elbe River in Hamburg, a product of the *Deutsche Werft* shipyard facility. Less than three years had passed, but she was already considered an old boat. This was her twelfth, and final, war patrol.

The double-hulled U-boat (or *unterseeboot*, meaning underwater boat in German) stretched more than 250 feet long, was 22 feet wide, and displaced between 1,200 and 1,800 tons submerged. Powered by a pair of 4,400 HP diesels, *U-505* could cut through the water on the surface at a top speed of 19 knots. She was much slower under the sea, where giant banks of batteries fueled electric motors that pushed the boat quietly at speeds of up to eight knots. The batteries had a limited capacity, which meant the U-boat had to eventually surface and run the diesels to recharge them.

Type IXs like *U-505* carried between 22 and 25 torpedoes (some in special containers outside the hull on the upper deck) that could be launched from six separate tubes, four forward and two aft. On and behind the bridge were anti-aircraft guns, which offered at least some protection against the deadly planes that had sunk so many U-boats.

U-505's commissioning ceremony on August 26, 1941.

Earlier in the war, a 10.5-cm. cannon had been mounted in front of the conning tower on the main deck to sink surface ships. The gun had long since been removed. Those "Happy Times" of riding waves and shelling merchantmen were a distant memory by 1944. The Allied control of the skies, radar, and the cracking of the German Enigma code—a secret the Germans never learned until long after the war ended—made travel on the surface a deadly proposition. Those boats that risked prolonged stays topside invited their own destruction.

No one was sure exactly how deep a boat like *U-505* could dive, because when crush depth was reached, no one returned to the surface to reveal the secret. The maximum safe diving depth was reported between 150 and 200 meters, but some boats survived much deeper plunges into the dark depths—usually not by choice—and were lucky enough to make it back to sunlight. Type IX boats like *U-505* rarely patrolled the seas in packs, preferring instead to sail as "lone wolves." U-boat Command usually assigned them to a geographical area of operations, but the captains were allowed considerable leeway to deviate from the patrol zone, if circumstances warranted.

Four officers (including the engineer), 15 senior and junior petty officers, and 29 ratings (enlisted men) made up the standard Type IX crew strength of 48. Extended missions often included additional personnel, such as a medical officer, war correspondents, cadets-in-training, extra gunners, and officers tapped to command a boat of their own, but who needed to acquire frontline experience before doing so.

With her lines removed, and with a small plume of bluish diesel smoke wafting above her stern, *U-505* eased into the channel leading to the Bay of Biscay off Frances' western coast. Heinrich Mueller was a helmsman sitting at his post in the control room, thinking back to the day in August 1941 when he and the rest of the young energetic crewmen had stood quietly on deck to listen while Kapitänleutnant Axel-Olaf Loewe, the boat's first captain, addressed them during the commissioning ceremony. "Comrades," began Loewe, "as commandant of *U-505*, I have come here to Hamburg in order, with your help, to take our boat to the front after our short shake-down and combat training exercises. It will be a hard life—have no illusions about that. But with a well-disciplined crew, we'll have our successes."

U-505 had enjoyed some success over the years, but by 1944 she was looked upon as a hard-luck boat. Patrols had been cut short when equipment failed to work as designed, neutral shipping had been accidentally sunk, and sabotage by French dockworkers had triggered mechanical failures that nearly sent the boat to the bottom. On one occasion, an aircraft dropped a bomb that ripped apart the top of the submarine. She nearly sank. How *U-505* managed to make it back to port stunned everyone who examined her once she reached Brest. And then there was Peter Zschech, the only captain known to have committed suicide during a patrol. He did so in *U-505*'s control room under what are still to this day mysterious circumstances. Seamen are a superstitious lot, and the men of *U-505* had a lot to be superstitious about.

U-505 was leaving Brest at 1835 hours under her third and last skipper, Harald Lange, a reserve officer with an undistinguished career. With him motored *U-373* and *U-471*, a pair of Type VIIC boats. There was still strength in numbers, even in 1944. The boats entered Biscay and separated from their escorts the following morning. The beginning of what was to be *U-505*'s last war patrol was officially underway.

The smaller Type VIIs running with *U-505* submerged to cross Biscay, which was known as the "Valley of Death" because so many boats and crews had been lost there to enemy aircraft and naval forces. Lange decided to increase his watch and make the journey on the surface as much as possible. To him, the risk of extended diesel sprints was better than inching along submerged beneath waters that were heavily patrolled by Allied aircraft and destroyers.

His plan worked. *U-505* emerged from Biscay on March 25. Lange turned his bow south and set a course for the hunting grounds around Freetown, a major shipping port off Africa's west coast. Although he hoped for good fortune, Lange's reward would be a fateful rendezvous with a United States Hunter-Killer task force.

Even though he was born in a small Hessian farming community north of Frankfurt in central Germany, Heinrich Mueller had been in love with the sea for as long as he could remember. Tales of sailing and exploration captivated him in his youth, which made his decision to join the German navy (instead of the Luftwaffe or infantry) understandable.

National Archives

Deep in tropical South Atlantic, some of *U-505*'s crew lounge above decks while a watch scans the horizon for enemy planes. Hans Goebeler (standing, center) wrote the only full-length account by an enlisted U-boat sailor, entitled *Steel Boat, Iron Hearts: A U-boat Crewman's Life Aboard U-505*. Something he and his comrades could not have envisioned was that in the not-too-distant future, many of them would come to know Gene Moore well.

His family had a rich military tradition that stretched back several centuries. His father, Erich Mueller, had been decorated for heroism during the First World War, just as his father before him, Jürgen Mueller, had for service during the Franco-Prussian War. An avid reader, the younger Heinrich especially enjoyed stories about the U-boats. As the world slid toward war in the 1930s, his thoughts were increasingly preoccupied with joining the navy and serving beneath the sea.

Turned away by recruiters in 1939 because he was only 16, Heinrich returned to school and completed an electrician's course and learned two foreign languages, one of which was English. Because learning to speak the language of one of Germany's enemies was viewed by some as unpatriotic, he quietly studied an English textbook in his spare time.

In August of 1941, at the age of seventeen, Heinrich was accepted for service in the Kriegsmarine. He received his training in occupied Belgium, where he had to learn to fight like an infantryman before he could learn the ways of the sea. When the training ended, Heinrich was invited to attend submarine school. Fewer than one in ten qualified for this elite branch of the navy. As he would soon discover, his short stature (5 feet six inches, with a heavily muscled chest and arms) would come in handy inside the cramped confines of a submarine. Grueling training followed in Wilhelmshaven on the North Sea and in Neustadt, on the scenic Baltic coast.

The top-ranked graduates, Heinrich among them, were assigned to frontline U-boats. His sleeve insignia designated him as a *Maschinengefreiter* (Machinist Second Class). His new home was in Lorient, France, with the Second U-boat Flotilla. It was there Heinrich first set his eyes on his new boat assignment: *U-105*. He was initially assigned there with another new U-boat sailor named Hans Goebeler. The pair barely had time to stow their gear and shake a few hands before being yanked from that boat and transferred to *U-505*, a new submarine recently arrived from Germany. Fate smiled on both men, for *U-105* was later lost in a depth charge attack. There were no survivors.

That same afternoon, Heinrich watched as *U-505* was being berthed. Her light gray paint was fresh, not a bead of rust was visible, and a stunning insignia featuring a lion wielding an axe graced the conning tower. To him, she was the most beautiful thing he had ever seen.

June 4, 1944

"Alarm! Aircraft spotted!"

Dozens of men coursed through the narrow U-boat, swinging through the hatches, spinning knobs, twisting dials, pulling levers, and yelling out commands. Heinrich sat on his seat in the control room, gripping the diving plane controls that helped drop the bow beneath the waves. The past few days had been filled with one emergency dive after another, fraying nerves, testing tempers, and wearing each of the fifty-nine officers and crewmen to the point of exhaustion.

U-505 had spent weeks patrolling off the coast of Africa with nothing to show for it. The long stretches of boredom and constant fear of attack from the sky were taking their toll. The Allied air cover in the region bewildered Harald Lange, who could not figure out where all the planes were coming from. As soon as they popped up to recharge his batteries, planes were spotted and they were forced under again.

"Take us down to 80 meters, Chief," Lange ordered Josef Hauser, the boat's engineer. Heinrich listened as Lange and his first officer, Paul Meyer, discussed the unfolding situation.

"I am beginning to suspect we have captured someone's attention, Meyer," offered the skipper. "I think an aircraft carrier group is hunting us."

Heinrich's blood ran cold at the thought. From what he had heard while ashore, once a submarine is located, the aircraft and surface destroyers hunt it to exhaustion. There was no way to escape.

"If we are suspected of being here," continued Lange, "the enemy group is probably west of our position—here," he said, leaning over the map table and pointing on the chart.

Meyer nodded in agreement. "Then we should turn east toward the coast," he suggested.

"Yes, I think that is the best course of action," concluded the skipper.

In fact, Lange's decision was the worst course he could have plotted. Instead of moving away from the carrier group, he was moving directly toward Captain Dan Gallery's American Task Force 22.3 and the USS *Guadalcanal.*

Dan Gallery was a seasoned hunter of German U-boats. His previous mission had sent two veteran boats to the bottom. One of them, *U-515*, had been temporarily captured with her skipper and Knight's Cross holder Werner Henke. Although the Americans had done their best, they could not prevent the heavily damaged *U-515* from sinking. Gallery, a native of Chicago and graduate of the Naval Academy, determined that if the opportunity ever arose again, he would send out a party of "stout hearted characters" to board the enemy boat and capture it.

Gallery's Task Force 22.3 was built around the Casablanca-class escort carrier *Guadalcanal* and its invaluable combat aircraft of Composite Squadron Eight. The group also included five destroyers of Escort Division Four: *Pilsbury*, *Chatelain*, *Flaherty*, *Pope*, and *Jenks*. Gallery put his command to sea on May 13, 1944, heading for his operational areas south of the Cape Verde Islands. His express purpose was to locate and sink or capture *U-505*. The Americans knew this boat was operating there because the German code, Enigma, had been cracked and was being read.

Although the group left with high spirits, the hunt turned up nothing but empty seas. Nearly out of fuel, Gallery ordered Task Force 22.3 on May 31 to head for Casablanca, Morocco. Even in retreat he saturated the skies 24-hours a day in the hope of spotting the elusive U-boat he was confident was lurking in the vicinity. Several radar contacts made by planes on the night of June 2-3 convinced Gallery to "stretch our fuel enough to spend one more night searching that area." The commander turned back and swept the area once more on the night of June 3-4. That decision, together with Lange's change of course in *U-505*, put the Hunter-Killer group on a collision course with the German submarine.

Heinrich was on duty in the control room when faint traces of a propeller were picked up by the boat's hydrophone operator, who spent his time in a small space tucked off the control room listening while submerged for other ships and submarines operating in close proximity.

"Perhaps an Allied convoy?" asked Meyer hopefully as he leaned in for a listen himself.

"No, I only have one ship—I think," he added, tapping the headphones. "Something is not working correctly."

Lange stood a few feet away, stroking his chin as he considered his first officer's optimistic wish. Maybe the patrol would not be a complete waste of time after all.

"Periscope depth, Chief!" Lange ordered, turning to watch as Hauser gave the command that would lift the boat close to the surface from their current depth of 80 meters. Heinrich felt his heart pound as he turned the wheel in front of him as ordered. The sound of air being blown into the ballast tanks, forcing out the heavy water, echoed throughout the boat. Slowly, *U-505*'s bow began easing its way upward.

"Periscope depth, Captain," Hauser announced a few minutes later. Lange had climbed up the ladder into the conning tower to take a seat at the attack periscope. An odd metallic pinging sound filled the control room—as if someone was throwing small rocks at the side of the boat.

"What's going on?" Meyer asked Hauser, who shook his head and began moving through the control room, checking dials and asking questions. Heinrich shot a puzzled glance of concern at Meyer, who refused to return his gaze. "I think it is a moored mine chain scraping across our hull," hissed the sound man, tapping his headphones.

The sound stopped as abruptly as it began, only to be replaced by a chilling word spat forth by the hydrophone operator: "Destroyer!"

Lange had just raised the periscope and was looking around when he caught sight of the light gray bow of a warship slicing through the water directly toward *U-505*. He let out a strangled cry of warning before spinning around 360 degrees and slamming the scope into its well.

"Crash dive, Chief! Down as fast as you can, 140 meters! Hard to port! Rig for silent running and prepare for depth charges!"

The strange metallic clinking sound was not a dragging chain but machine gun bullets from two carrier-based aircraft that had spotted the outline of the U-boat gliding beneath the surface. They were firing into the water to mark the boat's position for the approaching destroyers, which were steaming at flank speed to reach the submarine.

Heinrich took note of Lange's ashen face when the captain slid down the ladder into the control room. As men rushed through the room toward the bow of the boat, the skipper pulled Meyer and Hauser to the side and explained what he had seen. Given the cramped conditions, privacy was nonexistent. "There are at least two fighter planes, three destroyers closing fast, and in the distance, maybe 3,000 to 4,000 meters, an aircraft carrier."

Heinrich's heart fell into his shoes. They had been discovered by a Hunter-Killer Group.

Gallery's Task Group 22.3 was on its course to Algeria when USS *Chatelain* reported a sound contact three miles from the carrier's position. The contact was only 800 yards from *Chatelain*. The destroyer's captain changed course slightly and reduced his speed to ten knots. "What do we have?" he asked.

"Coming in loud and clear, sir, off our starboard bow," replied the sonar man. "I think it's a U-boat—but shallow."

The range to the target was now only 600 yards and closing rapidly. Two planes skimmed the surface, stitching it with 50 caliber machine gun fire to alert the destroyer where the U-boat was. When the contact was confirmed as a submarine, general quarters bells rang throughout the ship, which steamed over the diving U-boat and dropped depth charges in an effort to rip her apart or blow her to the surface.

Captain Gallery had found *U-505*.

Newly promoted Lieutenant Buck Nelson gripped the starboard railing of the USS *Pilsbury* as he watched *Chatelain* lean slightly to starboard as she increased her speed to reach the spot where the planes were tearing up the ocean. Fresh from the North African desert, and no longer coaching baseball, Buck still felt uncomfortable in his role as damage control officer. His months in training had taught him well and he enjoyed his posting, but nothing had been as exhilarating as routinely beating the Army team under a hot Tunisian sun. Until now.

Buck watched as the *Chatelain*'s "K Guns" fired 300-pound Torpex depth charges off the port and starboard sides of the ship. Massive 600-pound charges were rolled from the back of the ship. Buck watched with a slow smile spreading on his face when giant geysers of white and gray erupted 100 feet into the air. It took a few seconds for the sound of the explosions to reach his ears.

"Bastards," he muttered to no one in particular. "That's for Ron Callais." He squeezed his eyes shut for a couple seconds to try and erase the memory of the boy's corpse and bloody glove from his mind.

A seaman standing by his side turned and asked, "Did you say something, sir?"

Buck let out a long sigh and returned his thoughts to the present. "Just thinking of an old friend."

Aboard *U-505*, sentiments were a bit different.

The boat was angling steeply by the bow and passing the 60 meter mark when the soundman announced, "Wasser bombs!"

Heinrich gritted his teeth with the rest of his comrades as they waited for the depth charges to explode.

"Brace yourselves," advised Lange, who stood calmly with one hand gripped around a ceiling pipe.

A few moments later a faint but distinct click was heard outside the hull, followed by a strong series of explosions that vibrated the boat without damaging it. The next series of detonations were closer. The last pair, however, were ear-splitting eruptions that shook *U-505* vigorously from side to side. The blasts knocked men off their feet and seats, popped light bulbs, and opened a narrow but strong gush of water into the control room. Everything loose inside the submarine was sent flying against bulkheads. Blackness replaced the light as more explosions rocked the creaking hull.

Heinrich remained at his station, as he was trained to do, while others shouted out orders. The first round of charges was over, but the boat had been damaged—how badly remained to be seen. It took nearly a minute before the emergency lights were turned on. None of the electric equipment was working. Try as he might, Heinrich could not stop the fear rising within. It was easy to imagine the seawater filling up beneath the deck plates, adding tons of weight that would soon make it impossible to bring the boat to the surface. The ocean floor was a mile below them.

Additional bad news followed when flooding of a more serious variety was discovered in the aft torpedo room. The news that sealed the boat's fate also arrived quickly: the main rudder was jammed. The U-boat was running in a tight circle, out of control.

A quick conference of the officers confirmed the news and convinced Lange that there was only one choice available to him. "Blow all ballast!" he yelled. "Prepare to surface and abandon ship!"

Heinrich turned to his friend Felix Kals, whose stoic calm was always a welcome sight. "Well, Kals, the war will be over for us in a few minutes—one way or the other."

By this time, both the *Pilsbury* and *Chatelain* were steaming in wide circles around the spot where the pattern of well-placed charges had been dropped. "There she is!" yelled someone. "There's the sub!" Buck turned to see the bridge of a U-boat rise from a mass of churning water. Widening circles of thick bluish-black diesel oil bubbled to the surface around the U-boat. The powerful Torpex had done its job.

The *Pilsbury*'s 50-caliber guns opened fire on the crippled submarine as soon as its guns could be brought to bear. Heavier weaponry was also thrown against it. The bullets and shells ripped ragged holes in the superstructure from aft to bow. Thirty seconds after the submarine surfaced a lone figure appeared on the bridge, doubled over, and fell out of sight. Another man popped up, staggered toward the rear of the bridge, and disappeared. Another minute passed, and then several men, one after another, appeared topside. Unable to find sufficient shelter, they began jumping into the sea, more afraid of the bullets than of drowning.

Although he did not know it, the first man Buck had seen was Harald Lange. As was the tradition aboard German U-boats, the captain was always the first man out. Lange had pushed aside the watch crew to climb out into either certain death or a crippling wound. The brave commander had scurried up the ladder to the main hatch, spun the handle, and pulled himself out of *U-505* for the last time. Machine gun fire struck him in the leg and cut him down. First Officer Paul Meyer followed his skipper onto the bridge before he, too, was cut down.

Heinrich was now standing with his other control room mates, the hydrophone and sonar operators, and a few men from the forward torpedo room. About a dozen other men had crowded into the control room, yelling and pushing to get up the ladder. Panic was setting in and no one was around to instill order and regain control of the situation.

"Where is Brey?" Felix yelled out to Heinrich above the din. Second Watch Officer Kurt Brey was nowhere to be found—just at the moment when leadership was most needed.

"We have to scuttle the boat!" Heinrich shouted back, looking around the control room for the Chief. "Has the Chief set the scuttling charges?"

"I don't know!" exclaimed Felix. "I think I saw him climb up the ladder! How do we set the charges?" His usually calm voice had assumed a slightly hysterical pitch. At that moment the stern of the boat began to sink several degrees. The submarine seemed poised to slip beneath the waves. If she did, everyone still aboard would ride her all the way to the bottom.

"Go, get out!" ordered Hans Goebeler, another control room mate and one of the most experienced men aboard. Hans had made every combat patrol aboard *U-505*. He was a natural leader, and the men liked him. "I'll pull the plug on the sea strainer . . . that should sink her if the Chief did not set the charges! Get out while you still can!"

The mad rush of frightened submariners, already underway, now became a stampede for survival through a single hatch in the conning tower.

Felix grabbed Heinrich by the arm. "Come on Heinrich, let's move before it's too late!" Heinrich hesitated, looking back at Hans as he worked on the sea strainer.

Hans saw his reluctance and screamed, "Go Heinrich! I have this!" Hans removed the top of the strainer, held it up for his comrades to see, and threw it in the corner, confident his action had sealed the fate of *U-505*. "Let's get out of here!"

Heinrich nodded and pushed his way forward with Felix and then up the ladder. To their surprise, the conning tower was jammed full of men who refused to climb the last few rungs to the bridge—and for good reason. Screaming artillery rounds and thousands of bullets were slicing through the air and striking every foot of the U-boat bobbing above the waterline. Who wanted to trade the relative safety of the tower for the killing zone above or the cold sea below? Heinrich pushed his way up the ladder, believing that if he remained behind, the boat would take them all down. "Come on, Felix! This is our only chance!"

To Heinrich's surprise, he discovered Lange still alive on the bridge, but his leg was badly injured and bleeding profusely. Someone had tried to fashion a tourniquet out of a torn shirt. Several other wounded men were also there, but most had leaped into the water. Heinrich and Felix followed suit, holding onto the side of the U-boat to save their energy for what promised to be their final swim.

And then the firing stopped.

"I think she's sinking!" shouted a sailor on the *Pilsbury*.

Buck watched in rapt fascination with hundreds of others from several warships as the stern of *U-505* edged its way beneath the water. Soon, only the conning tower and most of the bow were still above water, and then only barely. "Yeah, she's done for," he replied. "Good. I hope she takes all those devils down with her. Save us the trouble of having to waste bullets to kill them, or for food to feed them."

That sentiment brought cheers from those standing nearby. To Buck's surprise, an order circulated to cease firing. It took a minute or o before every ship got the word, but the firing tapered fitfully to a close. Several whaleboats had been launched and were rowing toward the stricken submarine. In them were heavily armed sailors determined to capture *U-505*. "I'll be damned," he exclaimed. "Captain Gallery wasn't kidding."

Ten minutes later one of the boats was tied up to the submarine, and several of the sailors, small arms locked and loaded, scurried onto the bridge and inside the wounded machine. One was Machinist's Mate Zenon Benedict Lukosius. After stumbling below, expecting any moment to hit a booby trap or have the boat drop out from beneath him, Lukosius found the cover of the sea strainer Goebeler had removed and thrown to one side. Lukosius replaced it on the opening of the pipe and ratcheted it shut. One source of water flooding into *U-505* was sealed. To Lukosius' amazement, most of *U-505* was dry.

The Capture of U-505

History remembers Gottfried Fischer as the only German sailor to die during the harrowing capture and boarding ordeal. Heinrich Mueller, Felix Kals, Hans Goebeler, and 55 other crewmen were plucked from the sea and quickly stowed away inside the aircraft carrier. Their only comfort was in believing that *U-505* had sunk, and in doing so had probably taken a few Americans with her.

They could not have been more wrong.

U-505 was captured off the coast of Africa on June 4, 1944. Heroic efforts by engineers and specialists, who risked their own lives to preserve the boat, kept her afloat. At times, water sloshed up and over the conning tower and the stern threatened to drop away beneath the sea, risking those who labored inside. A line was hooked up to the USS *Guadalcanal* and *U-505* was towed to Bermuda. The submarine was the first enemy ship boarded and captured by the U.S. Navy since the War of 1812.

The capture of *U-505* was one of the most significant events of the war. Contrary to what most of the Germans believed at the time, the scuttling charges had not been set, and the ship was not mortally wounded. Flooding turned out to be minimal, and the rudder had not been severely damaged. The confusion in the attack left the entire contents of the boat available for Allied review. This included a working (and priceless) Enigma decoding machine, complete with current code books. The Enigma code was what the Germans used to transmit important operational information. Gallery's bold plan had worked perfectly.

The United States Navy kept the capture of *U-505* a state secret until after the end of the war.

Chapter 15

Norfolk

Two days after *U-505* was captured (which was the same day the Allies liberated Rome), the invasion of northern Europe began at Normandy. Hours before the dawn landings on the beaches, thousands of paratroopers were dropped from the skies or landed in gliders. The drop was a giant mess, but the confusion and scattered nature of the landings also confused the Germans, who had no idea how to effectively respond to the Allies.

The man tasked with defending "Fortess Europa" was Field Marshal Rommel, the same commander who had been flown out of North Africa by Hitler to prevent his capture or death. Everyone knew an invasion was coming. The question was where in northern France the hammer would fall. The most likely spots were Normandy and Calais. Rommel wanted to keep his armored divisions close to the front so they could respond quickly and drive the Allies into the sea. If a beachhead was formed and held, he knew that containing the Allied juggernaut would be impossible, and the war, for all intents and purposes, would be lost. Hitler and his theater commander, Field Marshal Gerd von Rundstedt, were of a different mind. They wanted the armor held in more central locations, and then rushed to the point of attack. Without control of the skies, however—superiority was decidedly in the Allies' favor—Rommel knew enemy aircraft would make quick work of slow moving tanks trying to roll their way toward the front along narrow French roads.

When the beach invasion opened early on the morning of June 6, the resistance along most of the Normandy landing areas was light or nonexistent. Fortune smiled on the Allies that day. Field Marshal Rommel had left Normandy for Germany to celebrate his wife's birthday. His armor remained concentrated far from the front. By the time the panzers were finally released later that day, they were too far away to do the Germans any good. Heavy fighting and serious casualties, however, were suffered along the stretch of sand tagged "Omaha Beach."

Unbeknownst to Allied planners, the Omaha defenses were manned by the 352nd Division, a largely veteran outfit with fighting experience from the Russian front. It took hours of bloody combat to secure the area and begin moving inland to expand the beachhead. Although Allied objectives for the first day passed largely unfulfilled, the tide had turned in Europe. The long hard slog to Germany, however, was only just beginning.

A nudge on his shoulder woke Gene out of a deep sleep. He jumped up, still dazed, stumbling over his glove and spikes lying on the floor next to his bunk. "Who in the hell are you?" Gene demanded, leaping to his feet in surprise.

"Shore patrol, buddy. Are you Motor Mechanics Mate Gene Moore?" the tall sailor in the white helmet asked.

"If I have to be."

"Get dressed, and follow me."

"Where and why?" Gene asked.

"You've pulled guard duty, and you need to watch our POWs."

Gene dressed in silence, wondering whether someone was pulling his leg. The war was far away, and they were in Norfolk, Virginia. "What prisoners of war could be here," he muttered as he laced up his boots. The sailor stood by without speaking. Gene stood up, looked in the mirror, and said, "Okay, lead the way!"

He followed three SPs across the parking lot to a quonset hut a few yards away. Inside were several of his teammates, each as confused as he was.

"Have a seat, men," ordered a young but serious looking lieutenant with the brightest and coldest blue eyes Gene had ever seen.

The baffled ballplayers sat down noisily on wooden folding chairs arranged in front of the podium while the officer took up station behind it.

"Gentlemen, what I'm about to tell you is top secret. You can share this information with no one. Does everyone understand what I've just said?" Everyone nodded in agreement. The lieutenant had their full and undivided attention.

"We have captured a large group of German sailors who will be transported to a remote camp in Louisiana with other Germans, mostly infantry. They will be held there, not as prisoners of war, but under a classified program that allows us to deny that we are holding them. They will not be allowed to mix with other prisoners, and they will not be allowed any contact with the outside world, period." The officer let the words sink in before continuing.

"As far as the krauts back in Berlin know, they are missing in action and presumed dead. I imagine by now that's what their relatives have been told. I can't tell you more than that now, but you have been selected to guard these men. We will be departing in two hours, so pack your seabag and prepare to move out. These German POWs will be arriving in Louisiana in less than one week. We will hold them there until further notice. Again, let me remind you this is absolutely top secret, and this intelligence is not to be shared with anyone—not your priest, not your mother, nobody." The officer paused again. "Are there any questions?"

Jim Riordan was not convinced that a practical joke was not being played on them. Over the past two years more elaborate hoaxes had been pulled on the team than he could count. "I smell a joke, here—sir. Where did you capture German sailors in Louisiana? Mardis Gras?" A few chuckles rippled through the room.

The lieutenant did not crack a grin. "I don't joke at this time of the morning. I am not authorized to tell you anything more, other than they are German, they are sailors, and they will be in Louisiana. You are sailors in Uncle Sam's Navy, and you're being ordered to guard them. We have prisoners, and you'll guard them. It's that simple." He looked at Riordan's teammates. "Any other questions?"

"Do they play ball?" Gene asked. The room erupted in laughter.

Even the blue-eyed lieutenant had to work hard to hide a smile. "Well, no . . . I don't suppose they do play ball. Do you?"

"He thinks he does, lieutenant," shot out Tim Milner, who reached out and punched Gene in the shoulder.

"I can't tell you anything more, gentlemen."

Gene's hand shot up. "Why us, lieutenant? We're the baseball team. I don't think I have held a gun the entire time I have been in the Navy. I wouldn't know how to load one, let alone shoot one, if a German tried to escape. I don't think anyone on our team knows how to shoot." Gene looked over at Ray, and asked, "Have you ever shot at anyone before?"

Ray screwed up his face into a scowl. "Are you kidding? Never."

"Didn't you boys go through basic training?" the lieutenant asked in disbelief.

"Well, not really, sir. See, for us the Navy made an exception and called it Spring Training," Ray replied. Everyone broke out in wild laughter. Even the lieutenant joined in.

The lieutenant waved over an ensign who had been standing at the door. "Ensign Lopez, please see that this ball team gets complete small arms training—including shooting lessons—first thing upon arriving in Ruston, Louisiana."

"Yes, sir."

"In the meantime," continued the lieutenant, turning back to face the ballplayers, "if any of these kraut-eating bastards try to escape . . . club them with your baseball bats." The joke triggered another round of hilarious laughter. Gene found himself wiping his eyes as he gasped for air. He was not alone.

It took the breakup of the briefing and the short walk outside to remind Gene it was still the middle of the night, everyone was tired, and they had just been told that, for the first time in the entire war, they would have to act like real sailors.

"So now what?" Gene asked the young ensign.

"Pack your seabags and report to the airstrip in two hours," he replied. "If there are no further questions, you're all dismissed."

The players walked slowly through the cold, pre-dawn morning air, chattering amongst themselves about the new curve Uncle Sam had thrown them. Ray and Gene lingered behind.

"These guys are real Germans?" Ray asked. "This ain't no joke, is it Gene?"

"Is there such a thing as fake Germans?" Gene responded. "I think this guy's for real." He looked at Ensign Lopez. "Ensign, come on, level with us. What's going on? What's the inside scoop?"

"Just what the lieutenant told you. These men are German submariners." He lowered his voice and shot a furtive glance behind him. "I'm not supposed to say more, but lots of guys are saying we captured a German sub somewhere and it was towed into the Caribbean. I don't know why, and I don't even know if it's true. That's what some are whispering. Supposed to be some great secret, but I know a dozen guys who believe it, and none of them have any clearance credentials—you know what I mean?" He looked Gene squarely in the eye. "If you repeat anything I've said, I'll make your lives so damn miserable, you'll wish I'd cut your hair and sent you to sea."

Two hours later, Gene and his teammates were packed into a cargo plane and ready to fly to Louisiana. As the aircraft taxied out to the runway, Gene forgot his geography and wondered whether they would fly over Sesser on the way. He missed his small house on Mulberry Street, he missed his friends, he missed playing at The Lumberyard. The military had been a tremendous experience for a young, small-town boy from the Midwest, but how could he ever go back home?

Gene drifted off to sleep dreaming about making the winning tag at home plate on the ramshackle ball diamond in Sesser. He was an innocent fifteen once again, the locals were screaming with delight, his father was smiling from the stands, and the hot sun felt good on his face.

Chapter 16

Camp Ruston, Louisiana

The unusual thing about Louisiana is that you always feel wet. Gene stepped from the outdoor shower in the morning and tried to dry himself off, but by the time he finished, parts of his body were damp again. The humidity never left, even at night. As the day progressed it became heavier, more oppressive. Climbing into his cot to sleep was like lying down on damp towels. The giant cockroaches scurrying across him at night, and biting mosquitoes that seemed to never sleep, only added to the general discomfort of life in the Deep South. Illinois had its share of humid days, but life in Sessser was never like this.

If the weather wasn't great, the landscape was at least attractive—or at least Gene thought so. He especially liked the trees that dripped with Spanish moss, a green lacy webbing draping the branches like an accessory. The moss, someone told him, only grew on what was called a Live Oak tree. He had no idea whether it was true or not. It was just one more thing to remind him that Sesser was a long way away.

After several days of training with small arms a few miles from the camp, and an intense course on how to interact with the prisoners, the ballplayers were introduced to Ruston. They were not sure what to think about the facility. Gene didn't know what to expect, and was a tad disappointed with the place.

By the middle of 1944, America was home to more than 650 camps designed for the sole purpose of holding Axis prisoners of war. Each had its own quirks, personality, and oddball characters. Camp Ruston was a sprawling complex in the northern part of the state. A host of prisoners were housed there, including infantry captured in North Africa and Kriegsmarine sailors from other U-boats that had been sunk. But these men were in the general prison. *U-505*'s crewmen were isolated from everyone else. Officially, they did not exist.

The camp's commander and several guards rode in a jeep behind two covered trucks carrying Gene and his comrades. All three vehicles stopped twenty yards from the barbed wire fence that marked the western boundary of the pen holding the men of *U-505*. The compound was a makeshift affair about one-half the size of a football field. Inside were several roughly constructed plywood barracks and tents—lots of tents. The complex had obviously been erected in haste in anticipation of the Navy's new and unexpected guests.

"Gentlemen, these are your charges," explained the camp commander, waving a hand toward the wire enclosure. "You have been fully instructed what you can and what you cannot do . . ." As he spoke, Gene stepped to one side and studied the enemy. Several of the Germans inside the wire had noticed their arrival and begun to gather in small knots to discuss what it meant. Some affected a defiant posture; others simply stood with arms folded across their chests, sizing up their new guards the same way the former ballplayers were taking stock of them.

Although he had spent months in North Africa in relatively close proximity to German troops, Gene had never met anyone from Germany before he arrived in Louisiana. The closest he had come was the Basso family in Sesser. Old man Basso hailed from Italy and ran the local grocery back home. The Bassos were dark complected with coal black hair, and the old man spoke German in addition to his native tongue. The language, harsh and guttural, delighted the children of Sesser, who enjoyed stepping into the store just to ask the old man to say something they could not understand. Gene considered the men standing in the small prison and was surprised by what he discovered. Although they were all dressed the same—blue dungarees and khaki shirts—they looked like everyone he'd grown up with in Sesser. He didn't know exactly what he had expected, but he hadn't expected that.

Four days later, after spending his time on guard duty walking the perimeter and ignoring the Germans standing inside, just as ordered, Gene decided it was time to say a few words to them. When the end of his shift arrived and Tim Milner relieved him from duty, Gene slung his M-1 Garand over his shoulder and stepped toward the fence. He caught the eye of the first man he could, a medium-sized fellow with sandy brown hair and large muscled arms.

"Hello," Gene offered, thinking the word was probably universally understood. He even smiled and nodded.

The man looked at him without changing his expression and walked away. Not knowing what to think, Gene tried again. And again, with the same level of success. None of them, it seemed, had any interest in talking back. The prisoners did not seem afraid; they just appeared uninterested. Perhaps they had agreed among themselves not to speak with the guards.

He had learned from his instruction that many spoke some English, and a few spoke better English than some of the guards. But when Gene tried to talk to them, they acted as if they had forgotten the language.

One afternoon, after relieving Ray Laws from his post, Gene was standing by the fence when he spotted a German prisoner walking along the inside track ringing the compound. Gene eased his way to the wire and motioned for him to stop. He did.

"What's your name?" he asked. "Do you speak English?"

The German looked around as if nervous that a guard would directly attempt to speak with him. "Ya. A little bit."

"What's your name?"

He squinted his eyes and replied slowly, "Mueller. Heinrich Mueller." It was obvious he did not trust the chatty American.

"My name's Gene Moore. I'm from Illinois. Do you know where that is?" Heinrich shook his head. "Where are you from, Mueller?" Mueller smiled and answered, "Germany," before walking away.

Gene shook his head and began walking around the perimeter of the compound. This guarding of prisoners routine was getting old quick. Worse, his baseball skills were rusting. He hadn't played in weeks, and he could feel the muscles in his arms and legs beginning to soften. It was time to do something about it.

When Gene returned to the barracks later that evening, he called for his friends to gather around.

"What's up, Gene?" asked Ray.

"I don't know about you guys, but I am tired of doing a whole lot of nothing." Everyone nodded in agreement. "So," he continued, "how about when we aren't on guard duty, we do what real Americans always do when they have some free time?"

"Chase girls?" asked Jim Riordan.

"No! He means find some cold beer!" exclaimed Tim.

Gene just shook his head and smiled. "Look how far we have fallen." When the rest of the guys just looked at him blankly, he said forcefully, "Americans play baseball!"

The sport was never far from any of their minds, but the new responsibilities, enervating humidity and heat, and a lack of a place to play had dampened their enthusiasm. They still checked newspapers and listened to the radio whenever they could to see how their favorite big league teams were doing. Although Gene's loyalties had changed from the Cardinals to the Dodgers, he was still thrilled to see that both the St. Louis Cardinals and St. Louis Browns were holding strong in first place.

"Baseball?" asked Jim. "You mean not just catching and throwing, but baseball as in baseball games?"

"Yeah. Why not?"

The idea excited the others, who all began talking at once. Someone produced a glove and another threw out a ball, and before long the guys were outside playing catch and discussing how and where to erect a ball diamond. Gene squatted down and Ray tossed him a few pitches.

"Don't worry, Gene. I won't hurt you!" Ray said with a laugh. "No forkballs. I know you want kids someday."

Gene waved him off with his right hand. "I need to get my gear on again, Ray. I feel naked without it." Ray nodded as he wound up and dropped a fast ball right into Gene's mitt. The pop brought a smile to both their faces.

"That sounds good, huh Gene?"

"Yeah, Ray. It sounds real good."

It didn't take Gene long to notice that the Germans seemed more than a little interested in American baseball. Every time their guards gathered outside the wire to play catch, a crowd of the enemy would do the same on the other side of the wire. They would stand there for hours, watching the players pitch, catch, and even hit once in a while.

One day, about ten days after the meeting to figure out a way to resume playing baseball, Gene was off duty playing catch with Dave MacIntyre. The ball sailed over Gene's head and landed inside the German pen. The prisoners stood and stared at the ball, unsure what to do.

Gene walked toward the fence. "Hey," he shouted. "Toss it out here." Gene waited, but no one moved. It was then he remembered a guy named Mueller spoke English. "Is Mueller there?" he asked. "Mueller, throw me the ball, please."

The group of prisoners shuffled about and Mueller stepped to the front. He nodded toward Gene and was walking over to pick up the ball when one of the other prisoners said something in German. Mueller stopped in his tracks. Gene asked for the ball a second time.

"I'm not asking you for any war secrets, buddy. I just want you to toss me my ball."

Mueller said something back to one of the other prisoners Gene could not understand and then bent over to pick up the ball. Instead of throwing it, however, he held it up and examined it carefully, like a jeweler might examine a precious stone. When some of the Germans began to chuckle, Mueller dropped the ball. Before it hit the ground, however, he began kicking it up and down in front of him. Up and down, over and over, never missing or dropping the ball. Several Germans began clapping and laughing, horsing around as Gene and Dave watched, mesmerized by Mueller's fancy footwork and coordination.

When it became apparent their guards were enjoying the show, Mueller stopped kicking and the ball dropped right where it had been to begin with.

"Thanks for the show, Mueller. Now, would you throw me the ball!" By now several other Americans had gathered to see what all the fuss was about.

Mueller turned and walked away. He lifted his left hand over his head and extended his middle finger–the universal language. The Germans began whistling and applauding with delight. Even a few of the Americans broke out in laughter. Gene was smiling too, scratching his chin as he pictured Mueller kicking the ball around in the air. That guy, he concluded, was likely one heck of an athlete.

When someone explained to the camp commander what had happened, arrangements were made to open the gate and retrieve the ball. Gene had never been inside the camp. He walked through the gate and across the yard. With the ball secure, he began walking out with it. Instead of leaving, however, he stopped and turned to face the prisoners. Gene extended the ball in front of his body and dropped it—just as Mueller had done. That, however, is where the similarity ended. The German had deftly kicked the ball from side to side, never allowing it to touch the ground. Gene, however, missed the ball entirely and nearly joined the ball on the ground. The Germans erupted in hoots of laughter. Smiling widely, Gene pointed at Mueller and gave him an approving nod. While the prisoners were still laughing he picked up the ball, laughed himself, held it up above his head like a trophy, and walked out.

That night, as he lay in his bunk sweating up a storm and slapping at the bugs buzzing around his face, the faint traces of an idea began to take root in his mind. "How would it feel being held in a prison pen in Germany, thousands of miles from home with your family thinking you were dead?" he wondered. The more he thought about it, the more feasible it seemed. "Maybe . . . just maybe . . ." he thought as he drifted off to a fitful sleep.

Although he had not slept that well, Gene woke up with more energy and excitement than he had felt for some time. He could not wait to get on duty. Later that morning, as he was pacing the perimeter of the wire, he spotted Mueller and tried to engage him in conversation, though without success.

When he saw Ray approaching he waved at him and trotted to meet the pitcher halfway. "Ray, I've got an idea!"

"What's new?" Ray chuckled while he studied the excitement visible on Gene's face.

"We're going nuts here in Louisiana doing nothing right? We're ballplayers, and there's no one to play ball with."

"Brilliant, Gene. I hadn't noticed. Who let you in on that secret?" Ray chided him.

Gene offered a half-mocking look in return and replied, "Just listen to me. I'm serious." When Ray nodded his understanding, Gene continued. "There are 15 of us, but at least four are on duty at any given time, and sometimes six, right? So the best case scenario is that we can only field eleven players for a game."

Ray looked perplexed. "Gene, field for what? We don't play games, and we don't have a ball diamond to field anyone on. Man, I have no idea what you're talking about."

"We don't have eighteen guys to play ball. We don't have two complete teams, right?"

Ray nodded slowly. "Right. So what's the point?"

A small smile creased its way across the Sesser native's face. "We have all of these Germans just standing around every day, more bored than we are . . ." By this time Gene was wearing a giant grin like a Halloween mask.

When Ray realized what Gene was proposing, he rolled his eyes and snorted with disbelief, "Gene, you losing your mind? Those guys are Nazis! You want to play with the enemy?"

Gene gave him a determined look. "Yeah, I do. Come on, Ray! You saw Mueller with that ball! He's a natural athlete. I bet lots of them are. We can find eight to ten more like him in that pen and then teach them to play baseball!" The idea energized Gene with a rush he had not felt in weeks.

Ray was not impressed. "Gene. You've lost it. As harmless as they might seem now, those guys really are on the other team! They don't just want to outscore us. They want to kill us!"

"I don't think so," Gene answered with a shake of the head. "They think the same thing—that we want to kill them. I don't wanna kill anyone. Do you?"

"Well, no."

"So, what makes you think they're any different than us?"

Ray raised his eyes in mock thought and said, "Well let's see. Poland, Belgium, Holland, France, Russia . . ."

"Ray, be serious, because I am."

"I know you are, Gene," the pitcher replied. "Tell me, how many men have you killed in your life?"

Gene frowned. "You know I've never killed anyone."

"Precisely. Can you say the same thing about the guys in the pen?" he asked, tilting his head toward the Germans. "They came from a U-boat. How many ships did they sink? How many American, French, or English boys did they kill without warning? Hundreds? Thousands? You and I have played baseball all our lives. They spent their lives learning how to be soldiers so they could kill people like you and me." The more he spoke, the more agitated Ray became. "Do you think they gave it any thought when they torpedoed ships and condemned people into the freezing ocean in the middle of nowhere? No! The only regret any of them have is that they got caught."

Gene shook his head. "I don't think so. They're sailors, Ray. They aren't SS, and they aren't even Wehrmacht. Nothing like that. As misguided and horrible as their cause is, they are just sailors, and they killed in the line of duty, just like us—or just like we would have if they had needed us to and we weren't baseball players."

"Gene Moore, you could not be more wrong. Take this Mueller guy, for example. He may seem harmless enough behind that fence, kicking that damn ball around. But don't you think he would slit your throat in a heartbeat if he thought he could get outta here and make for the coast?"

Gene sighed, his confidence lessened a bit after Ray's reality check. "Maybe you're right. Still, they don't make policy. I mean, do you sit and discuss strategy with FDR? I doubt any of these guys dine with Hitler and throw a dart on the map to see which country to invade next."

Ray shook his head and reached out and punched Gene on the shoulder. "Come on, buddy. We have a fence to walk."

Heinrich Mueller watched as the pair of Americans walked the wire, neither speaking to the other. Although he had been some distance away, he overheard enough of the conversation to know that if the American guard asked to speak with him again, he would gladly do so.

Chapter 17

Playing with the Enemy

After tossing and turning all night, tired but unable to sleep, Gene rose before dawn the next morning, showered quickly, and walked across the tree-lined path to the commanding officer's barracks. Commander William "Dirty Bill" Arbeiter was an early riser, and Gene was happy to see him standing in the doorway performing his trademark ritual: drinking a bottle of warm Coca Cola in the morning. It was about 6:00 a.m.

"Motor Mechanics Mate Third Class, Warren E. Moore, sir. Permission to speak."

The commander returned his salute and waved him inside. "Have a seat, sailor. What did you say your name was?"

"Thank you, sir," Gene answered as he walked inside and took a seat in front of the largest desk he had ever seen. It was littered with stacks of paper, empty soda bottles, several books, and a pack of Lucky Strikes that looked as though it had seen a boot heel. "Warren Moore, sir. They call me Gene."

"What can I do for you?"

Gene cleared his throat and began. "Sir, the mission our Navy baseball team has now is guarding these prisoners. Most of us are hoping and praying for a career after the war in the Majors, but we need to play ball, sir. I can feel my skills deteriorating every day I don't play."

To Gene's surprise, Arbeiter looked sympathetic about their plight. "That's right. You're the catcher. I love baseball, and used to play some in my day. There's lots of room around here. Can't you find a place to practice when you're off duty?"

"That's just it, sir. We can throw and catch, and bat a little, but we need to play real games, and we don't have enough players to do that."

The officer's face suddenly took on a hard countenance. "Well, I'm sorry son, but there is a war on. Guarding these prisoners is more important to your country right now than your career in the Majors. There'll be time for your career once this war's over."

"Yes, I understand fully, sir," Gene continued. "We all appreciate the fact that service to our country comes first."

"Good," answered the commander while nodding. He reached over and searched for a cigarette in one of the crushed packs, pulled out a crooked stick, straightened it gently, and then lit it with a chrome Zippo lighter, which he snapped shut with a click. A blue anchor was emblazoned on the side. Arbeiter drew deeply from the cigarette and exhaled two streams of smoke from his nose. The look on his face told Gene he was surprised the young sailor was still sitting in the chair.

Gene was not about to give up. "What I'm asking, sir . . . well, let me put it this way. These German prisoners, they're going as crazy as we are. Because of their unusual status, sir, their loved ones think they're already dead. They get no mail, can send no mail, and have no access to the Red Cross." Gene watched as the officer drew hard on the cigarette and blew the smoke out of the corner of his mouth. "I think the longer they sit around behind that fence, the more time they have to figure out how to escape, and the more bitter they become."

"Okay, Moore, so now you are an expert on POWs. Where you going with this? I have still not had my breakfast yet and I am getting hungry—fast."

Gene gulped and then blurted out, "We'd like to teach them to play baseball. You know, give us something to do, and give them something to do. It'll be great for our morale and it won't hurt theirs."

Arbeiter crushed out the smoldering Lucky Strike and leaned forward across the desk to glare at Gene. "Sailor, that dog don't hunt with me! It is completely out of the question! I don't care if they're bored, and I couldn't care less about their morale—they are lucky we rescued their Nazi butts instead of leaving them to feed the sharks. In fact, I care more about the sharks! If they try to escape, let 'em. You will shoot them. If you don't shoot them, I'll personally shoot you. Hell, son, this is not a resort or summer sports camp for bored ex-Nazi Hitler Youth who decided to see the world aboard a damn U-boat! I hope they die of boredom. There will be fewer of them I have to feed."

Gene was not expecting Commander Arbeiter to welcome the idea, but he was hoping he would at least be willing to take it under consideration. "Yes, sir, I understand completely. But they are sailors, sir, just like us— well, not just like us, but sort of like us. Their killing days are over."

"That's for damn sure," the commander replied, patting down the crushed cigarette pack a second time and pulling out a pair of Lucky Strikes. He put one behind his ear and lit the other. Reaching down behind his desk, he picked up a balloon made from a large cellophane bag. "Have you heard about this little stunt yet?" he asked.

Gene shook his head. "No sir." ˌ

"Last night, your sailors—you know the ones, the guys with funny names who are just like you except they speak a different language, invade friendly countries, and are now behind barbed wire—made this damn balloon out of cellophane and filled it with hydrogen gas!"

"Hydrogen gas?"

"That's right. They made the gas by mixing some cleaning chemicals together. They're not a dumb bunch, Moore." Arbeiter held the bag aloft. On each side was a paper Iron Cross with the words "U-505 lives!" written on it. "The Germans released several of these things over the camp fence hoping someone would see one, have some sympathy, and get word back to Germany they are still alive!"

Gene swallowed hard and said nothing. Arbeiter smiled at him, revealing a row of teeth stained from years of tobacco smoke and warm soda. "And you start my day out by marching in here and asking whether we can open an international school of baseball? Is there anything else, or was that your only brilliant idea for the day?"

"Sir, may I speak again?" Arbeiter nodded in reply, leaning over to set the balloon down. "Sir," Gene began, "it's not my intention to entertain the prisoners. My only goal is to keep the United States team in good shape. So, if you allow us to play, you would be doing our side a favor—a huge favor. And what can that hurt? I think it can only help us and American morale. Besides, there are many other American guards here, and they can watch us play when they are not on duty. So could the locals." Gene paused. "It's been a long war for them, too."

Arbeiter flicked the ash from the tip of his cigarette into the top of an empty Coke bottle. He offered the pack to Gene, who declined. He appeared to be softening. Gene could sense it. Arbeiter was warming up to the idea. "Moore, let me get this straight. You want to put a bat in the hands of one of these krauts? They would like nothing better than to see us all dead, and you want to put a weapon in their hands? Do you realize how many good American men these Nazi elites have killed, not to mention how many Brits, Canadians, and French? Moore, I understand what you are trying to do, but I don't see how I can do it safely, without my superiors coming down on me like a ton of bricks."

Gene leaned forward in his chair, excited by the small opening the officer was inviting him to exploit. "Only one at a time will have a bat, sir. And the guards around the field will be armed. I don't see them running into the woods or swamps. I think they're more afraid of the snakes than they are of us. They won't leave, and if any try, they will be shot and they know it. It's at least two hundred yards to the fence and the trees. I'll personally shoot them, sir."

The officer reached up with his right hand and rubbed his eyebrows. "This is the craziest thing I have heard in a long while, but let me think about it. If the Navy even thought for a moment I would entertain the idea of letting Jerries play baseball, they'd probably bust me down to seaman and transfer my sorry ass to the Pacific!"

"Yes sir, I understand."

Arbeiter's voice and manner, however, no longer matched his rhetoric. His tone had softened considerably. "Look, Moore, I'm sympathetic to your problem. Believe it or not, I'm even a little sympathetic"—he held up two fingers, with an inch of space between them—"to theirs. But they are still the enemy. Believe me, son, none of us wants to be in Louisiana. The war is over there," he pointed with his forefinger. "It's on the open seas. I'm bored silly, too." He slapped a mosquito on his cheek and looked at his hand. "The bugs that bite around here never take time off." Arbeiter picked the remnants of a large insect from his hand. "Do you know what the state bird of Louisiana is, son?"

"Ah, no sir, I don't."

"The mosquito." He shot Gene a glance. "Are we through here?"

Gene smiled and chuckled. "Commander, earlier you said you liked baseball and even played some."

"That's right."

"What position?"

"Look, Moore, don't bullshit me."

"Just give me a few weeks with these guys, sir, and we'll give you a good game to watch. I promise. Think of it this way, commander—we will be using Yankee ingenuity here."

Arbeiter stared at him. Gene noticed for the first time that the skin around his eyes was folded into jagged wrinkles, the result of years of heavy cigarette smoking. "Yankee ingenuity? How so?"

"We would be using the Germans to improve our ball game and help our side win the war—in our own small way," replied Gene, his voice rising in excitement as he spoke. His commanding officer was definitely weakening. "We would be playing with the enemy—sure—but we would be using the enemy, too."

"Hmm." Arbeiter stood up and walked to the window, where he spent a full minute staring outside without speaking. After toying with the cigarette behind his ear he turned around to face Gene, running a calloused hand over his tight brown crew cut. "This could be the end of my glorious naval career. You clear with me when and where you practice, and when and where you play. I—and only I—approve the logistics of this crazy idea. And I will pull the plug on this damn thing the minute anyone—and I mean anyone—gets out of line. On either side! Do you understand where I am coming from, sailor?"

Gene jumped out of his chair at the news. He saluted and smiled broadly. "Aye, aye, sir! I won't disappoint you."

"You damn well better not."

Chapter 18

The Berlin Bombers

It was only 6:30 a.m., but Gene was already dragging out the team gear toward the field with the biggest smile on his face anyone had witnessed in weeks. For him, it wasn't just a game—it was everything that went with it . . . the whole circus atmosphere in which baseball was steeped. He always looked forward to playing: going to bed early the night before, falling to sleep while imagining the winning tag at home plate, waking up early and putting on the uniform, dragging out the gear. Even hours of endless practice were fun in any weather, rain or shine. There was not a single activity associated with baseball that Gene Moore didn't love.

He dropped the dirty white heavy canvas bag full of balls, gloves, and bats next to the makeshift plate he and his teammates had installed the week before and looked across the ramshackle field to the pen where the enemy sailors—soon to be the opposing baseball team—were still sleeping. Gene had no idea whether these Germans would like or even agree to play baseball. He hoped they would be excited by the prospect of getting up early every morning and hitting the diamond. "Who knows," he thought, "this may be the beginning of the Germans adopting baseball as their national pastime!" He unbuckled the bag and began pulling the contents out. "They call it the World Series," his mind raced. "Maybe someday, there will be baseball all over the world, including Germany."

When the contents were spread out, Gene stood and stretched, looking again toward the prison pen. A few captives were already up and milling about. One was watching Gene. It was Mueller, the quiet one who could kick the ball. Gene had long ago sensed that German, in particular, was a leader and respected by his fellow prisoners. The others watched him and seemed to measure their responses to situations based on what Mueller said or did. And, he spoke good English, which was a real plus. Gene waved at him, and to his surprise, the German lifted his arm and offered a weak wave in reply.

Gene trotted back to the barracks, where everyone who was not on duty was still sawing logs. He took a big breath and yelled at the top of his lungs, "PLAY BALL!"

No one stirred or said a word.

Gene tried again, "Get up . . . rise and shine! Today, at The Lumberyard, it's the Brooklyn Dodgers, U.S. Navy Exhibition Baseball Team, versus the pride of Hitler's Germany, the Berlin Bombers!"

"Hey, Gene," Tim Milner mumbled, turning over and glaring at him. "Tell them to go play Stalin's Moscow Reds, and leave us alone!"

"What? Get up! Let's get some food and play ball. I did everything but beg to let us play, and you repay me with this kind of lip? Get your candy asses out of bed, and be out on the field in thirty minutes, with full stomachs. We are playing with the enemy, boys!" Gene ran from bunk to bunk, shaking each player, ducking a few swings, and laughing before heading out the door to the *U-505* pen. The last thing he had been expecting was a better reception from the Germans than his own teammates.

Gene approached the wire and looked around for Mueller. He spotted him walking the inside track, as he did every morning. The catcher trotted along outside the fence until he caught up with him. "Guden morgen, Mueller," he offered in German. Please, thank you, and a half dozen other words comprised his entire German lexicon.

Heinrich Mueller slowed his pace, and turned to look at the strange American who was always trying to get his attention. "Good morning to you," he answered in perfect English.

Gene smiled. "Can we speak in English? I can't speak German." Mueller shrugged and nodded.

"I've got some good news for you and your friends."

"The Americans have surrendered?" Mueller asked with a small smile.

Gene chuckled. "That's funny. You have a good sense of humor. No, we're still going at it overseas. I came to tell you we are going to play baseball!"

Mueller's expression lost its smile. "You can go play with yourself," he replied before picking up his pace.

Gene walked faster to keep up. "Mueller, wait a minute. Stop—please!" Mueller stopped and turned to face Gene. "You think I wanna be here in Louisiana, stuck with you?" continued Gene. "Let me tell you, we hate it here, too. These guys guarding you—me included—are baseball players. You know what that is, right?"

Mueller nodded slowly. "American baseball?"

Gene nodded. "Good. What about making the most out of this lousy situation, and having some fun? What do you know about the game?"

"About American baseball? It is a boring game. Very slow and nothing happens. Now football—German football—that is a real game. You Americans call it soccer. That is hard to play well, and moves fast. The world plays football. Americans play baseball alone because it puts the rest of us to sleep!"

Gene laughed at his answer. "Well, coming from you, that's a speech." Mueller furrowed his eyebrows to indicate he did not understand. Gene waved him off. "Never mind." He tried again. "How would you like to come outside the wire every day?"

Now Gene had his full attention. Mueller looked around, as if sensing a joke or a trick. "Outside? To work?"

"No. To play baseball."

"Why would I play baseball with you?"

Gene turned his outstretched arms over and replied, "Why wouldn't you? It's good exercise if nothing else, and it's also a lot of fun. You can hit, catch, throw the ball, run. We will teach you and your shipmates. Or you can sit behind the wire doing nothing and wasting away."

Mueller studied the American carefully, trying to gauge the sincerity of his offer. "Do you have a cigarette?"

Gene shook his head. "No, sorry. I don't smoke." He decided to ease into the program, step by step. "Tell you what. We are going to be playing more baseball now, more organized practices over there," he said, pointing to the open field. "You watch us. If you like what you see, then we will teach you. Okay?"

Mueller shrugged and nodded. "Ja, okay. We will watch."

Chapter 19

We Have Guns!

The members of the U.S. Navy baseball team spent the next ten days preparing the field, stripping away weeds, building up a mound, and practicing the game. Through it all the Germans watched from afar, standing or sitting behind the wire studying the Americans and their strange game played with a stick and a ball.

At first only a handful paid much attention, but when word spread that the guards wanted to teach them how to play, nearly everyone in the compound found a seat somewhere and spent hours at a time eyeing the proceedings.

After one particularly exciting practice ended, Gene took off his gear and walked over to where Heinrich Mueller was standing. "Mueller, we're going to do each other a favor," Gene began.

"You are going to let me go?" the German replied sarcastically.

"Yes, but only over to there," he answered, pointing in the direction of the diamond. "I was trying to explain this the other day, but didn't do a good job. Look, we aren't real soldiers or sailors."

Mueller's eyebrows shot up in amazement. "And those are not real guns," he asked, nodding his head toward a pair of guards walking around the fence with rifles slung over their shoulders.

"The guns are real, and we know how to use them—and we would if we had to," Gene continued. "What I am trying to explain is that these guys you see here each day playing ball are part of a baseball team. We were put into the Navy together to play ball. We spent months, for example, traveling all over North Africa playing baseball."

"Why? Why would you do such a thing? For what purpose?"

"For entertainment," replied Gene. "To give the real American soldiers—the guys actually fighting—a break from the front . . . to give them a taste of home."

"You Americans are not as smart as you think," Mueller said with a determined shake of his head. "You do it wrong. You should have been playing to entertain the German troops."

"Why's that?"

"Baseball could be your secret weapon," smiled Mueller. "You could have bored us to death and won the war already."

At that, Gene burst out laughing, "Well, if you find baseball boring, you've just been watching the wrong team."

"What does this have to do with me? I am your prisoner. We just want to go home."

Gene's voice took on a more serious tone. "Someday you will. We want the same thing. But since we are all here, there's no reason why we can't try to make the most of a bad situation, right?"

"Why do you keep speaking with me about this? I am not an officer."

"You speak English," Gene responded.

"Several of us speak English."

Gene caught and held Mueller's gaze. "Look, I saw what you did with that ball inside the yard. My guess is you're an athlete—a good one. Am I right?"

He shrugged and nodded. "I play football."

"And I bet you are a star, right?"

"I play very good football. If we were not at war, I would probably be on our German national team."

"I was right. I knew you were an athlete," Gene answered with enthusiasm. The barriers between them were beginning to break down. "Meuller, if it wasn't for this war, I'd be playing professional baseball. So would Ray over there," he continued, pointing to the pitcher who was playing catch with Jim Riordan. "In fact, everyone who guards you here was part of our team."

Mueller shrugged again. "What is the purpose to this interrogation?"

"This is not an interrogation. I'm asking you to play baseball with us. We want to teach you and your men how to play the game. It'll pass the time. We can get to know each other, and have some fun."

Mueller rubbed his light blond beard and thought about the offer. The idea that the enemy would invite him and his fellow Kriegsmarine comrades outside the fence to teach them baseball perplexed the German.

"Hey Ray!" shouted Gene. "Come over here a second." The pitcher nodded and trotted across the field to where Gene was talking through the wire with the prisoner.

"Mueller, this is Ray Laws. He's a pitcher. Ray, this is Mueller." The introduction was a bit awkward, and both men nodded in reply but said nothing. "Ray, tell this guy why we want to teach them baseball."

Ray replied, "Because we are all bored silly, love the game, and want to pass the time until we get the hell away from this place. And we need to field more players." Mueller bobbed his head and continued stroking his beard.

"We won't be talking about anything having to do with the war or your role in it," Gene assured the German. "In fact, our commander forbids it. Hell, I wouldn't even know what to ask you. We have no hidden agenda. We just want to play ball."

Mueller looked at Gene, and back to Ray. Ray looked at Gene, then to Mueller. Gene looked at them both and finally asked, "What do you think? Might be good for international relations."

Mueller sighed and replied, "I will ask around with my comrades. I mentioned it once, and several liked the idea. Many do not. But some do. A few are angry and think I am discussing things I should not be—what you call collaborating, I think the word is. I will explain to them." He turned away and took a few steps before stopping to turn back around. "What do I call you?" he asked.

"Call me Gene. Gene Moore."

"And you?" he asked, pointing at Ray.

"Ray Laws. Call me Ray."

"My given name is Heinrich," offered Mueller.

"Heinrich," Gene continued, "I have an idea." He told both men what he had in mind before leaving for the commander's office.

Felix Kals walked quickly up to Heinrich as he walked back toward his barracks. "Heinrich," he asked quietly so as not to attract attention. "What did those Americans want with you?"

Heinrich shared what he had been told. When Goebeler and the other crewmen joined them, he repeated the conversation. Felix shook his head. "I don't trust them. This is just a new interrogation technique. We can get in big trouble if we play with them. We could be shot for treason when we get home."

"When we get home, the war will be over and no one will be shooting anyone," another sailor interjected. "What do they want to say to us?"

Heinrich picked a tiny black biting bug from his arm and another from his ear. "Wait, you will see. You will not believe your ears when you hear. These Americans have lost their minds. I have been asked to interpret what they want to say to you—to all of us."

"What have you been telling them?" Felix asked.

"Nothing!" Heinrich adamantly declared. "I have said nothing and disclosed nothing. I have only listened to them, and agreed to be an interpreter." By this time several more crewmates had gathered around the men. Heinrich waited for their questions, which came fast and hard. He did his best to answer them.

"Please speak slowly, and in short sentences," Mueller requested. "My English is good, but slow."

Thirty minutes had passed. Gene and Ray were standing outside the wire with most of *U-505*'s crew gathered in front of them. Commander Arbeiter had listened, grumbled and complained, but ultimately granted Gene's request to allow the prisoners to approach the main fence in large numbers—something usually forbidden—so he could discuss baseball, and only baseball, with them. Extra guards stood outside, but at a distance, ready to respond if anything unexpected took place. The expressions on the German faces spanned the gamut, from friendly smiles to angry stares. It was also obvious several were quite upset with Mueller. Three had joined to listen, but had their backs to the man.

"Okay, this is most of our crew," Mueller said when the last few Germans walked up and sat down on the red soil. "I will interpret your words. I will not do more. If they want to play, I will play. If they do not, I would be viewed as a traitor to play with you, and I will not do that." He repeated what he just said in German. A few heads bobbed up and down in agreement. Others simply sat quietly and glared at Gene.

Ray looked at his catcher, and said, "Seems fair enough to me."

Gene nodded, cleared his throat, and began. "Thank you," he began nervously, his mouth suddenly dry. "My name is Gene Moore," he announced, loudly and slowly, as if the Germans were hard of hearing but spoke perfect English. He waited as Mueller translated his greeting.

"Your guards are part of an American baseball team." Gene stopped while Mueller spoke. Puzzled, the prisoners looked at one another but no one spoke.

"We would like to teach you to play baseball." Heinrich repeated the words, and several Germans started to chuckle.

With the preliminaries out of the way, Gene explained his entire rationale for wanting to teach them baseball, how he received permission from the camp commander, and that as far as he was concerned, they were all sailors doing their duty as they saw it. By the time Mueller finished translating, especially that last part about everyone doing their duty—every man's ears were up and listening. Duty was something the Kriegsmarine men understood.

Gene continued and Mueller assisted for another fifteen minutes. When Gene finished, he asked if there were any questions. A hand was raised slowly into the air. It belonged to Felix Kals. "We know nothing about this American baseball, so how can these teams be fair?"

"We understand they won't be fair, but we will not be playing as hard as we can," explained Gene. "The purpose is to have fun, get some exercise, and keep everyone busy." He thanked his translator and with Ray at his side, walked away.

When Gene shot a glance over his shoulder, he noted with satisfaction that most of the Germans were gathered around Mueller, jostling for position and asking questions as fast as they could get them out of their mouths. Gene elbowed his friend, who turned and looked back at the prisoners.

"Looks like you at least got their interest," Ray stated. "Think they'll actually play? Do you think we can actually teach them?"

"We have guns, don't we?" Gene chuckled. "We can force them to play." Both men laughed at the thought of making the Germans catch and throw at gunpoint. "Yeah, I think they will, Ray." He paused next to home plate, and Ray stopped with him. "Don't get me wrong here, buddy, but I think that Mueller guy is okay."

"Do I need to remind you who he is?"

"Nope," replied the catcher. "He's a German sailor, and our countries are at war. But let's face it, he knows they aren't going to win, and I tend to think the killing spirit is gone." Both men looked back at the compound when a loud cheer broke out of the large group of Germans kneeling around Mueller.

"Looks like you have your answer, Gene."

Gene beamed with pride and felt a lump in his throat at the same instant. "Think about it Ray!" he said, unable to contain the excitement rising in his voice. "Tomorrow, we will be playing with the enemy!"

Chapter 20

Kraut Ball!

"Okay, gentlemen," began Gene. "Listen up."

A few minutes earlier, 21 Germans had emerged slowly through the compound gate and walked, under armed escort, to the diamond, where they sat in a semi-circle behind home plate. Commander Arbeiter watched the initial practice session standing well down the first base line. Ten armed guards walked around the periphery of the diamond, giving it and the men gathered there a wide berth. It was 8:30 in the morning. It was hot. And it was time to teach these German sailors how to play baseball. Many others from *U-505* adamantly refused to participate at any level.

When Mueller interpreted Gene's first few words, some of the German sailors tilted their heads back and looked into the sky. Ray Laws laughed loudly and elbowed Tim Milner, who also chuckled. Arbeiter's face broke into a smirk. "No, no that's just a saying, Heinrich," explained Gene. "Just tell them to watch me and listen to whoever is speaking."

"Ja, okay."

"This," Gene continued, holding up a new white ball, "is a baseball." He picked up a Louisville Slugger. "This is a bat. We hit the baseball with the bat." Gene paused for Heinrich to catch up. The Germans shook their heads. "What's wrong," he asked innocently.

With a deadpan look, Mueller answered, "We are not stupid. We know what a ball is. Most of us have played the British game called cricket. We understand the basics of your baseball, and we have been watching you play now for some time."

"Well, sure. Okay." Gene glanced over at Ray. "This may be easier than we thought." He turned back to face the Germans. "We will divide in half. Half of you will go over there with Ray and some of our other teammates, and learn to throw and catch. The other half will stay here with me and these guys," he said while motioning with his arm to four players, "and learn how to hold a bat and swing it properly."

Gene looked at Mueller. "Let's go! Tell them to move!" Mueller barked out a few words in German and the men did exactly as instructed. Gene turned to look at Arbeiter and smiled. The officer arched his eyebrows in a "we'll see" look and pulled a cigarette from behind his ear. He nodded once toward Gene and returned to his office.

Arbeiter stopped at the entrance to his office and listened to the sounds of men laughing and yelling in two languages, and the crack of a wooden bat giving a hardball a ride through the humid Louisiana morning air.

The weeks passed quickly. As the Americans discovered, the Germans were quick learners and most of them were very good athletes. Like kids meeting for a practice or game on a sand lot, they just played ball and had fun.

Thankfully for everyone, there were no escape attempts, and no physical altercations. The only incidents were of a minor nature. Most had to do with one German telling another how or why to do something. They had grown used to a precise pecking order.

The one occasion everyone remembered was when Mueller was trying to help a former diesel mechanic, who was something of a hothead, properly swing the bat. The interpreter stood back with his hands on his hips and shouted, "Juergen! If you don't like me telling you how to step into a swing, then go back behind the wire! There is no rank out on this field!"

Juergen, who had been troublesome from the start, said something in his native tongue and stomped away to pout. Gene arranged for two guards to escort the mechanic back inside the compound. When he left, Mueller walked to where Gene was standing and said, "No big loss. He could not catch well anyway. We will be a stronger team without him." Gene marveled at the progress Mueller had made in such a short time.

Like Gene, he proved to be a natural athlete and was good at everything he tried.

"Hans!" Mueller yelled, striding away from Gene's side. "You must keep your elbow down when you catch a fly ball. You will never catch it like that! Let me show you." Gene looked over at Tim and both men laughed. Mueller was beginning to look and coach like an American ballplayer.

Because the Germans were so inexperienced and new to the game, Gene and Ray decided to mix the two teams together. This worked well and did not give either side a distinct advantage. After two months of practicing and scrimmaging, however, Mueller made a surprise request on behalf of the German prisoners.

"Gene, we do not want to play with you."

The statement, delivered forcefully, took him by surprise "What are you talking about, Heinrich? I thought things were going great. What's wrong?"

"Nothing is wrong. We do not want to play with you anymore."

Gene looked over at Ray, who stepped closer to get into the conversation. From the look on his face, he was as confused as Gene. "What's going on?" he asked.

Gene was about to ask Mueller a question when he noticed the German was wearing a big smile. "Okay, I'll bite. What?"

"I told you," Mueller chuckled. "We do not want to play with you anymore." There was a brief silence before he added, "We do not want to play baseball with you Americans. We want to play *against* you!"

Gene turned to Ray and they erupted in laughter. "You want to play against us?" Ray replied. "I don't think you know what you are asking."

"Do you not speak English, Ray Laws?" Mueller chided. "We wish to play baseball against you. Our German national team against your American national team."

Ray shook his head. "Heinrich, you wouldn't stand a . . ."

Gene interrupted Ray in mid-sentence, "Yes, of course! The Germans against the Americans will be fine."

"Gene," Ray protested. "They can't beat us, so what's the point?"

Before the catcher could explain it, Mueller proceeded to do so. "Germans are proud people," he began. "What you would call very nationalistic."

Ray opened his mouth widely and answered sarcastically, "Oh . . . I think we've noticed that."

Mueller ignored the pitcher and continued. "We have grown to like *some* of you as fellow human beings, but many of our team cannot tolerate the fact we are still at war, and you are still our . . . enemy. You must understand there is not a man on this field who wishes to harm another, not a single one. That was not true when you first brought us out here." Mueller let the words sink in. "Yes, it is true that we cannot compete against you in baseball and win, but some of my fellow sailors would rather lose to you as a team, than win with you as teammates."

It seemed reasonable to Gene, but Ray was obviously disgusted, offended that some of the Germans felt that way.

Mueller wasn't finished. "We have new rules of engagement to which you must agree."

"Whoa, there," began Ray. Gene cut him short by throwing up his hand. Mueller looked at Ray without moving an eyelash. The two respected one another, but had never become as friendly as Gene and Mueller had.

"Tell us," Gene urged him.

"When the Germans pitch, the Americans only get two strikes and they are out, but get five balls before taking a base." He paused and waited for their response. Ray had removed his hat to scratch his head, deciding to leave this to Gene.

"Go on. Name them all," Gene said.

"When the Germans pitch, the Americans only get two outs, and the inning is over." Once again Mueller paused for their reaction, and once again Gene told him to continue.

"When the Americans pitch, the Germans get four strikes before it is an out, but only two balls allow us to take a base. We also get four outs per inning, but as I said, the Americans only get two outs."

"Okay, what else?"

"When the Germans cross the plate, it is two runs. When the Americans cross the plate, it is only one run."

"I think that's fair, Heinrich," Gene said.

"Fair?" Ray protested. "Fair to who? Have we forgotten who's in charge here?"

"There is more," Heinrich continued.

"Of course there's more!" shot out Ray. "I think maybe after the third inning, the Americans should serve you cold beer and sausage sandwiches on dark German rye! Would you like that?"

Mueller looked at Ray for a moment and turned back to Gene. "Can we arrange such a thing?"

Gene shot Ray a sharp look and shook his head. "Ray is being facetious—making a joke. What other rules do you want to change?"

"The Americans can only score three runs in an inning; then you are out. We can score as many as we can," replied Mueller.

Gene pushed the rim of his cap up higher on his head. "Ray, I think this is great! It will even the sides and force us to be sharper."

"There is still more," Mueller said. Ray groaned. "All dropped strikes by the American catcher will allow the Germans an opportunity to take a base. A dropped strike by the German catcher will not allow the Americans to do anything. Passed balls by the German catcher will not allow the Americans to take additional bases or score."

Heinrich stopped and smiled. "Those are our rules. Do you accept?"

"We accept," Gene said.

"What do you mean, 'we' accept?'" Ray blurted out. "Don't you think we should talk it over with the guys?"

"No. They won't mind." He turned back to Mueller. "It's a deal, Heinrich. You go tell your team they have a deal."

"Wait, I am sorry," Heinrich interrupted. "I forgot something." Heinrich smiled at Ray. He was getting everything he wanted despite Ray's protests, and was obviously enjoying getting under Ray's skin.

"What now?" Ray asked. "We have to play blindfolded?"

"No," Heinrich said calmly. "That would not be fun. We want you to see us beating you at your own game. No blindfolds."

"In your wildest dreams," Ray mumbled under his breath.

"What's your final rule change, Heinrich?" Gene asked.

"The German pitcher pitches as in cricket. They call the pitcher a bowler. He can take a running start, but will throw from twenty feet closer."

"No way—NO!" Ray blurted out.

Gene was going to object, but changed his mind. "It's a deal." Mueller thanked him and turned away.

Ray looked at his catcher as if he had lost his mind. Gene smiled and said softly, "Ray, these rules will not change a thing. And won't it be more fun when we beat an entirely German team—I mean, really take it to them, with rules they set?" That got Ray thinking about the changes in an entirely new light.

The next morning was a Sunday. This time, for the first time, the teams divided up according to nationality, and began playing their own unique form of baseball. Some of the Americans referred to the new game as "Kraut Ball." The Germans called it an improvement on an otherwise boring game.

Word of the game spread quickly, inside and outside of camp, that the guards were playing baseball with the prisoners. Several dozen people from the small town of Ruston ventured out with their families on a Sunday afternoon to watch through the camp fence as the two most unlikely teams in America played a most unusual form of what would otherwise be called baseball. The Americans won the first game 17-2, and the second—a double-header that afternoon—19-4. The Germans didn't care one whit. They acted as if they had won both games.

Like kids, they played baseball nearly every day. They laughed, they argued, they yelled at each other. Occasionally, they even pushed and shoved one another, but at the end of the day, they walked off the field together, reliving a controversial call at second base, a long ball Mueller smacked into right-center, or a tag Gene missed at home plate. The catcher didn't have the heart to tell Felix Kals he had slapped his mitt into the dirt intentionally.

While Gene was in Louisiana, teaching the German sailors from *U-505* how to play baseball, Ward Moore was in central Europe teaching the Germans something else.

Chapter 21

Fighting with the Enemy

The fighting in Normandy to break out of the beachhead and drive inland consumed the rest of June and most of July, at the cost of tens of thousands of lives. Inland the fighting took on an entirely different characteristic, a yard by yard push through the old-growth hedgerows known as "bocage." Towering and thick, these hedgerows were nearly impossible to cut except by running a specifically equipped tank through them to clear a path for infantry to follow. The inability to break away from the beachhead and cut across France threatened to become a bloody stalemate.

For the Axis enemy, matters were much worse. Erwin Rommel was severely wounded in a strafing attack and sent away to recuperate, replaced by Field Marshal Günther von Kluge. Neither marshal would ever command in the field again. Both were implicated in the July 20 plot to assassinate Adolf Hitler. Rommel was forced to commit suicide to save his family honor and assets; Kluge did so voluntarily.

British efforts to break free in the north in early August attracted heavy German reinforcements, which made it easier for General Patton and his Third Army in the south to sweep around the German lines into Brittany. When a large German counterattack, ordered by Hitler himself, was thrown back with heavy losses, the stability of the entire Axis position in France was threatened. By the middle of August, Allied landings in the southern part of the country forced the Germans to begin withdrawing to escape a potential pincer movement that threatened the occupation force with annihilation.

The breakout of Normandy nearly destroyed the German Seventh Army and put the Allies on the fast track for Paris, which was liberated from a four-year occupation on August 25, 1944. With Patton bogged down in the south opposite Aachen, Germany, Montgomery was given permission to make a massive paratroop drop into occupied Holland to hold key bridges and roads, followed by a deep and narrow armored thrust, in an effort to break through and sweep toward Berlin. Operation Market-Garden, as the campaign was called, quickly fell apart when the Allies blundered into elite German units resting there, rather than the weak and green outfits Montgomery expected.

As the end of 1944 drew near, it was obvious Germany was losing everywhere—Italy, Russia, and western Europe. The Battle of the Atlantic had been lost more than a year before. That fall, Hitler proposed to mass Panzer and infantry divisions and launch an offensive through the Ardennes in Belgium. His goal was to capture the port city of Antwerp and sever Allied supply lines. Although his generals were adamantly opposed to the attack, which they did not think could possibly succeed, Hitler was determined to follow through.

The Americans manning the fifty-two miles of front were largely inexperienced or desperately in need of rest and organization. Intelligence suggesting a massive enemy build up was ignored. When the attack came on December 16, the Allies were woefully unprepared. German armor smashed through the lines on the way to Antwerp. A giant bulge was formed in the lines, giving the campaign its historic name. Heavy fighting took place around Bastogne and Saint-Vith, where the 101st Airborne and other units hung on, blunting German attacks and slowing down the advance. The bitter cold also took its toll on men of both sides.

Hard fighting, good luck, and a lack of sufficient German fuel and troops doomed the attack, which was finally contained and driven back with heavy losses on both sides. Although other Allies played a role, the campaign was largely fought by American troops. It was the largest battle in Europe waged during the war. More than 600,000 Americans participated; 80,000 were killed, wounded, or captured by the time it officially ended on January 30, 1945. Hitler had stripped troops and tanks from the Eastern Front to launch the unsuccessful attack—a critical strategic blunder that hastened Germany's demise.

Everyone was confident that the advent of spring would see the end of the war in Europe.

Ward Moore and his Sherman tank, together with others from the 45th Tank Battalion and infantry from the 16th Armored Infantry Battalion, all part of the 13th Armored Division, moved slowly across the German countryside on the way to a small village reported to be occupied by Nazi infantry. On Ward's shoulder was the triangular patch with the number "13" on top and the words "Black Cat" emblazoned across on the bottom, which gave the unit its nickname: the "Black Cat" Division. This was his first opportunity to see real combat. The loud noise generated by the rolling tanks, he thought, would surely announce their arrival to the enemy.

After leaving Gene in North Africa, Ward had remained behind for a few weeks before his outfit left for the Italian Campaign. Ward never made it to Italy. To his dismay, he was transferred to the 13th Armored Division, which trained in England before landing in Normandy at Le Havre, France, on the 29th of January, 1945. Instead of the action he was craving, two months of tedious occupation duties occupied his time. There was no action worth writing home about. In early April the division moved to Homberg near Kassel, Germany, where it joined General Patton's Third Army for an advance into enemy territory.

Ward was pleased with the assignment. After his breakout performance in France, and aggressive action in the Ardennes Campaign, Patton had become a household name. Many of the Germans considered him the finest Allied general in the field. He was given the nickname "Old Blood and Guts," which one of his soldiers proclaimed was earned by their "blood" and his "guts." Brash, loud, mouthy, dramatic, and a brilliant tactician, George S. Patton was a fiery warrior driven by his own desire to fill a destiny he believed was preordained. Ward was sure they were going to be in the thick of things soon. He may have doubted their ability to sneak up on the waiting Germans, but once they locked horns, Ward had no doubts about the outcome.

As the tank rumbled slowly along the narrow muddy road, Ward thought about how eager he had been to get into this war. His sense of duty and patriotism had driven him to be the first in line after the attack on

Ward Moore, U.S. Army, 1942.

December 7, 1941. Now, more than three years later, Pearl Harbor seemed a lifetime ago. Although he was still determined to do his part and defeat the enemy, his enthusiasm for war had long ago faded. Well into southwestern Germany and hopefully headed for Berlin, Ward's thoughts were less of glory and fame than of family and home. He knew he had a job to do and wanted to get it done as fast as he could. Like nearly everyone else, Ward just wanted the whole mess to end so he could return to Sesser and start his life over again.

His meeting with Gene in North Africa the year before had been a blessing, and an opportunity to apologize for having been such a jerk during the days leading up to his leaving home for basic training. He was happy his little brother was playing ball. Knowing Gene was in Louisiana guarding prisoners instead of walking around with a rifle in his hand and a life expectancy of a few weeks was very comforting. Ward knew one day, his brother was going to be an amazing ballplayer—probably one of the best in the country.

The 13th Armored Division had traveled quite a distance, but had yet to account for many dead Germans. The Black Cat outfit had occupied countless French villages, and even wrested a few away from light enemy resistance. The Germans had not put up the tough fight Ward and his comrades had expected, but everyone had been warned the level of combat would change once the Americans began driving into Germany.

As a tank driver, Ward was responsible for many things, including keeping the tracks on firm ground to prevent the machine from sliding into a steep muddy ditch. It never ceased to amaze him how easy it was to get a 30-ton tank stuck or throw its tread. When the order arrived to stop, he threw the tank into neutral and turned to Lieutenant Banks. "You think they know we're coming?"

"They should, unless they're deaf," the young lieutenant responded sarcastically. "Ward, get moving again. I think the staging area is just about half a mile that way," he added, pointing to and through the tank they were following.

All Ward knew was a village ahead of them was occupied by German infantry, and elements of the 13th Armored Division were serving as one flank of the attacking column. No one could tell him the strength of the enemy, but it really didn't matter. The Americans couldn't turn around, and they couldn't go around the town and leave the enemy in their rear. This village was directly in their path and on their way to Berlin, so defeating the Germans was the only viable option. "If the going gets too tough," their colonel had told them the night before, "there are plenty of reserves to call upon to help break the logjam."

"Moore!" Lieutenant Banks called out as he tapped Ward's helmet. "We're being waved over. Follow the directions of that sergeant. This must be the staging area."

As Ward maneuvered his Sherman next to the tank traveling in front of it, Lieutenant Banks climbed down and approached a group of officers congregating near the front of the line. Ward and the other three members of his crew also climbed off to stretch their legs and take a look around.

"Son-of-a . . . it's General Patton!" someone yelled. "In the jeep—look!"

The congregation of soldiers, some already parked and others still pulling up, were electrified by the news. General Patton had already assumed mythical proportions in the ranks. Ward didn't have much of a feel for history, but he sensed that being able to stand close enough to hear Patton speak, or even to set eyes on him, would be something he could tell his children and grandchildren about one day.

The general stood up in the back of his jeep and lifted one booted foot up on the top of the front seat, nodding in approval as the men gathered around him. The shine from his black knee-high boots caught the sun. Someone shouted out, "The general's wearing gold spurs!" Ward muscled his way to the front of the group of soldiers. Patton was a sight to behold. As he stood there surveying his tankers, Ward thought the entire setting was something straight out of a painting . . . a work of art.

Ward had once bumped into General Omar Bradley in a mess tent in North Africa, but didn't even realize who he was until someone pointed it out to him. Bradley looked like every other officer. General Patton was different. An energy moved with him when he walked.

"Hello, boys!" the general shouted as he jumped onto the hood of his jeep to address the troops. He was decked out in a green jacket and khaki riding pants. Ward edged to the left a couple feet to get a look at Patton's hips. Sure enough, ivory-handled revolvers were strapped there. Patton made quite a show of removing his black leather gloves. From out of no where he produced a riding crop.

"You have heard rumors about me. Some of them may even be true!" he shouted. Patton laughed aloud at his own joke; everyone around him joined in. "One thing no one will ever say about me is that I lead from behind! I am here today with you to tell you each, personally, how grateful I am for your service to your country. You men have performed magnificently. I am damned proud of each and every one of you. Damned proud! Up ahead a few miles we will be engaging the enemy. The village and terrain around it they hold is just one more obstacle standing between us," Patton paused, scanning the faces of the soldiers assembled before him, "and Berlin!" Another cheer and shouts of support erupted from the tankers.

"Our Russian allies are planning to take Berlin before we can get there and that is, quite frankly, horse dung. Berlin is ours. Hitler is ours.

The faster we crush the resistance ahead, the faster I can personally kick that rotten bastard Hitler in the ass!" Patton waited for the laughter to die down. "At that time, we will welcome our 'so-called' Russian allies into an American-occupied Berlin!" More laughter and applause. Patton's presence and words of encouragement instilled courage.

The general lowered his voice a bit and became more serious. "You know your jobs. You know what to do. And I know you will do it." With that, Patton jumped off the hood of his jeep and began walking from crew to crew, shaking hands and making small talk. Ward could barely contain himself. Patton was heading his way.

"What's your name, son?"

"Ward Moore, sir. Sergeant Moore."

"Where you from, Sergeant?" asked the general.

"Sesser . . . Sesser, Illinois, sir."

"Coal mining country!"

Ward was amazed. "Sir, yes it is."

"Are you a coal miner, son?"

"No sir, I'm not."

"What do you do?"

"I'm a sergeant in the 13th Armored Division of General George S. Patton's Third Army, sir. This tank is going to lead the way for you to enter Berlin, and we're gonna have a front row seat while you personally kick that rotten bastard Hitler in the ass. Sir!"

Patton broke out in a loud laugh and reached over and put his arm around Ward's shoulders. "Now here's a soldier who knows exactly why he's here!"

Patton stood back and looked at Ward. "Sergeant, will you take the lead into that village ahead?"

"You're damn right I will, sir," Ward proudly responded.

Patton turned to yell to all the assembled men. "Follow Sergeant Moore and his tank to victory! May God bless every last son-of-a-bitch in the Black Cat Division!" He turned back to Ward and nodded. "I'll see you in Berlin, son."

Lieutenant Banks climbed back onto the tank and began shaking his head. "Sarge, do you understand what just happened here?"

"Sir?" Ward asked.

"The rest of us watched a tiny slice of history unfold, but you got to play a part—you lucky bastard!" The lieutenant laughed. "I'm jealous. I can't believe it. I'm not talking to you until the war is over. I will probably have to, though."

Ward was laughing. "Why?"

"Because you volunteered our tank would lead the way."

"Could you say 'no' to General Patton, sir?" Ward asked.

"Of course not." The smile left the lieutenant's face, "We'll lead the way. Someone has to be first. Might as well be us."

The fighting began with light rifle fire when advanced infantry screens from both sides made contact outside the village. Thirty minutes later the tanks on both flanks arrived on the scene and opened fire, bombarding the nameless place for about an hour before the Black Cats were ordered to roll ahead. The streets in the village were strewn with debris and corpses, but the resistance was still intense.

Ward winced each time he heard a bullet ricochet off the front of his tank. "I thought we were meeting someone else here," Ward hollered over his shoulder up to the lieutenant. "Is anyone else moving in with us?" German Wehrmacht soldiers were running from building to building, crossing rubble-strewn streets, and shooting from windows. They were everywhere. "We are sitting ducks here!" yelled Ward.

Lieutenant Banks knocked on Ward's helmet. "Over there—there's the problem!"

An American tank had been hit by something heavy and slammed into a building, which had collapsed on top of it. There was just enough of the tank sticking out into the narrow street to block the armored units attacking from the other side of town. Ward was going to back up but another tank was ten yards behind him—way too close for comfort. He looked up at the Lieutenant, "Give me some cover with the machine gun, and I'll dig those guys out!"

"No! It's too dangerous. Back up and get that guy's attention that we need to get outta here!"

"Lieutenant, we can't back up, we can't move forward. It's more dangerous to sit here. Those guys are screwed if we don't help them!"

Banks thought for a second and said, "Okay—but not until I say go!" The lieutenant ordered the soldier manning the Browning .50 caliber machine gun to provide covering fire for Ward's mad dash to the crippled tank. Banks bellowed out another order and the turret slowly turned to the left front.

"Fire!" he yelled.

The building across the street from the trapped tank was full of German infantry. It erupted in a geyser of whitish-gray smoke and flying bricks and mortars.

"Go!" the lieutenant shouted.

Ward, already breathless and wondering what in the world he was doing, jumped out of the tank, hunched over, and ran down the street to the buried Sherman. Enemy bullets whizzed past his ears as he instinctively ducked and bobbed his way toward the trapped crewmen. It was as if he was moving in slow motion, his feet coated in heavy clay. He finally reached the tank, breathless but exhilarated; three infantrymen joined him there a few seconds later. While two provided covering fire, Ward and the remaining man dug through the rubble to reach the hatch.

When the hatch was exposed, Ward rapped on it with a brick to warn the men inside they were friends. At least, that's what he hoped they would think. The last thing he wanted was to have them open the hatch and start shooting. When the hatch popped open, a young soldier, his eyes wide with fright, looked up from inside the trapped tank. The tanker looked up, first with surprise, and then with a big smile pasted on his face.

"Ward Moore? What in the hell are you doing here?"

Ward was equally stunned, but the whining bullets whistling through the air cut the reunion shorter than either would have wanted. "I guess I've come four thousand miles to save your ass!" Ward replied as he reached down and helped the soldier and his buddies climb from the crippled tank.

The jaw-dropping coincidence was one the people of Sesser would speak of for decades to come. At the barber shop, in the grocery store, on the local ball diamond—everywhere there was talking that needed to be done, the story of how Ward Moore saved John Brown's life was mentioned. The grateful face beneath the hatch was another native of Sesser, Illinois. John Brown and Ward Moore had grown up and attended school together. John had played ball with Gene when they were pre-teens. And now, years later and thousands of miles away, with men dying all around them, war had brought the two hometown friends together again.

The rest of the crew bailed out quickly and crouched behind the remnants of a demolished wall looking for a way to safely withdraw without being cut down by the crossfire. When the firing slackened a bit, they ran as fast as they could toward the American lines.

Ward was a few feet from his tank when he stumbled and fell. "Ward, you okay?" John yelled, reaching back to help Ward to his feet as the two hobbled the last few feet and collapsed behind the Sherman.

John repeated the question. "Crap, no!" Ward winced, rolling to his side and grabbing his rear end with one hand. "One of the damn Nazis shot me in the butt!" The bullet had entered one of his buttocks and exited the other side. It was deep and bled quite a bit, but it was not serious. A few minutes later, another bullet grazed his back.

More American infantry poured into the area, but the fighting continued for some time until the Germans were finally cleaned from the village. John summoned a medic, who arrived to treat Ward's wounds and get him to a makeshift hospital tent erected outside the town. The injury in his rear end was more embarrassing than damaging. For the rest of his life, whenever he was asked how it was the Germans were able to shoot him in his behind, Ward would reply, "Because the Krauts weren't fast enough to shoot me in the front!"

Ward Moore was awarded the Purple Heart for his wound and the Bronze Star for his bravery.

Chapter 22

The Final Innings

The defeat of German forces in the Ardennes at the Battle of the Bulge was a clear indication that Germany had lost the war. Germany itself, however, remained to be conquered.

February and March of 1945 were bloody months as the Allies walked, fought, rolled, and died their way through and over a long series of anti-tank traps and fortifications dubbed the Siegfried Line, which marked the western border of Germany. Cologne was the first major German city to be captured by the Americans. It fell on March 5, 1945. The next advance carried the Allied troops into the Ruhr—the industrial heart of Nazi Germany.

The next and last major barrier was the Rhine River. By the third week of March, the Allies had a bridgehead across it thirty-five miles wide and twelve miles deep, though the fighting in many places was fierce. Once the Rhine was crossed, there was little to hold back the Allies in the west. The Russians were advancing from the East, their eyes set firmly on Berlin.

"Moore, come in and have a seat son," Commander Arbeiter ordered, motioning him to a chair.

"Thank you, sir," Gene replied, wondering why he had been summoned to the commander's office.

"How's the game going?" asked the officer, dropping himself into his seat behind the giant and as always, messy desk.

"Good, sir," Gene answered, studying the commander's face in an effort to figure out what he had in mind for this meeting. "We're all playing well, and the Germans, they've really caught on."

"You know, Moore, when I watch you play, it's often hard to tell who is on what side. Those Krauts are enjoying themselves." Arbeiter stood and began pacing. "I have to confess, this has been hard for me—hard. They are the *enemy*. We can't forget that."

Gene fidgeted but remained confident. "I understand, sir. I won't forget. I haven't forgotten."

"Good. The reason I've asked you in today is to talk about the end, how we wind things down here." Arbeiter flipped open his Zippo, flicked it with his thumb, and lit a Lucky. He was about to offer one to Gene when he thought better of it. "Forgot. You don't smoke."

Gene shook his head. "Wind what down, sir?" He looked at the commander with a puzzled expression. "The end of what?"

Arbeiter leaned over the desk and put his palms down flat on the only two clear areas available. "Moore, I guess you don't follow the war too closely, but the end is in sight. Our so-called Russian allies are knocking down the door to Berlin, Patton and other generals are advancing from the other side. This war in Europe could be finished next week. It wouldn't surprise me if Hitler's own men were trying to kill him right about now just to save their own sorry hides." He exhaled a cloud of smoke with the cigarette dangling from his lips. "Any way you slice it, the war will be over sooner rather than later."

A sense of panic began rising inside the catcher. "So what does that mean for us, sir? Here, I mean."

"I am just giving you a head's up. We might be closing down our operation and shipping the prisoners elsewhere. I doubt they'll be going home for a while, but they might not be staying here too long, either."

The news stunned Gene. He had not given much thought to the end of their time in Louisiana, and baseball with the Germans had been endlessly interesting and exciting. And now it could all end—sooner than any of them had expected.

"Is there something wrong, Moore?"

"No, sir. That's great news, sir."

"Well, you don't seem too damned happy about it!"

"I'm delighted, sir."

"The hell you are," he snorted. "I hope you're not feeling any attachment to these damned Nazis. You are still playing with the enemy, and we are still at war—for a while longer, anyway."

"Of course, sir. There is no confusion on that score, and never has been," Gene answered.

Arbeiter straightened up once more. "I just wanted to let you know that word could come down tomorrow, next week—hell, it could arrive this afternoon—that we are all out of business here." His voice softened before he spoke again. "I wanted to give you time to prepare, son. I know how much time you have put into this, and I never thought it had a prayer, frankly. You've done a good job organizing and motivating everyone. I know the locals have loved it, and the other guards—they can't get enough."

Gene smiled at the unexpected kind words, thanked the commander, saluted, and walked out. Arbeiter was a tough guy, but he had a kind streak in him a mile wide.

The end of the war meant returning home, seeing his family and friends again, and picking up where he left off with his baseball career. The prospect excited Gene. On the other hand, the end of the war meant Heinrich and his team would also return home. For the first time, Gene fully understood how much he had grown to like some of the Germans—Heinrich, especially—even if they were the enemy.

Two days later on May 8, Gene, Ray, Heinrich, and the two teams were finishing up a late afternoon game when a siren sounded. Someone started yelling something, and the call was taken up by others. Everyone on the ball diamond stopped playing. Ray Laws caught himself as he was throwing a pitch, and the ball dropped into the dirt.

"That's a ball!" yelled out Felix in German. "That counts! No one called time out!"

By this time no one was paying any attention to whether Ray had thrown a ball or strike. That was because everyone who could understand English was standing with their mouths open, shocked by the news some of the sailors were yelling: "The Russians took Berlin! The war is over!"

Ray took off running for the plate and leaped on Gene, who bear-hugged the pitcher as they rolled in the dirt. "Did you hear that?" Ray screamed. "It's over! The war in Europe is over!" One by one, the American players fell onto the top of the pile until nothing but a mass of squirming arms and legs was visible. Anyone watching the scene would think the American team had just won the pennant or the World Series. The celebration continued for a minute or two until Gene extricated himself from the pile. The first thing he saw made him stop mid-yell.

The Germans were gathered along the first base line, exchanging somber glances. A few looked as though they were crying. None spoke. They had not had any word of how the war was going for nearly a year, so the news that Berlin was in enemy hands floored them.

Gene walked over and stood a few feet from Mueller. "I'm sorry, Heinrich—for you and for these guys, I am sorry. But this is good for us both, right? The war is over and you get to go home."

Heinrich turned his head away. "Home to what?" he answered softly. "What could possibly be left of my country? The Russians have Berlin? I could never have imagined it in a thousand years. Part of my family had moved there before our last patrol. What are the odds they are still alive?" The German leaned over and said something to another from his crew who looked to be having a hard time with the news. "You have every right to celebrate your victory, Gene. You won. Your family is safe, your country strong and intact." Heinrich threw his glove to the ground and walked off the field. Every other German player followed him.

Dave MacIntyre heard the exchange between Gene and Heinrich. "Hey, Mueller, remember, we didn't start this war! We were dragged into this thing! The Japs bombed us on a Sunday morning, the cowardly bastards, and your Hitler declared war against us—remember?" Mac was walking after Heinrich now, who was still stomping away. "Yeah, walk away! We didn't invade other countries, either!"

"Mac!" Gene screamed, trotting after the pair. "Knock it off!"

Mueller, however, boiled over with emotion. He spun around and ran toward Mac, who reached down and picked up a bat and headed for the approaching German. Ray jumped in front of the American and grabbed him, while Gene tackled Mueller and knocked him to the ground.

"Heinrich, don't do this!" Gene yelled as he struggled to hold the German on the ground. Gene lifted his head and looked around, convinced the rest of the Germans would be leaping to Mueller's defense. Thankfully, Milner and Riordan had jumped in front of them and waved them off. The fact that sailors with rifles were running to the field also helped keep the argument from escalating into something much worse.

Gene jumped up and waved his arms. "Put the guns away, we're arguing over a bad call!" When the sailors hesitated, Gene said it again, not as loudly but just as convincingly. "It's fine! Put the guns away! The war is over, right? It would be stupid for anyone to get hurt now."

The guards lowered their weapons but surrounded the teams. "What the hell is going on here?" barked Commander Arbeiter as he trotted onto the field. "Moore! Where's Moore?"

Gene waved his hand to catch the commander's eye. "Actually, nothing's going on, commander. We were arguing a call and decided to settle it with a wrestling match, what with the war being over and all. Sir." Several of the American players lowered their eyes and looked away. Many of the Germans did the same.

Arbeiter wasn't a complete fool, but he didn't press the matter. "Okay, the ball game is over." He turned toward the guards. "Get these Jerries back into that pen, and if they so much as look at you funny, you have my permission to drill one as an example!" Mueller quickly translated for the men who did not speak English while the guards herded the prisoners toward the gate to the compound. Mueller caught Gene's eye and nodded briefly as if to thank him.

"What the hell got into them?" Ray asked.

"Probably the same thing that would get into us if we were in their shoes," Gene replied. "We were celebrating the loss of their country, and maybe even the death of many of their family and friends." He bent down to pick up his mitt and started walking toward the pen. "Damn thoughtless of us," he muttered.

"Moore!" It was Commander Arbeiter. Gene stopped, and turned. "Where do you think you are going? Get over here."

"Yes, sir," answered Gene, walking to where the commander was standing and saluting.

"Now what the hell really happened?"

"We started celebrating the news of the end of the war. They don't know about their homes or families, I guess we forgot about them standing here listening. That's all."

"Moore, don't go native on me," Commander Arbeiter shot back. "I don't give a rat's ass about their feelings or their families. As I have told you over and over, they are the enemy, and . . ."

"Not as of today, sir."

Arbeiter's eyes bulged and he looked like he was going to explode. "Damn it, Moore! Don't you ever interrupt me again! Am I making myself crystal clear?" Stunned, Gene swallowed hard and nodded. "Answer me now, or I will have you arrested!"

Gene stood there, unable to say a word. The American team gathered around him. The commander looked at Ray Laws, who stared back without saying a word.

"Moore, Laws—in my office. NOW!" Arbeiter stormed off.

When he was out of earshot, Ray asked, "Do you think he meant right now, Gene, or do we have time for a cup of coffee?" The entire team fought, largely without success, to stifle their laughter. Luckily, the commander was already out of earshot.

Gene shot a look at Mac, who fumbled his way through an apology. The catcher shook his head and waved him off. "Forget it, Mac. Just forget it."

"Do you think he's calmed down, Gene?" Ray asked during the walk to Arbeiter's office.

"Who knows," he answered. "I've never seen him so worked up, but he's a reasonable man." Ray shot him a look as if he had lost his mind, but Gene ignored him and knocked on the door.

"Commander Arbeiter, sir? Moore and Laws reporting as ordered."

"Come in and have a seat." Arbeiter's voice was calmer, his tone measured, but it was obvious he was still steamed.

Both players took a seat while Arbeiter remained standing near the window looking outside. An uncomfortable silence followed. The officer finally cleared his throat and began speaking. "I took a big chance on this baseball thing, Moore, and as I told you, it was not the fiasco I thought it might be. So you can imagine my surprise when I look out my window this afternoon and see what others might view as a prison revolt." The commander turned and looked long and hard at both men. "This is not the way I want to end my career!" he yelled.

The commander walked to his desk. One of his massive forearms pushed aside a stack of paper and two empty bottles so there was room for him to sit down on the corner. A full minute passed before he spoke again. "You know, Moore, overall, this has been a great experiment. I doubted it in the beginning, but you made a believer out of me. Except for today, there hasn't been a single problem—not one. No fights, no escape attempts, no sharing of unauthorized information—at least nothing

I heard about." He paused before adding, "A few months ago I almost shut the whole program down."

The ball players looked in surprise at the commander. "Why?" they both asked together.

"Either of you ever heard of Papago Park, outside Phoenix, Arizona?" The sailors looked at one another and shook their heads. "Large POW pen for krauts. They wanted to play volleyball, and got the tools to do it. Bunch of bleeding hearts there, too, I guess." He cleared his throat and continued. "Can you guess what they did with the tools?"

"Tried to escape?" guessed Ray.

"Now that's a shock, isn't it?" Shot back Arbeiter, his eyes wide in mock surprise. "They dug a 178-foot tunnel under the volleyball field! More than two dozen slipped free just before Christmas. Most were recaptured within a few weeks. Can you guess who the leaders were?"

Ray and Gene shook their heads.

"U-boat men." Arbeiter watched for their reactions. Ray looked over at Gene and raised his eyebrows.

Gene ignored him. "When will they be leaving, sir?" he asked.

"Who? Your German players?" Arbeiter scratched his head and then shook it. "I don't know. I'm sure there are many details to be worked out. If they don't close the camp and transfer them, they could be here months— maybe longer. Who the hell knows? The brass doesn't consult me on these things." Arbeiter looked lost in his thoughts. Another twenty seconds of uncomfortable silence followed.

Gene and Ray looked at each other, not knowing whether they should say anything. Finally Gene broke the silence. "Sir?"

"No more baseball."

Gene and Ray turned to look at one another. "Commander, did you say no more baseball?" Gene asked.

Arbeiter nodded. "I'd say baseball is over, wouldn't you? There's no reason to keep playing now that the war in Europe has ended. They will probably be shipping out soon—or you guys might be. Have you given any thought that all of us might be headed for the Pacific soon?"

Gene thought fast, trying to come up with a reason to continue playing. "With all respect, commander, I think there is a reason to keep playing." The catcher was buying time. He had no idea what he was about to say next.

"And what would that be—other than you want to play baseball?"

Flustered, Gene paused and looked at Ray. "Yes, of course, sir, there is every reason to keep playing," Ray chimed in, looking back at Gene for an answer.

"Sir, as you said, this has been good, and because it's been good . . ." Gene looked back at Ray.

"As Gene was saying, sir, as good as all this has been—."

"We thought it would be good to end with 'The Friendship Game,'" interjected Gene, whose smile and nodding was completely at odds with what he was feeling. "Where did I come up with that?" he wondered.

"The Friendship Game?" Arbeiter narrowed his eyes as if he smelled a rat. "Why haven't I ever heard of that?"

Gene stood up with excitement, but then remembered where he was. "Sorry, sir. The Friendship Game is something we have been planning for just this occasion, commander."

"Sit down, Moore."

"Yes sir, commander," answered Gene, dropping back into his seat.

"Now, fill me in on what you have in mind." Arbeiter sat down in his own chair and began hunting for his pack of Lucky Strikes.

Commander Arbeiter had informed his superiors that baseball was being played in the Louisiana POW camp. The initial reaction was disbelief, followed by anger. Eventually the brass warmed to the idea—especially because someone like Commander Arbeiter strongly endorsed it. That was something neither Gene nor his teammates ever learned.

When the rest of the camp found out about the American-German "Friendship Game," the idea took root and everyone looked forward to the event. All Gene had to do was sell Heinrich and his teammates on the idea. To his surprise, it was much easier than expected.

The game was scheduled for August 8, 1945. The news was that after the game, Mueller, Kals, Goebeler, and the rest of the Germans from *U-505* would be transferred elsewhere. Some said they were going to a camp in Canada; others claimed their destination was England, where they would be put to work cleaning up the ravages of war.

When they would return to Germany was a question no one could answer.

Chapter 23

The Friendship Game

The simultaneous advance of the American and British forces from the west, and Russians from the east closed a death-like vice grip on the German Third Reich. How the war would end was largely decided in early 1945 at the Yalta Conference, where President Roosevelt, Winston Churchill, and Josef Stalin agreed on terms that would change the world forever. Poland, Hungary, the small Baltic states, and Romania would be governed by the Soviets. Others, like Yugoslavia, Austria, and Greece, would be divided between "The Big Three." Additional countries directly affected by the Second World War—France, Holland, Denmark, Luxembourg, Belgium, and Norway—would remain under Western (American and British) control. Germany itself would be occupied by American, British, Soviet, and French troops, as would Berlin itself. These decisions seemed wise at the time, but were really a recipe for future conflicts that also voluntarily stripped freedom away from tens of millions of people for two generations.

With the war winding down, the Germans became increasingly anxious to surrender to American or British troops, knowing that capture by Russian forces meant either a death penalty or long-term captivity. Hundreds of thousands of Wehrmacht troops surrendered *en masse* in April and early May. During the deep Allied advance, evidence of horrific German war crimes became apparent when concentration camps were discovered. The barbaric treatment of the Jews and others in these camps shocked even the hardened Russians, who thought they had seen it all in a lifetime of hardship. After General Eisenhower walked through the camp at Ohrdruf, he wisely ordered every German civilian in the immediate vicinity to do the same, so no one could later deny what had taken place right under their noses.

Hitler selected Grand Admiral Karl Dönitz, the head of the German U-boat war, to act as the next Führer, and then killed himself in his underground bunker in Berlin. Dönitz did what he could to get hundreds of thousands of refugees west and away from Soviet forces before signing the surrender documents on May 7. Others surrendered to the Soviets the following day. V-E Day (Victory in Europe) was officially proclaimed on May 8. Many high-ranking German officers like Hermann Goering, Albert Speer, Alfred Jodl, and Wilhelm Keitel, were captured and eventually tried for war crimes. Many were eventually hanged.

The war in Europe was over. But the world war was not. On the other side of the world in the Pacific Theater, many hundreds of thousands would be killed and wounded over the next few months as the Japanese continued to wage a bitter defensive struggle to the death.

Gene and his teammates were always excited any time they put on their cleats, but playing Heinrich Mueller and his fellow prisoners was not much of a challenge. Mueller was a great natural athlete, but new to the game and thus unaware of its intricate complexities. The skill levels of the rest of the Germans varied considerably. Simply put, they did not have the experience or sense of the game to put up much of a battle. Mueller's "rules of engagement" made the game interesting and even more fun, but it never really put the Germans in a position to beat the American team.

The U.S. Navy baseball team was set to play the German prisoner team in front of all the other prisoners from the entire Camp Ruston, as well as most of the service men and women from the area and local townspeople. It was being billed locally as "The Friendship Game." The war was over, the German prisoners would soon be leaving for somewhere, and this was the last time they would play baseball together.

Gene knew that most people would enjoy seeing the game, but until it was ready to begin he had no idea so many people would place so much significance on it. They had been playing with the Germans in Louisiana for the better part of a year. Except for the first game or two, when Commander Arbeiter would attend to try and find a reason to shut it down, it had never been a big deal. A dozen people would show up—mostly other off-duty guards or a few local area residents. That was it. All Gene knew was that he was going to play a game and a crowd was expected, so he wanted to be at his very best.

On the morning of the big event, he was standing at the foot of his bunk getting dressed when a familiar voice spoke from behind him.

"Well, if it's not Sesser's favorite son, the Pride of the Egyptians."

Gene spun around and dropped his mouth in astonishment. "Mr. Boudreau! How are you?" He could barely contain himself as he shook hands with the man who signed him to play baseball.

"I'm doing fine, Gene. Please call me Frank." The scout looked the star catcher over from head to toe. "I didn't think you could get any taller, but you added an inch or two since I saw you last—what, four years ago now? How are you, Gene?"

"Yes sir, I think it has been four years. Well, the war's over and I'm still playing baseball. I'd say all in all, I'm doing just fine." Gene could not wipe the grin from his face. Neither could Frank.

"Gene, I have been talking with Commander Arbeiter about how you and the boys are playing ball with the enemy. I heard this whole thing was your idea!"

Gene's broad smile turned into a sheepish grin. "Well, I don't know. It just evolved out of an idea to keep our own skills as sharp as possible, that's all. It's no big deal, really."

Frank nodded and grinned back. "I always said you are a sharp kid—sorry, you're not a kid anymore! I'll let you finish getting ready, and you can tell me more about what it's like to play against the Germans. Any good prospects out there I should keep my eye on?" Both men laughed at the suggestion. "It's good to see you, Gene."

"It's good to see you, too, Mr. Boudreau—I mean Frank. So you'll be around after the game?"

Frank nodded. "I have already talked with the commander, and he said we can have dinner together off base, if you like—my treat, of course. They still don't pay you enough for me to expect you to pick up the tab, but I have a hunch you'll be buying me dinner soon enough!"

When Frank arrived at the Camp Ruston ball field, he was amazed to find a sizeable crowd of people had gathered to see a local baseball game. From what he could tell, people were still arriving, parking long distances away, and walking in with picnic baskets and kids on their shoulders. Some even brought their family dogs. The Brooklyn Dodgers' scout took a seat behind the American bench on some scaffolding set up for the occasion. He didn't expect much, but "The Friendship Game" was obviously a local event not to be missed.

When the game was ready to begin, Commander Arbeiter walked onto the field and introduced the umpire for the game. The "ump" explained the unusual rules—the same rules of engagement Heinrich Mueller had outlined months before. Gene got a kick out of watching the expressions of the people in the crowd when they realized how unfavorable they were to the American team. None of them seemed to realize that many of the Navy sailors were getting ready for a career in the big leagues.

When the umpire was done explaining the game to the fans, Arbeiter signaled to a young sailor standing near third base. He walked slowly onto the field carrying a trumpet under his arm and stopped between the pitching rubber and second base, where he lifted the shiny instrument to his lips and began playing the National Anthem.

While the anthem was being played, Gene looked down the line of his teammates. Each was standing proudly with his cap held over his heart, lined up along the third base line. Gene thought for a moment about Buck and hoped that wherever he was, he was safe. "If only he could see us now," Gene dreamed wistfully. His mind drifted to Ward, and then to his mom and dad, other siblings, and finally to Ron Callais. He wished they could all be here to see this.

As the anthem was nearing the end, Gene shot a look across the field to Mueller and his German teammates lined up along the first base line. It was hard to read their mostly stoic expressions, although one or two looked angry—or at least that is what it seemed like to Gene. Maybe it was just sadness at how everything had ended.

As the final notes blew, Gene could not help but think how much he had grown to like some of the Germans. Together, they had made life in Louisiana not just bearable, but fun. He knew them well enough now to know that if they had grown up in the same town, they would have been good friends.

"PLAY BALL!" yelled the umpire. The crowd erupted in cheers.

As the teams trotted back to their respective benches, an electric pulse seemed to be heavy in the air—everyone was excited and ready to play ball. Although energized, the Germans were also a bit intimidated by the crowd; several were visibly nervous.

Gene made a beeline for Mueller and the pair shook hands firmly. "It's been my honor to get to know you, Heinrich. Have fun and we'll celebrate after the game."

The German nodded his appreciation for the kind words. Gene trotted back to his bench and heard him shout back, "Thank you, Gene Moore. It is my honor, also!"

As the visiting team, the Germans were up to bat first. After Ray Laws threw his last warm-up pitch, Gene lifted his mask and trotted to the mound. "Ray? I have an idea. Let's let them get a few hits. Let 'em play with us a bit. You know, make a game out of it for them and the crowd."

Ray shrugged and replied, "Sure thing, boss." He took off his glove and began rubbing the shine off the ball.

Martin Ackermann was the first batter. Ackermann played second base for the German team, and was by far the shortest man on the team. Under the rules of this game, this was especially significant because a German could take his base on only two balls. Ackermann's diminutive stature decreased the size of the strike zone.

Gene called for the first pitch and Ray sent it off, slower and higher than normal. Martin swung hard and missed. "Strike one!" shouted the umpire.

"Wait for your pitch, Martin," Gene coached. "Release and don't take whatever he gives you. Be patient. Patient batters tend to get on base." Gene laughed as he threw the ball back to Ray. Ackermann didn't understand a word of English, and so had no idea what the catcher had just told him. The German shot Gene a strange look, but politely acknowledged his comments with a nod of the head.

The second pitch came in high for a ball. This time Martin didn't swing. "Ball!" shouted the umpire. The batter turned to Gene and smiled.

"Way to go, Martin. Wait for your pitch."

Ray stepped off the mound and looked over at Mac. "Whose side do you think Gene's on?" he asked with a grin. The entire infield broke out in laughter. Ray stepped back onto the mound, took the sign from Gene, and sent the ball hard and low over the plate.

"Ball two!" the ump yelled. "German rules of engagement—batter takes his base!"

As Ackermann trotted to first, he thumbed his nose at Ray and looked back at Gene for approval. The catcher burst out laughing.

Ray glared at the German and turned toward home plate. "Hey, ump," he yelled. "I think our catcher's on the wrong side! Kick him in the backside to remind him he's with the Stars and Stripes, would ya?"

The ump pretended he didn't hear Ray, but he did lean in and ask quietly, "Whose side *are* you on today, Gene?"

"I'm on baseball's side today, ump," answered the catcher. "You know these guys can't beat us. What's wrong with putting on a show for the folks, and letting these Germans earn some of their dignity back?"

The ump just shook his head at the thought and yelled, "Let's keep the game going. Next batter!"

The second batter was Rudolf Steinhart, the German third baseman. When he connected with the ball, it usually sailed deep into the outfield. Steinhart was one of the Germans who really enjoyed the game, and he was a natural athlete with a tremendous swing. But he also liked to pretend he hated everything about American baseball.

"Okay, Steinhart," Gene said. "Show us what you've got." Gene liked to use the opposing players' first names, but Steinhart seemed a better fit for the third baseman.

As usual, Steinhart completely ignored Gene, glared at Ray, and stepped into the batter's box. Gene set his glove for a low and outside pitch.

Steinhart swung so hard he missed and fell down. The crowd roared with laughter as the umpire called out the strike and the German jumped to his feet, angry and embarrassed.

"Nice swing, Steiny," Gene joked as he threw the ball back to Ray, "but that ball was about two feet outside the strike zone. Wait for it." Steinhart understood some English, but there was no way he was going to acknowledge the catcher's remarks. He shot another look at Ray and stepped into the batter's box.

Gene set his glove in the same spot, and the German swung hard a second time. "Strike two!" shouted the umpire. This time Gene didn't say anything. Instead, he called time and trotted to the mound.

"Ray, let's let this guy get a hit or walk him. It would do them good to score a run. Give 'em some confidence and maybe make a game of it."

"You know, Gene," Ray replied, "it's hard for me to purposely allow a hit or walk some guy. Would you purposely strike out?"

Gene thought for a moment before answering, "No, I suppose not. Can you at least take some of the edge off the ball? We won't let them win—they can't win and you know it. If they get too far ahead, send in the heat. Let's just give them the opportunity to stay with us and put on a good show."

Ray sighed. "Okay, Gene. You got it."

The outfielders were playing tight because few Germans hit the ball deep. If Steinhart could make good contact, he might send the ball over their heads. Gene set himself behind the plate, dropped his mask, and called for a change-up. Ray delivered perfectly.

The crack of the bat could be heard by everyone as Steinhart sent the ball straight over the center-fielder's head. He ran hard to first base and headed for second, where he stopped and smiled as he watched Ackermann score easily.

Gene smiled, too. The German bench came to life. The prisoners had started the game nervous and intimidated. After only their first two at bat they led—under their rules—2-0!

Next up was the German third baseman, Norman Hoffeditz, or "Stormin Norman" as the Americans called him. Hoffeditz was one of the best German athletes. He took to hitting as though he had been doing it all his life, and he was coming to the plate with no outs, a man on second, and a 2-0 lead. He walked to the plate, staring down Ray with every step. Gene loved his confidence; Ray always found it offensive.

"Alright, 'Stormin Norman,' let's see what you've got!" Gene said, beating his fist into his mitt as Hoffeditz took his place in the batter's box. "Wait for your pitch. Be patient."

"Ya, ya, no need for Moore you to tell me what I do," Hoffeditz uttered through clenched teeth. Ray had been working with Hoffeditz on his English. He still needed a lot of work.

Ray stepped off the mound and turned his back to the plate. Gene knew what that meant. He would turn back in a moment, his face ice cold, and be all business. Ray was turning back around when Gene yelled "Time!" and trotted back out to the mound.

Ray rolled his eyes and scowled. "What in the hell is it now, Gene?" he asked in frustration. "I'm trying to concentrate and get a rhythm going. You keep acting like this is little league."

"Come on Ray. I know what you're thinking. Don't knock this guy down. Give him your best stuff if you want, but I know that look. For the first time, they're really into this game, Ray. They won't win—they can't win and you know it. But don't throw at them."

Ray stared at Gene for several moments before loosening up a bit. "Okay, boss. But I am not gonna let this guy hit. If he gets on, he's gonna have to earn it. And there is no way he can earn it."

Gene nodded. "Fair enough. Just promise me you won't throw at any of them. You could really hurt these guys. They don't really have a clue how to avoid a fast pitch."

"Okay, okay, I get it! Get back to the plate and stay there, would ya? I don't want you back on this mound the rest of the inning!" Gene chuckled and trotted back to home plate.

Ray's next pitch was so fast Hoffeditz barely saw it. He had never seen anyone throw that fast. By the time his eyes picked up the ball and he wanted to swing, it was snapping into Gene's mitt. He swung anyway.

"Strike one!" shouted the umpire, dancing one step to the right as he pumped his fist out to the side. The pitch electrified the fans, who jumped to their feet and cheered. They had never seen a pitch like that, either.

The next three blew past Hoffeditz for the first out. He smacked his bat in the dirt, muttered something in German, and stomped back to the bench. The next batter was their catcher—Heinrich Mueller.

"We are winning, no?" Mueller said as he smiled at the American and took a practice swing.

"You are winning, yes," Gene responded with a smile. "Can you knock your man in from second base?"

"I believe I am up to that challenge."

"Then let's see what you can do. Ray's not happy, so you'll have to earn your hit."

"I want it no other way," replied the German as he swung his bat a second time and stepped into the box. "It is more fun when Ray is not happy."

Gene gave Ray the sign, Ray nodded, went into his stretch, and delivered his forkball in hard and low. Mueller swung and missed. He was not even close.

"Strike one!"

Gene threw the ball back to Ray and turned to Mueller. "Do what I always tell you," he reminded him. "Be patient and wait for your pitch. Patient batters tend to get on base more. He's not going to make it easy for you."

Mueller nodded, having now played enough American baseball to know that Gene's advice was sound. "And it is my wish not to make it easy for him."

He stepped back into the batter's box and focused his eyes on the pitcher. Ray wound up and sent a fastball in at the letters. He did not have as much on it this time. Mueller swung and connected, sending the ball high to right field, where the American player easily made the catch. The base runner on second tagged up and ran for third.

There were now two outs and a man on third. According to the German rules of engagement, they still had two outs left. The next batter up grounded out to the second baseman, but the man on third scored. The score was now 4-0, with one more out to go.

Ray was still visibly angry. He motioned for time and waved Gene to the mound. The catcher lifted his mask and laughed. "Me? You want me at the mound? I thought you said you didn't want to see me again for the rest of the inning? Or was it the rest of the game?" The look on Ray's face convinced Gene it was wiser to pay a visit to the pitcher, so he stood up and trotted out to the mound.

Ray had a new ball and was doing his best to rub the shine off it, together with its coating. "This is no fun, and it's damn embarrassing!" he complained, working his hands as hard as he could over the ball.

Gene shook his head and replied, "Ray, this is just a silly game, for crying out loud. Loosen up and have fun! Let's get this last guy out and we'll catch up next inning."

"Try again, buddy. The score is 4-0, but under Mueller's stupid rules, we can only score three runs an inning. We can't catch them until the second inning."

Gene shrugged. "Second inning, third—who cares? They can't win! Let's get this last guy out. We'll limit them to only two runs an inning, and we'll score our three. We'll talk it over around the seventh inning, and see what needs to be done then. Deal?"

"I'm tired of your deals, Gene. No offense, but I'm not holding back any more. Frank Boudreau is here. I don't want him to think I have lost anything, you know? I'm gonna pitch to the best of my ability or as our unofficial manager, you can put someone else in. How's that deal?"

Gene put his hand on Ray's shoulder, and answered, "Fine, Ray, but loosen up and have a little fun. This is a game you can tell your grandchildren about, buddy. I think you will remember more about it if you actually enjoy it!"

Gene looked over at the German bench as he trotted back to the plate. They knew they had gotten to Ray and they loved every minute of his discomfort. They had lost the war, but the prospects of returning home after winning this last little battle—regardless of how long the odds against them were—was exhilarating.

Ray retired the next batter on four pitches and four swings of the bat. The Americans batted in their two runs easily. The Germans scored again in the top of the second. And so it went as the innings flew past.

When the Germans stepped up to bat in the top of the ninth inning, the score was a surprising 13-12, with the Americans barely in the lead. Gene had done his best to keep the score close, dropping catches, letting a few pitches slide past, making an occasional bad throw to second, and even striking out twice. The Germans managed to score once in the ninth—which meant they ticked up two runs under their rules—to take a 14-13 lead.

The first Navy batter up in the bottom of the ninth was center-fielder Tim Milner, who was hitless for the day. As he picked up his bat Gene hollered over, "Tim, what do you think about a pinch-hitter?"

"Not much!" he yelled back, taking a practice swing. "Who got the first hit this team ever had?"

"You did!" Gene responded with a smile.

"Then let me get one of the last. I can get on, Gene." He winked and stepped toward the plate.

It was a little tricky hitting the German pitcher because none of them had ever played cricket. The throwing style was a bit unnerving and it was sometimes difficult to pick up the ball. Tim took the first pitch for a strike.

"Come on, Milner! You only get two strikes!" Mac yelled from the bench. Mac shot a look at Gene, and added, "Damn it, Gene. You should have pulled him."

The next pitch came in fast and high and Tim tagged a high line shot over the shortstop's head. The man who got the first hit—a double—in

North Africa repeated his performance with another two-base hit. The crowd erupted in cheers.

"Okay, guys, we only need two runs and this one's in the history books!" Gene yelled, clapping his hands as he paced in front of the bench.

Chuck Ellens was up next. He took two pitches and fouled both. According to Mueller's terms, he was out. Ellens gnashed his teeth and sighed heavily. The last chance for the Americans was Gene. He picked up his bat, grinned at his teammates, and headed for the plate. One man was on second. There was no margin for error. At the very least he had to get on base, but a home run would end the game.

Gene took the first two pitches. Both were high and wide. He fouled away the third. Under the rules, another strike or even a foul ball, and he would be called out.

Gene stepped out of the box, took a practice swing, and stepped back up to the plate. He locked his eyes on the pitcher as every spectator stood to watch. Gene felt his heart racing and felt his skin tingling. This sort of moment was exactly what he lived for.

The German pitcher took a few steps toward the plate and then let it fly. The ball came in waist high right across the plate. Gene swung hard and sent the ball sharply between the left and center fielders. The Navy bench went wild as Gene rounded second and Milner scored the tying run at home. The third base coach motioned for Gene to keep running. Gene glanced back and smiled when he saw the center-fielder fumbling for the ball. Gene rounded third and headed for home as the ball reached the shortstop. The winning run or final out of the ninth inning would be decided at the plate.

As soon as he left third, Gene began doubting the wisdom of trying to score. The third base coach waved him on, but the throw to the shortstop had been perfect. The ball and Gene would arrive at about the same time at home plate, where Mueller was waiting for them both. The German caught the ball as Gene began his slide. Mueller turned to make the tag—just as Gene had taught him to do. As he dropped his arm for the tag, however, the ball popped out of his mitt. Gene's cleats caught the lip of the plate, but his forward momentum carried his body hard against it. The umpire was already signaling safe when a loud and sickening "snap" was heard by everyone within 100 feet.

Most of the crowd was now on its feet, cheering the Navy team for winning in dramatic fashion 15-14. But those closest to the plate,

The Slide

including the umpire and Mueller, knew something bad had just happened. The German popped up on his knees and looked at Gene. His body was twisted funny around home. Mueller's eyes traveled down Gene's left leg. He gasped when he saw Gene's ankle. It looked as though it was on a hinge, bent completely back and to one side. Part of his bone was sticking through his bloody sock.

Mueller threw off his mask and stood up. "Mein Gott! Medic, Medic! Mein Gott! Help! Gene needs a doctor!" he screamed, moving in and out of German and English.

Gene grimaced in pain and tried to sit up. He propped himself up on his elbows and looked down at his ankle before falling back to the ground with a loud groan. "Damn!" he muttered through clenched teeth as a sudden sharp pain began pulsating through his body. "This didn't happen! I can't believe this happened!"

"Don't move, Gene," said the umpire as he knelt down beside the injured player.

Gene tried to lift himself up again, but Mueller dropped to his knees and eased him back down. "Don't look, Gene. Everything will be alright. Just lay still." Gene nodded and used a hand to wipe the tears running down his cheeks. The pain was becoming unbearable.

A stretcher crew arrived to part the crowd of ballplayers who had gathered around the all-star catcher. Frank Boudreau was with them. "Gene," he said as others moved aside so the scout could speak with his favorite ballplayer. "Oh . . . Gene . . . Just lay still, son. We will get you to the doctor right away. It looks like it's only a broken ankle. You'll be fine, Gene."

"Hi Frank," Gene managed through the rolling waves of pain. He groaned aloud before willing himself silent. "I'm alright. I'm alright," he repeated over and over. He took a deep breath and tried to compose himself before uttering, "Tell the Dodgers . . . I'll be ready to play."

"I know Gene, I know. I'll call Brooklyn right away. I'm sure they'll want their doctors to see you." The medics examined the ankle and carefully eased Gene onto the stretcher. Even that was sheer agony. Gene cried out again. "Just lay back, slugger," Frank said, lightly gripping his shoulder. "I don't want you to worry about anything. You'll be fine."

Gene arrived in the small camp hospital ten minutes later. The doctors gave him a shot of morphine, straightened his ankle out as best they could, and braced it. They wanted to operate right away, but a representative from the Brooklyn Dodgers had contacted the Navy. The team wanted Gene flown immediately to a surgical hospital in New York City. Who was going to treat him? Even with the morphine the pain was tough to bear, and his mind was so muddled now from the pain and the drugs he could not think clearly.

Through the fog Gene made out a familiar voice that grew louder with each word. He watched as Frank walked up the porch steps and smiled at him. "Do you have any lemonade, Gene? Are your parents home?"

"Sure, I have lemonade. You want a glass . . . Mr. Boudreau?"

"What's he talking about?" asked Frank.

"It's the morphine," answered the doctor. "It's not unusual. We gave him more."

Frank knelt down a few inches from Gene's ear. "Gene, it's Frank. Can you hear me? Do you know who is speaking?"

Gene nodded and opened his eyes. "Hello . . . Mr. . . . Boudreau."

"Gene, the Navy has agreed to move you to the Veteran Hospital in Brooklyn. The Dodgers' doctors will not be allowed to treat you, however . . ." Frank shot a glance at the Navy doctor standing next to him, "because you are still the property of the United States Navy. They will, however, be able to consult with the Navy physicians and decide together how to get you catching and hitting as fast as possible. Do you understand?"

Gene nodded slowly. "I think so."

"Gene," the Navy doctor began, "I'm not going to pull any punches with you, son. Your ankle's a mess. It nearly broke off from the rest of your leg. We straightened it some to hopefully prevent any nerve damage, but you need surgery. In my opinion, waiting to move you to Brooklyn is a mistake. You need attention sooner rather than later." He shot a look at Frank. "Much sooner. For whatever reason—and I can guess what it is—the Brooklyn Dodgers want you in New York, even though I have assured them we can repair your ankle every bit as well as they can."

"Thanks, doc," Gene whispered as he closed his eyes. The morphine made him feel as if he was floating toward the ceiling, and the men gathered around him were holding him down.

"Gene, it's Frank," continued the scout. "We just want to know you're getting the best care possible. Are you okay with this? Ultimately, it's your leg, son. You need to make the final call."

Gene smiled and forced his eyes open again. "Whatever you say, Frank. I . . . trust you. Just . . . I want to play . . . ball . . . again . . ."

"Okay, Gene, I understand. I'll be back as soon as I have some news." Frank touched Gene's shoulder lightly and left.

The pain was now completely gone, and Gene was starting to slip off to sleep when his doctor returned. "Gene?"

"Yes, doc."

"Two armed guards are here, and they have someone who wants to see you. I said no, but Frank Boudreau insisted it would help you. You have two minutes—if you can stay awake that long—and then you get some sleep."

"Hello, Gene," a formless voice whispered in a thick German accent. Gene forced his eyes open and smiled. Above him was Heinrich Mueller's sweat-stained grimy face.

"Heinrich," Gene responded weakly. "You . . . played . . . well."

The German shook his head in genuine sadness. "Gene, I am sorry. Mein Gott, I did not mean to injure you."

Gene shook his head slowly. He felt like he was on the top of the Ferris Wheel he rode each summer back home at the Franklin County Fair, as a wave of euphoria rushed through him. "My fault . . . not yours. My cleats. . . . Stupid."

Mueller sought out the American's hand and gripped it tightly. "We are proud of what you have taught us—all of us are. We are grateful to you and your team, Gene."

The catcher nodded his understanding but did not reply.

The doctor tapped Mueller on the shoulder and motioned with his head. It was time to leave. The sailors stood by to escort him back to the camp. Heinrich looked down at Gene as he drifted off to sleep. "We will meet again, Gene Moore. I am sure of it."

The next day, Gene was in a truck driving on some stretch of lonely highway. It took him nearly three weeks to reach the hospital in Brooklyn, New York. Why, exactly, he was never able to fully determine. By the time he arrived in the city, his toes had turned a darkish color and his ankle and foot were grossly swollen. He was alone on a train, balanced on crutches waiting for someone to help him get to the hospital. He waited in vain. No one was there to meet him.

Gene gritted his teeth as he climbed down from the train and made his way to the street, where he found a cab driver who offered to take the feverish sailor to the hospital. When Gene explained that he did not have enough money left to pay the fare, the driver waved him off and helped him into the back seat. He was operated on the following day.

Two weeks later, Heinrich Mueller and his German teammates were sent by train to Canada, and then shipped to England, which they reached in December 1945. Their excitement about returning home fell away when they learned they "had been sold to the British," as Hans Goebeler later put it, and would be working in Scotland.

The crew members of *U-505* toiled there for two years before being sent back to Germany in December 1947.

Chapter 24

The Broken Purple Heart

Life at the Brooklyn VA Hospital quickly became unbearable. Gene slept every night in a hospital ward with twenty other men. But Gene just wanted out. His surgery had gone better than expected, his leg was healing, and he was told the cast would come off any day. What made lying there insufferable, however, was his roommates. Their injuries were real war wounds. Most were the result of gunshots, but everything from shrapnel injuries to parachuting accidents were represented. He felt deeply guilty, being in this room with men who had real wounds, inflicted by an enemy who had been trying to kill them, not tag them out at home plate.

Gene could leave during the day on crutches, and the Dodgers were kind enough to provide him with free tickets to every home game. The bus trip from the VA Hospital through Brooklyn was quite an experience. Each city block held more people than all of Franklin County. As he took in the hustle and bustle of the city, he wondered where he would live while playing in Brooklyn. It never ceased to amaze him how many people there were walking the streets. "What did all these people do for a living?" he once asked the bus driver. His only answer was a shrug.

A sign leading into the city proudly announced Brooklyn as "the 4th largest city in the USA!" Gene had no way of knowing whether that was true. Brooklyn reminded him of Chicago: big, busy, and crowded. Everything Sesser was not.

Gene fluffed the pillow behind his head and sighed. He could move about the city and see some games, but he desperately wanted to be released and restart his life in baseball.

"Motor Mechanics Mate Warren E. Moore?"

"Yup, that's me," Gene answered turning his head to find the voice. When he saw the officer standing by his bed he lifted a hand in salute and began to sit up.

The officer returned his salute. "Stay there, sailor. I'm Captain Robert Shirk. I am pleased and honored to be here today to present you with this symbol of your country's immense gratitude for your service performed, and sacrifice made while defending your country." The captain leaned forward and pinned something on Gene's T-shirt.

"What's that, sir?" Gene asked, pulling his chin down to see what was affixed to his chest.

"Moore, you have been awarded The Purple Heart."

The entire ward erupted into laughter. Gene's own heart sank. "Sir," he answered sheepishly, "I'm afraid there's some mistake."

"What's that?"

"I wasn't wounded. I broke my ankle sliding into home plate in a baseball game." From what he could tell from the look on Captain Shirk's face, his explanation didn't matter at all. "Maybe he doesn't understand," thought Gene. He tried again. "Sir, I wasn't wounded."

The captain looked around and when he spotted all the men listening to their conversation, he leaned toward Gene, who was now sitting up. "I know, Gene," Shirk whispered. "I heard. You catch one hell of a game. Your government recognizes that you were injured while serving your country, and has paid you this high honor. Don't question it." He paused and then lowered his voice even more. "It comes with a small pension for the rest of your life, so shut up about how you were injured."

The captain backed up, snapped to attention, and saluted Motor Mechanics Mate Warren Eugene Moore. Gene slowly returned the salute, irritated by the unwanted attention. Captain Shirk smiled and smartly stepped from the room.

A few of the men in the ward hooted and teased the Sesser native, who felt a mixture of embarrassment and pride. He played baseball during the war. He did what he loved to do while his brother and millions of other men had braved the fury of combat. On the other hand, he knew he had entertained thousands of troops, and that his play had raised morale and resolve of the men who shouldered the rifles, drove the tanks, flew the planes, and cared for the wounded and dying. Hundreds had told him so, personally. He was injured while playing for the United States Navy. Gene smiled as he unpinned the medal and held it up to study it. "Wait 'til the guys at Bruno's get a load of this!" he exclaimed. The entire ward erupted in laughter once again. He joined in. For the first time in weeks Gene felt really good.

He was just leaning back to read a magazine and maybe take a nap when another visitor arrived. "Moore? Gene Moore?" the young messenger asked, as he stood at the foot of Gene's bed.

"Now what?" someone teased from another bed. "The Congressional Medal of Honor?"

Laughter once again shook the room.

"Yes, I'm Gene Moore."

"Sign here," instructed the stranger. "I have a registered letter for you." Gene signed and the man stuck a letter in his hand. It was from the Brooklyn Dodgers. Gene smiled wide and said out loud, "This is turning out to be a great day!"

Gene opened the letter, and began reading:

Dear Mr. Moore:

We regret to inform you that, due to your injury, we find no alternative but to release you from your contract with the Brooklyn Dodgers Baseball Club effective immediately.

Regretfully,

Walter G. Blankenburg
Director of Player Personnel

Stunned, he read the single sentence over and over, trying to make sense of it. Just minutes earlier he was awarded the Purple Heart in gratitude for his contribution to the war. Now, moments later, the Brooklyn Dodgers were expressing their gratitude for his service by telling him he was no longer wanted.

The other soldiers and sailors in the ward knew Gene had been signed by the Dodgers, and baseball had been the hot topic of conversation for weeks. Everyone could tell the news, whatever it was, was not good.

"Gene? Is everything okay?" asked one of the guys.

"What's the letter say?" asked another.

"The Dodgers . . . they cut me from the team because of my ankle." A flood of boos and cries flooded the room.

Gene shook his head as he fought back the tears welling up in his eyes. He slowly folded the paper, slipped it back into the envelope, and set it on the small table next to his bed. There had never been anything in his life but baseball. He loved it, lived it, and breathed it. And now this. He fell back onto his bed as the room fell into a stunned silence.

A young nurse, her heels clattering on the tile floor, walked into the ward and made a beeline toward Gene's bunk. "Congratulations! I hear you got something special today!" she said, snapping gum as she spoke.

Gene closed his eyes, scooted down in the bed, and rolled away from her, pretending to go to sleep.

Chapter 25

Branch Rickey

Frank Boudreau rarely visited Brooklyn. It was even rarer for him to be called into Mr. Rickey's office. He had met Branch Rickey several times, but as a scout, Frank was far below the radar of the legendary general manager of the Brooklyn Dodgers.

Branch Rickey was known in baseball circles as the "Mahatma," partly because of his overpowering presence and partly because he had been around for so long. Rickey had managed the Cardinals and served as the general manager for that organization before moving to the Dodgers.

It was Rickey who invented the "farm system," which allowed for young players like Gene Moore to be signed by Major League teams and then "farmed out" to minor league ball clubs owned by the Major League teams. There, young players got a chance to play steady ball at a high level and develop their skills with the chance of making it to the Major Leagues.

The general manager's office was unlike anything Frank had ever seen. Walls of dark cherry wood, trimmed in a colonial dentil crown molding and wainscoting, gave the room a rich warm feeling. When he stepped onto the carpet, Frank felt as though he was walking on expensive bedding, sinking an inch or two in with each step. Branch Rickey has a history in baseball worthy of this office, Frank thought.

"Frank, thank you for coming to see me," smiled Rickey, stepping out from behind his desk. He was in his mid-sixties, but he still had a thick dark mane of hair brushed up and over. Horn-rimmed glasses gave him the look of a college professor, as did the bow tie he almost always wore.

"The privilege is mine, Mr. Rickey," Frank replied. "I was surprised, and of course honored, to get your call."

"Frank, you have been a very important member of the Dodgers organization through the years. You are a trusted employee and have proven in the past to have a sharp eye for young talent."

"Thank you, Mr. Rickey, I'm grateful, and . . ."

The general manager cut him off. "No, wait, Frank. Let me finish." He motioned to a chair and took his own again before continuing. "This is a hard job. I feel as though I hold careers and futures in my hands and, in fact, I do. My future, the Dodgers' future, is often in the hands of our scouts. Unfortunately, like Major League ballplayers, scouts seem to have a career that at some point goes south. Frank, as grateful as we are to you for your past performance, I unfortunately today have the job of letting you go."

Frank's mouth dropped open. "I don't understand, Mr. Rickey. Have I done something wrong?"

"Frank, please don't make this harder than it is," answered the general manager, his face cold and expressionless. "Just look at your signings over the last few years. Frankly, they have not performed as we had hoped."

"Mr. Rickey, there was a war on and the pickings were very slim. I've had little to work with, and there was literally no one to scout except 15 year olds who could barely swing a bat and old men who could barely run the bases without getting winded." Frank paused, but Rickey remained silent, his expression unchanged.

Frank cleared his voice and continued. "Mr. Rickey, now that the boys are coming back from the war, I can get you the most talented ballplayers around! Remember Gene Moore, the young catcher from Sesser, Illinois? He's going to be the best in the majors—the best the Dodgers have ever had suit up!"

Rickey frowned and shook his head. "That didn't work out either, Frank. Unfortunately, Moore's leg didn't heal as well as we had hoped. It was a bad break Frank—bad. One of the worst our doctors had ever seen."

"What are you saying?" Frank asked, even though he already knew what the general manager was telling him.

"We released Gene from his contract."

Frank leaped to his feet. "You're not serious?" his voicing raised in surprise and frustration. When Rickey remained silent he shook his head and began pacing. "Mr. Rickey—you can't be serious! That kid is better with one leg than most of your big leaguers are with two! He can out-slug your best hitters and has a rifle for an arm. If you release that kid, it will be a decision you will regret—of that I am confident." He sighed. "Thanks for the opportunity you gave me with this organization, Mr. Rickey. It's the best, and I hate to leave it—especially this way."

Frank started walking toward the door, but paused with his hand on the doorknob. Without turning, he said, "Mr. Rickey, I love this team, this organization." He let go of the knob and turned to look directly into the general manager's eyes. "Permit me to say that I believe you have made two big mistakes. First, you let Gene Moore go, and second, you let me go. I think we just might make you sorry on both counts. As for me, well, I have had a wonderful career in baseball, and I know it's not over yet. I'll get another job with a good organization—it's not like I don't get offers as it is. But, Mr. Rickey, that kid is the best I have ever seen. Someone else is going to get him."

"Maybe, Frank," Rickey replied, "but I don't think so. Moore's through." Frank walked out through the big cherry door, shutting it harder than he otherwise would have under different circumstances.

Frank caught a cab outside the business gate at Ebbets Field. "Brooklyn VA Hospital," he said as he took a seat in the back. Numb and confused, he leaned against the uncomfortable seat and closed his eyes. He knew scouts came and scouts went. Same thing with players. Heck it was common. Frank Boudreau just never thought he would be one of them. When a horn blew loudly outside his window he opened his eyes and took in the passing buildings as they raced by. He was not really all that concerned about his plight. He had enjoyed a great career, had money saved up, and was still employable. It was Gene Moore who Frank was worried about.

The cab pulled up to the hospital at the base of the Verrazano Bridge. Frank paid the driver and walked through the doors. The elevator was full, so he walked up the seven flights of stairs. Motor Mechanics Mate Third Class, Warren E. Moore, was in room 702, bed number 7.

Frank hesitated at the door, forced a small smile on his face, and stepped inside. His smile vanished. Bed 7 had been stripped down to the bare blue and white pinstriped mattress. Two pillows were stacked at the foot of the bed.

"Can I help you, sir?" asked a young nurse.

"Yes, I'm looking for Gene Moore. He's a sailor. He was here with a broken ankle."

"Oh, Gene. Sure, he's a nice fellow. He went home this morning. Indiana? I think that's where he's from."

"Illinois," corrected the scout. "He's from Sesser, Illinois." His words came out more sharply than he intended.

"Okay . . ." she answered. "It was Illinois. My mistake."

"How was he when he left?"

The nurse's eyes narrowed as she studied the stranger. "Who are you?"

Frank produced a card—the same one he had shown Gene six years earlier. As he handed it to her, he realized it was no longer legit. He no longer worked for Branch Rickey. "I'm a baseball scout. I've known Gene since he was fifteen."

The nurse nodded her approval. "Mr. Boudreau," she began, looking up from his card. "To be honest, yes and no. Gene left much better than when he got here. He's still on crutches, of course. He was the funniest guy in the building. He was always laughing about something, and trying to make everyone else laugh, too. Something changed a few days ago. I heard he got a letter, and he was never the same. He didn't even say goodbye to us when he left. Probably a 'Dear John' letter, I guess. Lots of the guys get them. Did Gene have a sweetie?"

Frank sighed. "Yeah, his one and only true love."

The nurse looked sad. "That's a shame. What was her name?"

"Baseball."

Chapter 26

Home, Again

The war in Europe ended in May 1945, but the war in the Pacific continued without respite. The bloody battles on Iwo Jima, fought in February and March of 1945, were followed by even more gruesome fighting on Okinawa from April to early July. Nearly 12,000 Americans lost their lives during the assault on the latter island stronghold. Another 34,000 were wounded. Japanese losses were several times higher.

By July 1945, Japan's once mighty empire was gone. Only the home islands remained, and neither side looked forward to the invasion both believed was inevitable. Allied troops from Europe were transferred to the Pacific to prepare for the final showdown. A pair of atomic bombs, one over Hiroshima and the other over Nagasaki, broke the will of the Japanese and compelled their capitulation. The bombs prevented an even bloodier battle for the Japanese mainland. V-J Day—Victory over Japan—was proclaimed when Japan surrendered on August 15, 1945.

The Navy provided Gene with train fare from New York to Illinois. The ride was long and uncomfortable. Like so many other men on the train, Gene was returning from the war with metal in his body. Most carried shrapnel or bullets. His were metal bolts in his ankle. Everyone had a story to share, a dream to confide. Gene had not said more than a few words during the entire trip.

Feeling defeated and rejected, Gene crutched his way off the train when he arrived in Carbondale and hitchhiked back to Sesser. No one knew he was coming home. His mom had sent a couple letters when he was in the hospital, but none of his family had paid a visit. No one had the money to travel. He had spent years dreaming of his triumphant return to his hometown, the war behind him, and baseball waiting for him. Reality was a bit different. He was returning to Sesser on crutches, depressed and embarrassed. He had been cut from the Brooklyn Dodgers without having played a single game for the Major League team. The people of Sesser held him in high regard because they believed in his future success. Gene could only imagine what they would think of him now.

The farmer who had picked him up was passing within a few miles of Sesser, but was kind enough to drive him all the way home. The man's son, a sergeant, had been killed in North Africa during the closing days of the campaign. As the prideful father recounted his son's exploits, Gene recognized the soldier's unit number. In all likelihood, he had watched Gene play baseball there. North Africa seemed like a lifetime ago.

"You don't need to drive me all the way into town, sir," Gene said.

"Least I can do for a crippled war hero," he replied.

Gene mumbled his thanks and turned his head to look out the window lest the man see the tears welling up in his eyes. A few minutes later Gene pointed his finger and the pickup truck rolled to a stop. He thanked the stranger as he climbed out, picked up his seabag, threw it over his shoulder, and began limping his way up Mulberry Street. Nothing had changed. It was as though he was stepping back into time.

The first thing that struck him was the smell. After all those years away from Sesser, he had forgotten what a hog farm—even a small one—smelled like. The house looked the same, only a bit more run down than when he had left. The trim had yet to be painted. One of the first things he had planned on doing when he started making big money with the Dodgers was send his mom and dad away for a couple days on a vacation—something they had never done, even once—and have the barn and house trim painted while they were away. He sighed. It was just another dream that would never come to pass.

His younger sister Erma was sitting on the porch swing, talking with his youngest sister, Hilda. He set his seabag down and limped toward the stairs. Erma lifted her eyes and stared at him for several seconds, unsure who he was. When she finally realized it was the brother she had not seen in almost five years, she flew off the swing and bounded down the steps.

"Gene! Gene! You're home! Momma! Gene's home!" She squeezed him as tightly as she could and then pushed him back. "Why didn't you let us know you were coming? I thought you were playing baseball in New York!"

Gene hugged her close again, and choked back words he had never spoken before: "I don't play baseball anymore." Erma pushed him away again and gave him a puzzled look, but Gene just smiled and made his way up the steps to the swing where Hilda was still sitting.

"Who are you, mister?" she asked innocently.

"Sweetie, I'm your brother Gene. You're really growing up, Hilda. And real pretty."

Her eyes grew wide as she took in the man who had required several seconds to kneel in front of the swing. "You're my brother? The big league baseball player?"

Gene nodded his head, shook it, then nodded again. "Well, sort of. I'm your brother. I just don't play ball anymore." He had been home less than a minute and baseball was on everyone's lips.

Gene opened the screen door leading from the porch to the kitchen. His mother was in her apron, as she always was, standing at the kitchen sink cutting lemons for lemonade. It was as though he had stepped away five minutes earlier to get a newspaper, lived an entire year during each minute he was gone, and stepped back through the front door.

He took a long, slow breath and sighed. "Mom. I'm home."

Allie stopped in mid-cut, the knife halfway through a lemon. She slowly turned toward the door, as if afraid of what she might see. Her eyes widened when she saw her son, now a grown man, standing in the doorway. "Gene!" she screamed, wiping her hands on the apron and running into his outstretched arms. "Oh, dear God, thank you for bringing my boy home to me." And then she wept.

"Mom, don't cry. I'm home and everything's fine. You look good."

Like Erma, his mom suddenly realized she had not been told of his pending arrival. "You didn't tell us you were coming!" she scolded, pushing back and looking him in the eye. Something was wrong. She could sense it. "But I'm so glad to see you! Your father will be so happy. He is with Tommy Thompson looking at some new sows."

It felt better to be home than he imagined it would. Even though he was now an adult and had been to places he had never heard of, there was something special about standing in your boyhood kitchen and embracing your mother that just seemed to melt his problems into the shadows of his consciousness.

"You must be starving! Sit down and let me make you something to eat." No matter what the circumstance, everyone was always hungry, and food cured everything—at least that's the way Allie looked at things. She made her son a cold meatloaf sandwich and glass of lemonade, and sat down to watch him eat. She never took her eyes off her son.

Between bites, Gene filled his mom in on everything—except for the baseball news. He was telling her about his reunion with Ward in North Africa when a voice from out front asked, "Is Gene in there?"

Gene recognized it immediately. He pushed away from the table and looked out to the porch to see Willy Kerbovac, a former teammate from the Sesser Egyptians. Gene walked to the door, doing his best to hide his limp from both his mom and Willy.

"Gene! Holy cow, it is you!" Willy pushed the screen door open and hustled inside, giving his old friend a hug and slap on the back. "Boy, you are a sight for sore eyes! When did you get home?"

"Willy, it's great to see you too," he answered. Gene looked out at his seabag that was still sitting on the front sidewalk. "A little while ago."

"Grab your cleats and glove and let's go," Willy said, talking loud and fast. He was always excited before a game. "In thirty minutes we play Anna-Jonesboro. Last time they kicked our butts! Won't they be shocked when they see the Great Gene Moore walk onto the diamond at The Lumberyard?"

Willy stopped to catch his breath and spotted the pitcher of fresh lemonade. Allie followed his eyes, smiled, and stepped to the counter to pour him a glass. "Half the town's there already," he continued. "When news spread you were home, old man Basso closed his store and ran next door into Bruno's screaming, 'Gene Moore's home! Gene Moore's home!'" Willy laughed out loud and slapped Gene on the shoulder. "What do you think Bruno did?"

Gene shrugged and shook his head. "What?"

"He pushed everyone out the door and closed up! Can you imagine Bruno ever closing that place up like that? Ever?" Without waiting for a response, he continued. "Everyone's headed down to The Lumberyard, yelling, 'Gene Moore's back in town!' Man everyone missed you here, buddy." Willy looked at Allie and laughed, "You'd think General Eisenhower himself was in town. Actually, this is better. Ike can't catch!" Willy winked at both Moores and laughed at his own joke.

Gene's blood throbbed at his temples while his heart pounded in his chest, breaking a bit with each thump. He felt dizzy, torn between wanting to tie on his cleats and run to the field, and telling his friend and the entire town of Sesser that his ankle was shot and that his baseball days were over. He took a deep breath and began. "Willy, I just got home. I'm really tired. And my ankle, well, I don't think . . . I don't think I can play baseball anymore."

"Oh bologna sausage!" Willy replied, waving his hand in the air. "We all know about your ankle, but I bet it's all healed up by now. We'll just stand you up at the plate and you can knock it out over the old Huie Lumber sign, Gene. Hell, I'll run out and carry you around the bases." Willy stopped when he saw the look in Gene's eyes. Allie's face had gone white. It was the first serious inkling she had that Gene's ball-playing days were over.

Gene shook his head. "It's not like that, Willy. I don't think I can play anymore."

"Now, wait a minute ," began Willy. "What's going on here? You're Gene Moore, damn it! You were born to play baseball! Of course you can play!"

Allie studied her son closely. She had known something was not quite right. Now she knew exactly what it was. When Gene looked at her, almost as if for guidance, she smiled and replied. "You go do whatever you think you can, Gene. Sit in the stands, play if you want. Supper will be ready when you get home. I'm making chicken and dumplings and I've got a banana cream pie for dessert."

Gene cleared his throat. "Willy, I don't even have a uniform."

"Are you kidding? They've had your jersey hanging on the wall at Bruno's since the day you left!" Willy laughed, "The old guys down at Bruno's, they raise a toast and salute that damned thing every night! We'll get Bruno to pull it off the wall!"

"Okay," he sighed. "Let's go play some ball—or at least try to."

Allie followed Gene and Willy out onto the porch. She raised one of her hands to her mouth to stifle a gasp. His limping was noticeable now.

Gene and Willy pulled up in front of Bruno's. "Damn, Gene, I forgot he closed up. I'll find an open window and be right back," Willy said, slamming the car door.

Gene reached down and was taking off his shoes when he heard glass breaking. A few minutes later Willy came running back to the car. "Had to break a window to get it!" he explained. "Just one pane. We'll chip in and buy Bruno a new one."

"Willy! It looks like half of Sesser is here," groaned Gene as Willy turned into The Lumberyard.

"Yeah, and the other half's gonna be real disappointed," laughed Willy. "Did you really think anyone would miss your return?" Willy didn't wait for Gene's response. He was out the door and heading toward the field yelling, "Gene's here! Gene's here!"

"Oh, Lord," Gene mumbled as he got out of the car, still only half-dressed and wondering what in the world he was doing. Seconds later a mob of people had gathered around him. Most were familiar faces, beaming with pride and trying to shake his hand to welcome him home. Many were complete strangers.

By the time they arrived the game was already underway. It was the bottom of the first inning, and the Egyptians were up to bat.

"Willy, I haven't even swung a bat for months. This is just plain stupid."

"Don't worry about it. You'll be fine, Gene."

"Who's managing the team now?" he asked.

Willy laughed and slapped Gene on the back. "I am!" he grinned.

Gene only recognized a few faces on the Egyptians as Willy introduced him to each player. The welcome was abruptly interrupted when the umpire stepped up. "Welcome back, Gene!" he said, shaking his hand and patting him on the back. Hope the ankle is alright. I hate to stop the party, but I have to get a batter up there. Willy, who's up?"

"Are you kidding? Gene Moore's up!"

"No way, Willy! I already told you I haven't held a bat in something like nine months!"

"Well, then you're really overdue for a hit!"

Willy yelled for a bat and the bat boy handed Gene his favorite. "We've saved it for you, Mr. Moore," he said nervously as he handed him the Louisville Slugger bat. "No one's used it since your last hit."

Gene held the bat tightly. It felt good, like he was shaking hands with a dear old friend. No two bats were exactly alike, and he had missed this one while he was gone. As he caressed the wood, Willy was pleading with the umpire for a few minutes' delay so Gene could stretch out. "Okay, okay," he replied. "This ain't the usual situation, I guess."

Gene stood to one side and began slowly swinging the bat stretching his arms and shoulders and loosening his muscles. Although he had not been on a ball diamond since the injury in Louisiana, he had done all he could to keep his muscles in shape and limber.

"How's the pitcher?" he asked Willy.

"Fast. He'll probably pitch you low and away. But if he makes a mistake and crosses the plate, it's all yours."

When he finally walked out toward the plate the fans in the weathered old bleachers—which had also not seen a coat of paint since he had left—exploded with applause. Gene's heart swelled with pride as he watched several hundred people standing and cheering for him. He tipped his cap and the crowd yelled even louder.

Gene approached the batter's box, but stopped short and took a couple of practice swings. "Are you Gene Moore?" asked the catcher from Anna-Jonesboro.

"Yeah, I'm Gene."

The catcher extended his hand. "I've heard a lot about you. It's good to meet you."

Gene shook his hand, smiled, took one more practice swing, and stepped into the box. "This feels good," Gene said under his breath. "Maybe it's not over. Maybe I can still do this."

The pitcher wound up and delivered it hard, low and outside.

"Ball one!" the umpire yelled.

Gene stepped out and tapped his cleats with his bat, took another swing, and stepped back in. The pitcher wound up and threw. It was low and away a second time.

"Ball two!"

Gene stepped out and looked back at the catcher. "He throws hard."

"Yeah, he does," agreed the catcher.

Gene glanced into the bleachers behind home plate. The crowd was still on its feet. "They don't want a walk, you know."

The catcher chuckled. "That's for sure."

"Get him to pitch me something decent. He's not afraid of me, is he?" chided Gene.

"Nah. No way," spat the catcher. "Let me see what I can do for you. Bet you a buck if he throws a strike, you won't hit him."

"You're on." Gene responded.

The pitcher stared down at his catcher, shook his head, shook his head a second time, and then nodded and smiled. He began his slow and deliberate wind up and let it fly. The ball looked outside, but curved right across the center of home plate, just above the knees.

Crack!

"My God!" shouted the catcher as he jumped up and flipped off his mask. The pitcher did not even turn around to watch the ball as it sailed over the Huie Lumber sign. But everyone else at The Lumberyard did. Willy jumped up and pumped his arms in the air, but when he looked for Gene he was nowhere to be found. The crowd gasped and grew quiet. Willy looked back at the plate. Gene was lying across the plate.

"Gene!" Willy ran to his prostrate friend. The catcher and umpire were helping him to his feet. "Are you okay? What happened?"

"It's my ankle, Willy," Gene spat through clenched teeth. "It gave out." Gene tried to stand on his own, but the pain was too sharp. Willy and the catcher set him gently onto the ground.

The umpire turned to Willy. "Someone needs to run the bases if you want this run."

Willy waved a couple of the players over. "Give me a hand," he said. "I told Gene at his house that if he couldn't get around the bases, we would carry him. He didn't want to play, but like a fool I talked him into it." Willy looked over at the other Egyptians standing around Gene and nodded. "Help me carry Gene around the bases."

Gene looked up in embarrassment. "No, Willy, just help me get out of here," he said. "This is damn humiliating."

"Did you hit that ball out of this park?" Willy asked with a smile, mixed now with eyes rimmed in red.

"Yeah, but . . ."

"But nothing! No one is running these bases without you."

The bench emptied, the Egyptians hoisted Gene onto their shoulders, and they carried him around the diamond. When they crossed home, half of Sesser was there to meet him. There was not a dry eye in the house.

Gene Moore was home from the war.

Chapter 27

Reality

John Moore was as happy as his wife to see his son home again. He let Gene take a few weeks to get settled in and figure out what he was going to do with the rest of his life. He had come late to the realization of the gift for baseball Gene had, and knew the ankle injury had taken a lot out of his boy—and not just physically. Pop Moore was fond of saying that life was tough, and whatever cards a man was dealt, he had to get on with his life. As the days passed, he didn't like what he was seeing, and he hoped this period of Gene's life would be short-lived.

After moping around the house for the first week or so, Gene began spending his evenings drinking at Bruno's, where customers bought him beers in exchange for stories about the war and baseball. He spent his mornings sleeping in late. Each day began with a bad hangover, an unshaven face, and bloodshot eyes. Once he managed to shake himself awake, Gene would down a few cups of coffee, snack on whatever his mom had cooked for breakfast, and hang around the house for hours before even washing his face or dressing. The rest of the day he wasted sitting quietly on the front porch, smoking cigarettes and rocking on the swing, thinking thoughts he refused to share with anyone. When the late afternoon slipped into early evening, he would head back to Bruno's and the process repeated itself.

Gene Moore was on a downward spiral and the bottom was still a long way away.

Allie and John "Pop" Moore during their later years (1966),
sitting on a swing in their yard in Sesser.

After several weeks John and Allie Moore had seen enough. It was time to sit down with their son and have a heart-to-heart talk about what he was expecting from life, and how he was going to get it.

"Gene," began his mom one afternoon after his hangover had faded away, "We got a letter from Ward yesterday. He's doing fine. Homesick, of course, but doing fine." She sat down on the porch swing and offered her boy a big smile and a hug.

Gene hugged her back and smiled. "Last time I saw Ward, we were in North Africa, and he told me he was heading for Berlin."

"According to his letters, he didn't get there," Allie continued. "They stopped along the way and ended up making their headquarters in the home Hitler was born in—Austria, for heaven's sake. That Hitler, that man was pure evil, and I guess not even German! That's what happens to you when you start believing you have the right to do just about anything. Start a war that sucks in the world and kills millions of people. I guess Ward just marched right in with his buddies and took over his house! Sounds like your brother, doesn't it?" she laughed.

"Yeah," Gene chuckled, lost again in his thoughts. "I can believe Ward would do that." He turned away and looked into the distance.

"I told you about how Ward saved John Brown, didn't I?"

Gene was silent for a few moments. He slowly turned back, as if he had just realized what she was asking. "Yeah, you told me. Pop told me. Erma told me, too. In fact, I hear about it every night down at Bruno's," he replied. There was jealousy in his voice, and bitterness, too. "Ward is quite the hero around here now."

"John's sister told Erma that John is back in the States and will be home next week," Allie continued, trying to ignore the tone she was hearing from her younger son. "I can't wait for Ward to come home, too. Our family is so blessed. He was shot twice, both times in the back, but never seriously. God was watching out for him."

"I guess he was watching out—for Ward."

The screen door squeaked open and John Moore stepped onto the porch. He had been listening to the conversation from inside the kitchen. "They gave him the Bronze Star for bravery," he proudly chimed in. "You are right, Allie. Lots of families in Sesser and Franklin County whose boys aren't coming home."

"I sat with Margaret Neville when she got the news that her Bobby was killed in the Pacific," Allie said. "Even though he was lost at sea . . ."

"He went down on the USS *Indianapolis*," John interrupted. "Did you hear about that?" he asked his son. Gene nodded but didn't speak.

"Anyway," Allie continued, "they put a stone up at Maple Hill Cemetery and had a service at the church, just like his body was there. It was so sad, Gene. Such a loss. But Ward is coming home, you're home, and you both have your lives ahead of you. We are truly blessed."

Gene tilted his head back and looked up at the peeling paint on the ceiling of the porch. "I'm not feeling very blessed, mom," he answered. "My ankle's a mess. I can't play ball. I walk like I'm seventy years old and I'm not yet twenty-two. I don't think I'll ever be able to play again—even for fun."

Allie pulled out a hanky and dabbed her eyes. "You're alive, Gene. Your brother is alive. Both my boys survived the war. That's all your father and I care about." Gene looked away again. Allie gave her husband a nod, the signal that it was his turn to join the conversation.

"So, Gene, you've been home three weeks now," began the older Moore. "What do you think your next step should be?"

"I don't know, Pop," the younger Moore replied. "This is all new to me."

"What's new to you?"

"Not playing baseball," he shot back. "I never gave a thought to what I would do if I didn't play ball." Gene paused while looking down at his hands. He rubbed them before using one to run his fingers through his uncombed and unwashed hair. "I don't know what to do."

John raised his eyebrows as he looked at his wife. "Well, you'll just have to give it some thought. You're a man now," he continued. "You need to make a life for yourself. Baseball was much better to you than nearly everyone who ever picked up a glove. But it's just a game, son, and you had fun playing. And you did a lot of good for a lot of people."

John hesitated and cleared his throat. Allie held her breath. Gene turned to look into his father's eyes. "If it's over, it's over," John finally said. "You just have to accept it. I'm sorry things didn't turn out for you, but I agree with your mom. We are very lucky. Some of your friends came back from the war none the worse off, some are much worse off than you, and a lot of 'em aren't ever coming home, and there wasn't enough left of 'em to bury."

Allie nodded. "I can't stop thinking of the poor Samples family. Billy stepped on a mine in Italy two days before the war ended. His younger brother Joe was killed a year earlier in France." Gene's mom choked up just repeating the story.

John continued for her. "Two days after they got the telegram, the old man kissed his wife one morning, walked out into the barn, and shot himself between the eyes. Now that family has suffered. We haven't." John sighed and scratched his ear, waiting for a response from Gene. None was forthcoming.

John took off his hat and turned it over in his hands, studying it as if he had never seen it before. "Get yourself together, son, and go on. I don't see any other choice. Do you?"

Gene nodded and turned away. "No sir, I know, Pop. I know."

John pulled his cap back on his head. "Gene, the damn depression is finally over and things are getting back to normal here in Sesser. It's been a long, dry spell. If I could rent a few more acres, we could plant some corn and maybe pick up another fifteen or twenty pigs. We could work this farm together. It's not much, I know, but it's a living. It's an honest living. Feeding people, farming, it's a good high calling for your life. Something you can be proud of."

The last thing Gene wanted to do was spend the rest of his life farming and raising hogs. "Thanks, Pop," he finally answered. "Sure. We can do that. I don't know what else to do. The mine isn't hiring, and I don't really have any other skills. By the time I got out of the hospital, most of the other men were back and the good paying jobs were gone. Bruno said he might be able to use me tending bar at night."

"Oh Gene, no!" Allie said. "Nothing good ever happens at Bruno's, or at any tavern. You're spending too much time there now, and I am worried sick about you. Please don't take a job there."

Gene looked over at his mom and smiled. "Okay, I won't tend bar. I'll find something else. For now, I can help Pop." He leaned over and gave her a kiss on the cheek. "I'll be fine. Stop worrying."

Once his parents went into the house, Gene stood up and headed for Bruno's.

The Sesser folk loved Gene—even if he could no longer play baseball. Sesser was a small town and, like his parents, many people in it worried about how much time he spent drinking and feeling sorry for himself. They, too, had expected Gene Moore would lead a different life—a special life. They never imagined it would consist of drinking away his health in Sesser's local tavern.

The people of Sesser had always looked at Gene as their way out of a run-of-a-mill life—even if they only experienced it from afar. Everyone knew there was more to life outside Sesser and Franklin County, but few got the chance to experience it. Gene's shot at professional baseball had given them all—young and old alike— something to look forward to. Gene Moore was going to put Sesser on the map. His strong legs, powerful arms, and unyielding spirit had always given them hope. His success had given them a genuine sense of pride.

All of that was gone now. Like the good people of Sesser, Gene was back home for good.

Chapter 28

Return of the War Hero

"Gene! Think fast!" The loud voice came from the doorway of the barn. Startled, Gene turned to see Sergeant Ward Moore, decked out in his dress uniform, finishing his wind up and hurling a corncob at him—hard and fast.

"Ouch! Shit!" Gene yelled as Ward's pitch hit him squarely in the nose.

"What the . . . Gene! You missed!" Ward laughed as he trotted toward his little brother.

Gene shook his head. "I guess I wasn't ready," he replied, leaning his head back and holding his bleeding nose.

"I'm sorry—really. I am. You've never missed one of those before—ready or not!"

"You boys didn't get enough fighting during the war?" asked John Moore as he walked into the barn. "You're back five minutes and you're already punching each other?"

"No, Pop! I didn't punch him," pleaded Ward. "I hit him with a corn cob—but I didn't mean to."

Pop looked at Gene in surprise. "You missed?"

Gene rolled his eyes and looked at his bloodstained fingers. The bleeding had nearly stopped. "Holy cow! Let's not make a federal case of it," shot back Gene. "Yeah, he caught me by surprise. I missed. So what? Just forget about it." Gene wiped the remaining blood from his nose with his sleeve. And then it hit him: his brother was back from France. "Jeez, Ward! When did you get back?"

"Like Pop said, about five minutes ago!" he laughed. The brothers exchanged a hug and slaps on the back. "Pop said you were out here feeding the horses and chickens, so I thought I'd come and surprise you."

"Well, you did that."

Ward took a step back and surveyed his brother. "Besides the bloody nose, you really look like crap! You been sick?" Ward asked.

"No," Gene replied, waving off Ward's inquiry. "Hail to the conquering hero! The guys at Bruno's have been talking about your exploits for a year. You'll be a big hit once they realize you're back in town." Gene paused when he spotted the Bronze Star pinned to Ward's uniform. "Is that it?"

"Is that what?" Ward asked.

"Is that the medal they gave you for saving John Brown from that trapped tank?"

"Yeah," Ward smiled. "That's it. They made a big deal out of it, but it really wasn't. That kind of thing took place all the time. Most guys never even get a mention, let alone a medal. You just do what you have to do, right?"

For Ward, the casual manner in which he spoke of his bravery was out of the ordinary—at least, that's how it struck Gene. "Saving the lives of three men trapped in a tank, under heavy fire and getting shot twice before you come home, I'd say that qualifies as a big deal," Gene replied, nodding his head as if he had been evaluating military exploits all his life. He looked over at his dad and smiled, "Don't you think, Pop?" John just nodded. He was proud, too.

"Well, it's about damn time another Moore got some attention in this town!" Ward waited for his Pop and brother to laugh, but only silence greeted his joke. Ward looked at them both and squinted. "So, is something wrong? Gene, you back playing ball yet? I am dying to see you play again. Ever since North Africa . . ."

"Nope," Gene answered, cutting him off and turning around to the grain bin.

"Nope what?" Ward looked over at Pop. "What did I say?"

"I'll leave you two boys alone to get reacquainted," was all John was willing to contribute to the uncomfortable situation. "Come up to the house when you're done and we'll have something to eat."

When John left Gene turned to Ward. "You did this last time we were home."

"I did what?" Ward asked.

"Bloodied my nose."

Ward threw up his hands in disgust. "Gene, what's going on?"

"Nothing," he replied, shrugging and turning away. "I'm feeding the chickens."

"You know what I mean. With baseball." Ward waited for a response. Instead of answering, Gene turned and carried the bucket through the door and out into the chicken pen. Ward was following hard on his heels when he stopped in his tracks. Gene was limping. Ward let out a sigh and kicked his way past a squawking chicken as he hurried after his brother. "Gene, I didn't get much news from home. All I heard was that you hurt your ankle—that's it! I didn't know it was serious. Damn it, tell me! What's going on?"

Gene stopped, set the bucket down, and turned back to face his brother. His face was angry, his lips trembling. "I did more than hurt it, Ward. I broke it, really bad. It's really screwed up." Gene bent down and began pulling handfuls of grain from the bucket and tossing it on the ground for the chickens, who gathered around to peck at the tiny yellow bits of ground corn.

Ward swallowed hard. "I assumed it would've healed by now, but I guess it hasn't," was the best he could come up with.

"Nope."

"What did the doctor tell you?"

"They don't know much, really. One kept telling me everything would be fine, but another told me I would never play ball again—at least not at the level I was used to playing at," Gene replied, throwing more grain on the ground.

Ward chewed his lower lip and exhaled through his nose. Loudly. "Gene, something else is going on. I haven't been home for years. Just tell me."

"Alright, I will," Gene shot back. "They had to put two steel bolts in it. The Dodgers released me, Ward. *They released me.* No one took the time to even visit with me. Some guy I had never heard of sent me a . . . letter." Gene raised his arm to his face and pretended to wipe dried blood from his nose, but Ward could see he was really wiping away tears. "I came back home," he continued after a few seconds. "That's it. That's all there is to tell."

"Okay," Ward said, nodding his head. "Okay." His brother's world had come crashing down, and he had not been here to help him. "So these Dodgers people—they're wrong, right? There are other teams that will want you. I'm sure of that, Gene."

"When I came home, I tried to play a game with the Egyptians and my ankle gave out my first time up to bat," admitted Gene. "It was damn embarrassing—and painful, too. Everyone turned out to see me. They expected one thing, but they saw something else."

"Is that it?" Ward asked. "Is there anything else you want to tell me?"

"Isn't that enough?"

"Yeah, I suppose so, Gene." Ward didn't know what else to say, so he patted his brother twice on the shoulder and watched as he continued feeding the chickens. His brother, the best catcher baseball could have hoped for, was limping through chicken shit and throwing grain on the ground. Ward felt like crying himself.

"Is Gene okay?" Ward asked his parents after he stepped through the back door, kicked his shoes off, and made for the kitchen.

Allie looked at John, who answered for them both. "I don't know, Ward. He just needs to get that game out of his system, that's all."

"That ain't gonna happen anytime soon, Pop," Ward answered. "He thinks the only reason he was put on this earth was to play baseball. Pop, let me tell you, I never paid much attention and only caught a few of his games, when he was about 10. But after seeing him play in North Africa, I can understand why he would think that."

"I know, Ward," John replied. "I saw him that day with the scout, Frank something or other. Gene was mighty good."

Ward looked back and forth between his mom and dad. "He needs to play ball, somehow. He has to."

"Ward," his mom began, speaking softly as she wiped down the counter around the sink. "Sometimes the mind and heart are willing, but the body just isn't able. Gene needs help adjusting. I'm not sure that kind of talk is going to help him."

"Do you really think he's never going to play ball again—ever?" Ward asked.

"You are not going to help the situation talking like that," his father said sternly. "No one else in this town is feeling like they've gotta play baseball. He's a man, now. He's been to war. He's home, alive, and it's time for him to go on with his life. It's as simple as that. Feeling sorry for him is only going to feed the problem."

"There's no problem, Pop," Gene said as he walked in from the porch. Ward winced when he saw his brother. "I think in the future, any discussion about me . . . should include me." Gene walked through the kitchen and into the living room.

"Mom, why don't we get an early supper on the table and give Ward and Gene the first good meal they've had together since the beginning of the war?" John suggested. Allie nodded and headed for the ice box.

It's just like old times, Ward thought as he finished eating, finishing off the white beans and ham and homemade cornbread. He wiped his mouth and tossed his napkin on his plate. "Mom, you have no idea how many times I've dreamed about your cooking. And you know what? It's even better than I remembered."

Allie smiled. "You have no idea how I missed feeding my boys."

The dinner conversation had been nothing but small talk—Ward's trip home, what had happened to so-and-so, the price of baby pigs.

Once the girls left to do their chores, Gene turned to his brother. "Hey Ward. Wanna go down to Bruno's and see everyone?" Gene asked.

"Sure, just let me go change out of this uniform."

Gene shook his head. "I think at least once, everyone needs to see Sesser's war hero in all his splendor. A war hero has an image to live up to, don't you think, mom?"

Allie nodded in agreement. "He sure looks handsome. Can you believe I never got to see Gene in his uniform . . . not even once?"

"Go put it on Gene! If I'm wearing mine, it's only fair that you should wear yours," Ward insisted.

"I left it," Gene sighed, shaking his head as he helped his mom clear the table.

"Left it where?" asked Ward.

"When I left the VA Hospital in Brooklyn. I just walked out with the clothes on my back and left it there. The only thing I brought home were my dog tags."

"And his Purple Heart," John added. "He brought that home too."

"Well if Gene's not wearing his uniform, I'd feel like a peacock in mine. Let me go change and I'll be right back. I'm out of the Army. Once I take it off, I'll never put it back on again, and I'm taking it off right now."

"Ward, that's exactly why you need to leave it on for your triumphant return to Bruno's!" Gene exclaimed, grabbing Ward by the arm and ushering him toward the door.

"Wait! What's the big deal?" Ward asked, pulling his arm away from Gene. "Just let me change." Ward's patience was beginning to wear thin.

"Ward, just humor him. He's proud of you and wants to show you off," John lectured.

A sheepish look crossed Ward's face. "Well, all right. One last night in the uniform. I guess that can't hurt. Let's go."

The brothers were walking toward town, headed for Bruno's, when Ward observed. "I bet that old place hasn't changed. I can't believe I'm gonna say this, but I missed that old dump. Is that picture of the Alamo still there?"

"Yeah, it's there," Gene answered. "Nothing's changed. The picture frame has the same dust on it from before you left." He laughed. "In fact, there's a few added layers on top!" Gene slowed to a stop. When Ward realized his brother was no longer by his side, he stopped too and look back. "Why would you ask about that, of all things?" Gene want to know.

"You mean the painting of the Alamo?"

"Yeah, it's been there for twenty years—at least."

Ward suddenly looked distracted, his thoughts far removed from Sesser. "When I was in Germany, Gene, there was this little village," he began slowly. Gene thought his voice sounded detached, as if it was not his own. "I opened my big mouth to General Patton and he asked if our tank would take the lead in the attack. What could I say? So like an idiot I said sure. As we rolled slowly into town, the Krauts were everywhere—everywhere, Gene—firing with everything they had."

Ward stopped and took a breath. It was only then that Gene realized his brother had his own demons. "Keep going," urged Gene. "What happened next?"

"We saw another tank ahead. It had come in from another direction. Part of a three-story building had collapsed on it, so I jumped out of the tank—ours was jammed up and couldn't move anywhere—and started digging out the crew."

A sudden realization hit Gene. "Was that John Brown's tank?"

"Yeah, it was. Can you believe it? But what was odd was when John and his crew had climbed out." Ward looked around, as if worried someone else would hear. "We ducked behind what was left of a stone wall . . . I'm not sure, it might have been a rubble pile. Anyway, that's not important. Gene, we were standing there, and not 50 feet away were a dozen Krauts, some in windows, some standing on the open street, all spread out. They were firing rifles and machine guns, MP-44s, I think they were, at the tanks and some infantry guys who were covering us. It was weird because they were ignoring us—like we were invisible." Ward stopped for a moment and shook his head, remembering how close death had come to touching him. "I know standing here in Sesser that this sounds a bit nuts, but all I could think about was the men in that painting, standing behind the walls of the Alamo and waiting to be killed. It was the safest place to be at that time, but only for a short time—you know what I mean?"

Gene nodded vigorously, enthralled with the story.

"I kept thinking about that painting, Gene. I knew how the Alamo ended. All the good guys were killed. The rubble or wall, or whatever the hell it was we were standing behind wasn't going to protect us for long, just like it didn't protect Crockett, Bowie, or Travis. So I grabbed John by the collar and we started running back to my tank. All I could think about was that I didn't want to end up as the subject of a painting in some bar—one of many guys who were killed doing something stupid."

Gene nodded slowly. "I understand, Ward. I mean, I didn't see combat like that, but I think I understand what you mean. Running back to your tank. That's when you were hit, right?" Gene asked.

"Bastards shot me twice. Once in the ass, and again across the back. A few weeks later they got me again, just for spite, a few inches above the back wound. Nothing that serious, though." A smile crept across his face.

"What? What's so funny about being shot?" Gene asked.

"Damn Nazis weren't fast enough to shoot me in the front!" Both brothers laughed. Gene grabbed him by the arm again and started moving him along.

"Gotta keep moving," Gene said as they headed down Main Street. "We don't want to be late!"

"Late? Late for what?" Ward asked, but Gene remained silent until they stopped in front of Bruno's.

"We're here," he said with a smile. Gene knocked on the door before announcing in a loud voice, "Let's go in and see if anyone's here!"

Gene pulled the door open and the crowd jammed inside erupted into cheers. A stunned Ward stood there with his mouth open, reading the sign hanging above the dusty old Alamo print: WELCOME HOME WARD!

John Brown walked out from the crowd and handed Ward a beer. "Hello, buddy. We both made it back. Here's the beer I promised you."

"We did, John. We did," Ward responded with a smile, clicking his glass against John's. "Pretty cheap payment for pulling you out of that tank." Both men laughed, stood there awkwardly for a moment, set their mugs down, and embraced.

"I wouldn't be here if not for you, Ward," John said gripping his friend tightly.

"You think you'd still be stuck in that tank?" replied Ward. "Someone else would've dug you out." Ward was flattered, but obviously uncomfortable with John's expression of gratitude.

"No, it took a heroic son-of-a-gun like you to jump out of your tank, run down the street—under heavy fire—dig us out, and then pull me back to safety. Not to mention the fact that you got shot twice." John stepped back. "You saved my life, Ward Moore, and I'll be forever grateful. Thank you."

Dozens of other patrons swarmed around the pair welcoming Ward back to Sesser. "Bruno!" shouted Ward. "You still keep your tools under the back counter?"

Bruno nodded from behind the bar, drawing draft beer as fast as he could pour them. "Sure, why? You want to build something tonight?" Everyone laughed.

"Nope. I brought a souvenir home for you. Can you bring me a hammer and a few nails?"

Bruno shot Ward a puzzled look, filled the mug the rest of the way, closed the tap, and turned around to find his hammer. When he handed it to Ward with a pair of nails, the former soldier walked to the wall at the far end of the bar. The other patrons fell silent as they watched Ward closely in an attempt to figure out what he was up to. Ward examined the wall, rubbed a spot with his hand, and turned back to face the crowd.

"What?" Bruno yelled. "What are you up to?"

"No good, I bet!" someone else yelled. Laughter followed.

Ward smiled and reached in his pocket. He pulled out something red, held it up to the wall, drove a nail through it, and stepped back. The bar erupted in loud cheers. He had nailed to the wall a black swastika on a white circle, sewn on a swath of red cloth.

"I don't think that murderous Hitler ever wore this!" Ward shouted. "But I got it from his birthplace. There's one thing I know for sure!" Ward paused, the crowd waiting quietly for the punch line so obviously coming. Ward yelled at the top of his voice, "That bastard will never wear it again!" The crowd cheered as it rushed toward Ward. Everyone wanted to shake his hand and buy him a drink.

"Ward Moore . . . let me get a look at that Silver Star!"

"T-Bone Mygatt! How are you?" Ward asked, glad to see his old friend. "It's just a Bronze Star."

"Well, it's a pretty medal, and well deserved. I am swell, just swell. I was in the South Pacific. Got home a couple months ago. I'll tell you, I missed this old bar and town. I guess there really is no place like home."

Ward Moore was home from the war and Sesser had a genuine war hero. Through it all, Gene remained in the shadows, proud of his older brother. This was his night. His triumphant return.

By the time he was polishing off his third beer, Ward had picked up enough bits and pieces about what Gene had been up to over the past year to worry him. Gene wasn't the same brother he'd left in Sesser when the war broke out, and he certainly wasn't the same sailor and ballplayer he'd seen in North Africa. When he spotted Gene across the bar standing alone staring at the old Alamo print, Ward picked up his beer and joined him.

"Hey, little brother." Ward put his hand on Gene's shoulder. He lifted his mug toward the painting. "Here's to you, gentlemen. I now know what it felt like."

Gene looked at Ward. "What are you gonna do now?"

Ward shrugged and took another gulp from his lukewarm beer. "Not sure. Maybe open a bar. I was thinking about Benton, but maybe Mount Vernon. I thought about it all the time I was over there." Ward smiled and asked, "Where's Jamie Reid? She still in town?"

"Yeah, she's working over in Benton, I think," replied Gene. "She asked about you when I saw her last."

"She wrote me two letters, and then I never heard from her again," Ward said with a wistful sigh. "She married yet?"

"Not unless she got hitched since last week." Gene smiled. "You thinking about looking her up?"

"Maybe. She still pretty?" he asked, shooting his little brother a sideways glance.

"Yup."

Ward motioned to a small table and the brothers sat down. "Let's get back to you, Gene."

Gene waved a hand in objection. "Ward, my problems are so small and trivial. I can't play baseball. I really realized how trivial it was when you were telling me about saving John's life. So many people died or were seriously injured. Remember that red-headed kid from Mount Vernon who always wanted to play ball but could never hit? I hear he is in the nut house—they call it shell shock or something. Just completely lost his marbles." Gene lifted his mug, took a long drink, and set it down again. "How can I complain about two screws in my ankle, which I got trying to slide into home plate!" He lowered his voice when he realized he was yelling. "I'm helping Pop on the farm now." Gene paused and glanced over at John Brown. "Your new biggest fan over there offered me a job at his service station. I'm in demand. Don't worry about me. You're home, all is as well as we could have hoped for, really." Gene lifted his eyes and stared at the old print he had looked at hundreds of times before.

Ward was once again left with nothing to say. "Gene, I'm not good with words, you know? I'm so damn sorry. You were the best. I never realized that until I watched you play in Africa. I know now I cheated myself out of years of good times by refusing to walk to The Lumberyard and watch you play. I can be a stubborn mule sometimes."

"Well, I'll agree with that!" Gene nodded. Both laughed in response. "It could be worse."

"You're damn right it could be worse. I saw too many dead men. Trust me, it could be much worse."

Gene offered a crooked smile. "I guess that's one way we're different, Ward. You look at your life now and say you wouldn't want to end up the subject of an old picture hanging on the wall of a bar."

Ward, Gene, and John "Pop" Moore (from left to right) on the porch of the small Moore family house on the corner of Matthew and Mulberry in Sesser, Illinois (circa 1946-1949).

"So?" Ward furrowed his forehead.

"I would trade my life for that," Gene continued, pointing to an empty space on the wall across from the painting.

Ward shook his head. "I don't know what you're getting at."

"That's where my old uniform hung while I was away. Had I died during the war, it would still be hanging there, and everyone here would remember me for who I was, not what I am. Now, I'm no different than anyone else, only I have a limp."

"No way, you'll never be like everyone else," Ward replied, setting his mug down and pointing his finger at Gene. "You're a Moore, and that's something to be proud of. You're my little brother. Your father is John Moore. That alone makes you special."

Instead of answering, Gene stood up. Ward followed his lead, and the brothers embraced. "I'm damn glad your home, Ward."

"Me too, brother. Me too."

Three weeks later, Ward moved to Benton, secured a loan, and eventually opened his bar. He also married Jamie Reid. Their firstborn was a son. They named him John, after "Pop" Moore.

Chapter 29

The Letter Arrives

Mornings in Sesser were unlike mornings anywhere else Gene had ever been. The early sky, the air, the sunshine of Sesser, invigorated him. Perhaps it was all about being home, surrounded by family and friends.

Another spring had arrived. Gene walked out the back door of the small home at Matthew and Mulberry on his way to the barn. The old screen door made a sharp cracking noise as it shut behind him. For a moment it reminded him of the sound a bat makes when hitting a ball. He sighed and looked across the state highway and the green fields beyond. The mist had settled gently, as it often did, between the rolling hills, whose peaks rose and fell like some sort of giant serpent, its back glistening in the morning sun. The morning was particularly beautiful. He took a deep breath of fresh air and exhaled. Although Gene hated farming, he could not help but feel the comfort that only home can provide.

As he crossed the short distance from the small leaning three-room home to the even smaller barn, his mind drifted back to his time in North Africa. How he had missed Sesser while stationed there—especially early in the mornings and late at night. Now that he was back in Sesser, he keenly missed North Africa, baseball, and the camaraderie of his teammates. Had he really been there, playing ball during a war with some of the greatest friends he had ever known? Gene sighed. He had been home for more than two years. Baseball, North Africa, Camp Ruston—it seemed more like a dream than an experience.

That particular morning, Gene was headed out to the south forty, a field just on the other side of the blacktop road leading to Rend City. John planted these forty acres in corn to feed the hogs. Gene was going to begin plowing.

Although Gene hated plowing, Eleanor and Franklin were well suited to the task. Both were stocky draft horses that not just tolerated, but seemed to enjoy, pulling a plow through the rich black soil. It was good the beasts liked the work because Gene despised it. There was no sport in it at all. No challenge. It was just work.

Gene stroked Franklin's muscled neck and rubbed his soft muzzle. He was still in Sesser, still farming, and his baseball career had ended before it began. The Egyptians had asked him to play several times, but he had moved on. He had tasted the sport on a high level. Playing for the local team with no future to hope for would be more painful than not playing at all. At least, that's how he rationalized it. His opportunity had come and gone. His life was now in Sesser, with his hands on a plow.

He smiled at Franklin and slapped his neck playfully. "Come on, buddy. We've got work to do today."

Allie was at the kitchen sink cleaning a chicken for that night's dinner when she heard a commotion on the front lawn, followed by a knock on the door. She wiped her hands on her apron and walked quickly for the door. She drew up short of the screen and stared. It seemed like half of Sesser was standing on her small front lawn but, after closer examination, she realized it was only Jack Cockrum, the mailman, and ten or twelve of the morning crowd from Bruno's.

"Where's Gene?" one of them yelled.

"He's plowing across the blacktop in the south forty," Allie replied. "What's wrong? What's he done?"

"Nothing, Allie," replied Jack as he held up an envelope in his hand. "He's got a letter."

"Okay, leave it here, and I'll see he gets it," Allie replied.

Jack winced. "Well, Allie . . ." It was obvious Jack didn't want to leave the letter with her.

"Mrs. Moore, will you open it and tell us what it says?" another man yelled from back by the street.

"Of course not!" she said with contempt. "Gene is a grown man. Why would I open his mail?" Her eyes narrowed with suspicion. "What's your business with this letter?"

Jack handed the envelope over to Allie. She looked at it and smiled.

Pittsburgh Baseball Club
Forbes Field
Pittsburgh, Penn.

Mr. Gene Moore
Matthew St.
Sesser, Illinois

"You boys are slipping," Allie laughed. "You missed the first two."

"First two what?" Jack asked.

"First two letters from the Pirates. They contacted Gene last winter, and he agreed to go down south somewhere to play, but when it came time to leave in March, he didn't go." Allie's voice trailed off. She sounded sad.

Allie handed the letter back to the stunned postman and said, "You know where he's plowing. Why don't you take it to him yourself? Maybe your encouragement is what he needs to play again."

The men delivering the mail formed the core group from Bruno's. They had never gotten over the fact that Sesser's "favorite son" was not going to play ball at Ebbets Field—or any professional ballpark. Like the rest of the town, they had few hopes left for their own future. If Gene succeeded, they could succeed through him. Gene had given up, but they had not yet given up on him. The fact that the Pittsburgh Pirates were sending letters to their native son inspired them to press on.

The group moved down Mulberry and crossed the old blacktop highway, walking down the gravel road that led past the monument engraver's shop, just before Huie Lumber. As they reached the crest of the hill, the Bruno's dozen spotted Gene, his hands on the plow, walking behind Eleanor and Franklin.

"Hey, Gene!" yelled Jack. "Gene!"

"Whoa, Eleanor, Franklin. Whoa, now," shouted Gene, bringing the plow to a fitful stop. Gene wiped the sweat from his brow and looked to see who was calling him. He saw Jack trotting toward him, waving something in his hand while the early morning gang from Bruno's followed in his wake. "Now what could they possibly want that's so important to stop us in the field," he asked the horses as he patted Eleanor on the side and took a few steps toward Jack.

"What can I do for you?" Gene shouted.

"We have a letter for you!"

"Yeah? When did you all go to work for the United States Postal Service?" Gene chuckled and slipped off his dirty work gloves. He wiped his brow a second time and waited for them to reach him.

"We have deputized ourselves, and we want to know what exactly is in your letter!" said one of the patrons named Winfield.

"Deputized? Let's see the badges?" The group erupted in laughter as Gene reached for the envelope. When he saw who it was from, his expression did not change at all.

"The Pirates must be a hell of a lot smarter than those snooty boys from Brooklyn, Gene!" Jack offered. Everyone voiced their agreement. Gene looked at the letter a second time.

"Please open it, Gene!" begged Winfield. "We walked all the way down here to find out what it says!"

Gene was unsure what to tell them. "Look guys, hear me out. You know how much I appreciate your support. Really, I do. But my baseball career is over. I still limp, my ankle hurts every day, and I don't want to go through all that again. It's over for me. My time has come and gone."

"Fine," Jack said. "We heard you out. Now open the damn letter and tell us when you leave for spring training!" Everyone erupted in laughter again, slapping one another on the back.

Gene sighed and reluctantly opened the letter.

Dear Gene,

We were sorry that you decided not to report to spring training with our Greenville team. We are still very interested in giving you the opportunity to build a career with our organization. If you will reconsider, please let me know at your earliest opportunity and we will make arrangements to receive you in Greenville.

Sincerely,

Ted McGrew

Gene handed the letter back to Jack. "Here, now you can read it for yourself." He turned back to the plow. "I have work to do."

Jack excitedly read the short letter to the group. "Gene, what are you going to tell the Pirates?" asked Winfield.

"Thanks, but no thanks," he replied, pulling his gloves back on his hands.

"What?" another man cried out. "Gene, you can't really mean that! They don't send those letters out every day!"

Gene put his hands on the plow. The old familiar feeling of anxiety mixed with self pity was rearing its ugly head again and tearing at his insides. He looked down at the ground and kicked the dirt beneath his feet.

"Gene, what is there to think about?" Jack offered. "You are the best damn baseball player ever, and you're from Sesser! Pack your bags and get going. The Pirates want you!"

Without looking up, Gene began speaking. "Look, I know you mean well. I know you're concerned about me and want me to play ball. I'm grateful—I am. But what you don't understand is that my ankle is shot. I have a couple of steel bolts holding my leg bone together. I feel them every time I take a step. I can't run like a major leaguer needs to run. The Pirates contacted me in January, and in the excitement of the moment I agreed to report. A Navy friend of mine is there. He pitches for them."

"So why didn't you go?" inquired Jack.

"Because wishing won't make it so. Reality set in. Why waste their time and mine? If I had two good ankles, I would be there. But the truth is I just can't do it. The old heart's willing, but the flesh . . . that's another story."

Jack sighed and nodded, as if he just realized, after all this time, that Gene could no longer play the game.

"You don't know what I've been through. I was in a bed in the VA hospital in Brooklyn while they put those bolts in my leg. I was there with men who had been injured in the war—I mean really injured. Some had lost their arm or leg . . . one guy lost both arms and a leg! These guys gave more for their country than you can imagine. You know what I was doing during the war?"

"What?" asked Jack.

"Pissing away my time playing a game. While real men were killing the enemy and having their limbs removed with saws in towns with names they could not pronounce and could never find on a map. I had my heart torn out by a letter. For . . . me," Gene hesitated as his voice began to waver. He took a moment, regained his composure, and continued. "For me, the pain was more than I ever want to bear again."

No one said a word. Gene chuckled softly. The sound surprised the assembly. Winfield asked, "What are you laughing about, Gene. This ain't funny. I nearly cry every time I think about it."

"What do you mean 'nearly cry,'" shot back Jack. "I do."

Gene offered a grim smile. "I guess, in some ironic sort of way, I deserved what I got. I sort of felt sorry for the German sailors standing inside the prison wire, and went to a lot of trouble to get permission to teach them how to play baseball. And I broke my ankle doing it. Had I just done as ordered and guarded them, I'd be playing in Brooklyn right now instead of plowing this damn field. My best friend is in Nashville, living his dream. I know some of my old teammates are playing professional ball in the big leagues because they send me letters once in a while. Most are married, starting families, and have a long career in front of them. Me? I have less than when I started. I'm back where I was, living with my parents and working on the farm. Only I can't even play well enough to keep up with the boys on the local team." Gene suddenly looked embarrassed, as if he had said too much. Without another word he dropped the letter onto the ground, slapped the horses on the backs with the reins, and resumed plowing.

Jack and the rest of the men just stood there as he slowly moved away from them. No one said a word. Jack reached down and picked up the letter as everyone began walking back toward town.

"Damn shame," he said to himself as he set the letter on the Moore front porch.

A few seconds later, a light breeze picked it up and carried the letter into the front yard. Like Gene's baseball career, an invisible hand skipped it easily down the road before blowing it into the ditch.

Chapter 30

Dark Night of the Soul

Gene walked into Bruno's and wiped the raindrops from his face. The drizzle began falling a few minutes before he arrived. When the door closed behind him, a flash of lightning lighted the sky through the window, followed a few seconds later by a loud clap of thunder. The walls shook and rain began to pour. Gene had made it inside just in time.

"It's really coming down," Bruno said as he glanced up at his ceiling, listening while the driving rain pounded the roof of the old building.

Gene nodded as he walked past the regulars gathered at the bar to the stool at the far end and took his seat. This was now 'his stool' since returning home from the war.

Several years had passed since the war ended, with hardly a change in routine. It was not the life he had imagined as a kid, and not at all what the townspeople of Sesser had believed he would become. The topic of baseball was no longer popular at Bruno's, and hadn't been for some time now.

Bruno still felt sorry for Gene. Every night he showed up to drink, smoke, and sulk until he could barely hold his head up. He had become little more than the barstool he sat on, a lifeless fixture.

"Gene, you just don't talk much anymore," Bruno observed as he set his first bottle of beer down on the bar.

"I can go down to Marlo's if you don't want me here," Gene answered sharply, looking Bruno in the eye as he took his first gulp of beer.

Author

Gene Moore at the end of the bar in Bruno's, beginning another night of heavy drinking. Behind him is Willy Kerbovac, a former teammate from Gene's days with the Sesser Egyptians.

"No, Gene," Bruno smiled, and then said in a softer, warmer voice, "I love having you here. I'm not complaining. I just wish . . ." Bruno paused.

"Wish what?"

"I don't know, Gene. I wish for something better for you. That you had come back from the war different, that's all."

"I guess I am different. I left a ballplayer and came home a . . . well, I don't know what I came back as." Gene paused and emptied his bottle with a few large swallows. "A pig farmer, I guess. Everything I ever wanted—everything I ever worked for—is now gone. Hell, Bruno, it's been gone a long time. Why do we keep having this conversation?"

"I'm sorry," Bruno muttered. "I'll try to never mention it again."

Gene lit a Camel straight and glanced up at the empty space on the wall where his uniform once hung. He had only recently taken up smoking. Bruno walked away and returned with another bottle of beer. Gene nodded his thanks. "You remember when you used to tell me that baseball wasn't something I did, but was something I was?" he asked.

"What and who am I now, Bruno? I don't know the answer to that question."

Bruno sighed. Gene complained about having the same conversation nearly every night, and yet nearly every night he asked Bruno that same question. Usually it came after his fourth of fifth beer. Tonight it had taken only one. "I don't know Gene," replied the bartender, "but I don't think a man's life is determined by what he does for a living."

"Bruno, can I get a house specialty—the fish sandwich?" asked Gene.

Bruno nodded and walked toward the kitchen. Tonight was no different than all the others.

Gene would drink a few beers, have something to eat, and then continue drinking until closing time, when he would stumble his way home. He had become an ordinary drunk.

Three hours later Gene was slumped over a half-empty bottle. The dark circles under his eyes told everyone that this lifestyle was taking its toll. "What time is it, Bruno?" he mumbled as he rubbed his eyes.

"Nine," Bruno answered, wiping down part of the bar with a white rag. The bartender walked to the front of the bar and looked out the big window facing Main Street. "It's really storming out there." He looked back at Gene, who was yawning deeply. "Gene, when you came in a few hours ago, you said you used to be a ballplayer."

Gene glared at Bruno, fumbled for his pack of Camels lying on the bar, and lit one up.

"Obviously, someone still thinks you are a ballplayer. How long are you going to sit on that letter from the Pirates? It's been what—three weeks?" Bruno waited in silence. "No response, Gene?"

He exhaled a cloud of smoke before accidentally dropping his cigarette on the floor. Another patron walking by picked it up and handed it to Gene. "Bruno, if I thought I could play ball, I would." His words were slightly slurred, his demeanor argumentative. "I lived to play baseball. Did I ever tell you that sometimes at the end of the day, my ankle is so swollen I can barely get my sock off?"

Bruno nodded. "Yeah, you told me that last night."

Gene squinted at the bartender through the smoke. "What position did I play?"

"You played catcher, Gene."

"That's right. Catcher." He moved to snuff out his cigarette, missed the ashtray, and used the bar instead. "Have you ever crouched behind a plate. No? It's tough, even in good shape. My ankle wouldn't hold up an inning, let alone a game—or a season. Trust me, Bruno," he concluded, "if there was any chance at all, I'd be playing ball."

Bruno leaned over the bar just a couple feet from Gene. "I appreciate your business. I love having you here . . . at least I used to, anyway . . . but I miss the old Gene Moore. I know war changes people and all, and I know you been through a lot. But it's like one person left and a different one came back in your body. Everyone tiptoes around you. You don't talk to anyone . . . no one talks to you anymore. Don't you think it's about time you snapped out of it?"

"Ah, give me a break," he shouted, waving his palm like he was swatting at a fly. "Yeah, everyone liked the old Gene because he could play ball. No one really ever cared for me for any other reason."

"That's not true," Bruno said defensively.

"The hell it's not!" Gene yelled as he slammed his fist on the bar, tipping over his now empty beer bottle. "I grew up over on the other side of the tracks, dirt poor. My dad shoveled shit at the sale stock barn just to feed us. He's a good man, Bruno . . . better man than me, but no one in this town ever gave him the time of day. So why would anyone care about me . . . the son of a shit shoveler? I'll tell you why. It was only because I could catch, throw, and hit. I could catch better than anyone who ever pulled a mask over his face. But looking back now, I was nothing more than entertainment for you people. Now that I can't play anymore, why does anyone care if I talk or not?"

"Because you aren't talking. Seven beers are doing the talking for you. And what you just said ain't true."

"It is true, Bruno! I was no more than a damn dancing bear."

"I'm sorry I brought it up, Gene, but you're drunk. Again. Why don't you go home and sober up?"

"I'm not drunk, I'm right, and you just don't wanna hear it. Nobody wants to hear it!"

A loud clap of thunder interrupted Gene's outburst. The lights at Bruno's flickered off. "Ah, damn. I knew it," Bruno sighed. "Every time it storms." The bartender grabbed Gene's matches and began lighting the candles he had pulled out just for this contingency. The weak light they provided was just enough for Gene to make out the silhouette of a man standing at the other end of the bar. No one had seen him come in.

"If I'm not interrupting anything, I'll have a beer," the stranger asked in an accent no one could quite place. "Whatever you are pouring on tap is fine."

Gene squinted to get a better look at him. He was soaked from the rain, wearing a gray flannel suit and white shirt and tie, which had been loosened around the neck.

"You know, I was in this town years ago, before the war," the man continued, wiping the rain from his shoulders. "I don't remember seeing any dancing bears," he chuckled. "But there was a kid here. I do remember him. That kid, he could hit like Babe Ruth—knock a ball a country mile. He was a joy to watch. You knew you were seeing the purest form of baseball in that youngster."

Bruno handed the man his glass of beer. He was speechless. So was Gene.

"When that kid hit the ball," continued the man, "the crack was so sharp and loud you could feel it in your bones. The ball soared like it had been shot out of a cannon. And he could throw the fastest guy out at second base from his knees—the ball sizzled through the air, almost like it was on fire. Any time I saw the second baseman catch it, I expected to see smoke rising from his glove."

Gene tried to get a glimpse of the man's face, but he could not make it out in the semi-darkness. He had heard the voice before.

The stranger took a long pull from the glass of beer and sat down on a stool. "That kid, he controlled the game like no one I have ever seen, before or since. It was truly magical. Watching him play was poetry behind the plate."

"What happened to that kid?" Bruno jerked his head around and looked at Gene. The former catcher was wide awake now, but his question was barely louder than a whisper.

The stranger sighed. "From time to time, I wondered what happened to him. I hear he went off to war—in the Navy, I think—suffered some sort of injury, and then ran home with his tail between his legs. Rumor has it he sits every night drinking himself into oblivion. Self-pity, I guess. Now, I don't believe everything that I hear, so I thought I would come back to the 'home of the Egyptians' and see for myself."

The stranger picked up his glass, eased his stool back, and walked toward Gene. Three steps later the familiar face of Frank Boudreau, the man who scouted and signed him for the Dodgers, was bathed in the light of several candles.

Gene's heart pounded. He didn't know what to feel when he saw him. Happiness? Anger? Gratitude? "Well, you seem to know everything, Frank. What do you see?" Gene asked sarcastically. Bruno groaned.

The scout took the stool next to Gene. "I see the best damned ballplayer I have ever known in my entire life, sitting alone in a bar. He looks a little older," Frank smiled. "He probably shouldn't be smoking, and I guess he could lose a few pounds. But you know, I think there's still a ballplayer in there. That's what I see, Gene Moore." Bruno nodded his head in vigorous agreement.

"Ha!" Gene barked. "Look again, Frank. I'll tell you what you see. You see a small-town farmer who had a shot at greatness and blew it. You see a guy who, instead of defending his country, played his way through a war that everyone else fought on his behalf. You see a guy whose brother was shot three times on two different occasions, while his kid brother you're talking about was playing a game instead of fighting. And at the end of it, it was all for nothing. He let everyone down."

Frank smiled into his beer. "Hmm. That kid—you know, the one we're talking about? Maybe he's not here anymore. He never would have said anything like that. You see, this kid, he had a wonderful, outgoing and friendly personality. He was unique. He didn't recognize failure. He only saw opportunities to play. He knew that this game he played—it is something special. And when he walked onto that field . . ." Frank paused and looked away, lost in the image his mind was creating to keep up with the word picture he was painting aloud. "When he walked out there, he honored the game." Gene just turned away and lit another cigarette.

"Gene Moore!" Frank Boudreau barked out. "Get up off your sorry ass and look at me like a man! Sitting on that bar stool is not the way I want to see you. You're talking like a damn loser, and you're starting to look the part."

When Gene stood up his stool fell over and clattered on the floor. The few patrons left inside Bruno's were also standing now, well away from the bar. "Well, Frank, if you know so damned much, tell me why you didn't make it in the majors as a player? Why is it you've been making your living off the talents of others?"

Frank shook his head at the pathetic question. "Gene, you really have changed. You are determined to tear down your life and make yourself feel better by swiping at me." The scout leaned forward. "Let me tell you how I see my life and what I do. I have spent my time in baseball helping kids make their dreams come true. Some have the heart to overcome the obstacles standing between them and the 'bigs,' and go on to live their dream. Some do not. I can find them, and I can sign them. But I can't play the game for them. And frankly, I'm proud of my career in baseball." Frank took another sip from his beer. "What about you, Gene? Are you proud of what you've become?"

Gene turned away and hung his head, reaching for his empty beer bottle that Bruno had already picked up. "Bruno, get me another bottle."

"No," answered the bartender. "You've had enough."

Frank's voice softened and warmed at the same time. "Listen to me, son. That kid I was talking about earlier? You remember—that boy who loved to catch? I want to tell him something." Frank paused. "If you see him, can you give him a message from Frank Boudreau?"

The words touched Gene deeply, unlike anything had for months—perhaps years. He smiled for the first time in a long while. "Yeah," he replied, nodding his head. "If I see him, I'll tell him. What do you want him to know, Mr. Boudreau?"

"Tell him the Brooklyn Dodgers fired me the same day they released him. And tell him that I, too, was hurt. Tell him the Pittsburgh Pirates hired me, and they want me to help them build a World Championship team. Tell him he is the first person I came to see. You tell him, if you see him, that I'm staying at the Hotel Benton, over on the square. You tell him I have a train ticket for him to Greenville, Mississippi, and a potential career with the Pittsburgh Pirates. Will you give him that message?"

Gene looked up, barely able to contain his emotions. He had never been so embarrassed in his life. "Yes, Frank. If I can find him, I'll give him the message. I'll look real hard for him too, but he may be gone."

"He's not gone!" whispered Bruno between clenched teeth. "He's not gone!" No one heard him.

"I think this kid's worth looking for. If you find him, tell him Frank Boudreau passes along his regards, and that even with a bad ankle, he might still be one of the game's greats. You tell him that for me, okay?"

"Hey, bartender," Frank called out.

"Yes?" Bruno responded.

"Where's the best place in town to have breakfast?" Frank asked.

"Around the corner, across from the Custard Stand and about two blocks down, a little white-washed concrete-block building called Heavy Turner's Café," Bruno replied without having to think about it.

"I'll have breakfast there tomorrow morning, say nine o'clock—just in case anyone wants to see me before I leave." Frank winked at Bruno and glanced over at Gene, who was unable to meet his gaze.

The scout threw a dollar bill on the bar, knocked on the bar with his knuckles twice, looked at Gene for one more long moment, and then turned and walked out the door into the night.

Chapter 31

Resurrection

Heavy Turner's Café was exactly as Bruno described it. Everyone who ate there passed through a rickety screen door with a rusty metal sign advertising "Bunny Bread." Frank was originally from the Midwest, and so was not unfamiliar with small-town America. But Sesser was so small, so different. Heavy's was just one more reminder of that fact.

At 8:45 a.m., Frank walked through the door and could not help but smile. Behind the counter was a man who stood five-feet-nothing, but weighed well over three hundred pounds.

"Let me guess," Frank laughed. "You must be Heavy?"

"And you must be Albert Einstein," answered Heavy.

"Right," Frank replied, slightly embarrassed. "I deserved that."

"Yup," nodded the fat man. Frank couldn't help but notice that the entire top half of his body shook as his head bobbed up and down.

Heavy's had a breakfast counter, a concrete floor, and a set of mismatched tables and chairs. It was not the kind of eating establishment Frank was accustomed to, but this was Sesser, Illinois, and the Southern Illinois town had a personality distinctly its own.

"I know who you really are," Heavy said. "You're that baseball scout." Frank nodded. "You gonna get Gene to play ball?"

Frank shrugged. "I came here thinking that baseball needs him. Now, after seeing him, I think he needs baseball more."

"Yeah, that's for sure," Heavy replied. "But I'll tell you, we need him to play more than Gene or the Pirates need each other. Maybe you

Tom & Janet Mygatt

Ezra "Heavy" Turner, his wife Edith, and an unidentified visitor inside Heavy Turner's Café in 1951.

haven't noticed, but this town has nothing going for it. We have been stripped of our pride, our dignity, there's no reason to come to Sesser, and no reason to stay." Heavy reached over and wiped the sticky counter in front of Frank and handed him a menu. It was greasy and stained with coffee. "Gene gave us something to look forward to," he continued, "something to hope for. Now, well, we watch him sit on a bar stool and drink his life away."

Frank sighed. "I know. I saw that last night."

Heavy seemed lost in thought for a moment. "You know, I guess he's become one of us, when we were hoping he would make us like him."

Frank's trip to Sesser began to seem more like a mission than a scouting assignment. Gene needs baseball, Sesser needs Gene, Ray Laws needs Gene, and the Pirates need Ray. Frank realized there was much at stake here. It was a mission that had to succeed.

"Absorbing the ambiance, Frank?" Gene asked, as he walked in through Heavy's screen door.

The scout answered without turning to look at Gene. "Well, I'll tell you. Heavy and I have been just sitting here talking about life."

"Be careful," Gene replied. "Heavy's the town philosopher. He'll make you think—hard. Around here, that sort of thing can only get you in trouble." Gene smiled at the man behind the counter. "Morning, Heavy."

"Morning, Gene. You know, this is the first time I've seen you smile since before you left for the war." Gene ignored the observation and joined Frank at a table.

Each man studied the other for several seconds. It had been several years since Gene had seen Frank. His hair had more gray, it had receded a tad in front, and his forehead was no longer wrinkle-free. Otherwise, the ball scout had not changed that much. Frank was thinking something quite different about the young man sitting across from him. The morning light revealed just how much Gene had changed in such a short time. It wasn't just the additional weight. He looked several years older than twenty-four. Dark circles pulled at his once-youthful eyes, which were sunken and bloodshot. Even his hands looked old.

Gene looked at the scout, his voice barely above a whisper. "You never came, Frank."

For a moment Frank was unsure what he meant. And then it dawned on him. "Gene—I did. I got to the hospital the same day you left. It was the day I was called into Branch Rickey's office and let go. I didn't know until that meeting they had released you. I told Mr. Rickey as I was walking out that he had made two mistakes. The biggest was releasing you, and the second, well, without sounding prideful, was releasing me."

"I never knew you came," answered Gene. "I thought you had forgotten about me. I guess that explains a lot." Heavy set down two mugs of steaming black coffee. He stood there to listen in on the conversation, but a look from Gene sent him back behind the counter. "I'm sorry you lost your job."

Frank smiled. "Well, we have a new lease on life, you and I. I have been hired by the Pittsburgh Pirates, and they want me to help them build a world championship team."

"Congratulations, Frank. That's great," Gene said. He meant it.

"And it's a very small world, Gene. The Pirates have an outstanding pitching prospect who is languishing in the minors, partly because no one can catch him. Have you ever heard of such a thing?"

Gene sipped from his mug and nodded, wiping his chin with a napkin. "Yeah, I have."

"Have you ever caught a forkball? Frank asked.

Gene smiled. "You know I have. Ray Laws throws it better than anyone, or at least he used to."

"He still does. Ray is in Greenville, Mississippi, and he is in desperate need of a good catcher. Ray needs you, Gene."

In desperate need of a good catcher. Ray needs you, Gene. The words echoed in his mind as his thoughts slipped back to his time in the Navy, when he wanted nothing more than to squat behind the plate and catch Ray's forkball. Gene sighed wistfully. How he missed those days.

"Here's the long and short of it, Gene," Frank said, cutting to the chase. "Every kid dreams of getting his shot. For the few, the very few who get it, it's usually their one chance at greatness. But it's even rarer to get a second chance. Gene, you have a second chance." He paused and locked his gaze on Gene's bloodshot eyes. "Can you make it? I don't know. You're older, you're certainly out of baseball shape, but the constant work on the farm has kept your muscles hard and strong. Sure, you have a couple of metal bolts in your ankle. But let's face it, speed was never your forte."

"I can't argue with you there, Frank," smiled Gene.

Frank smiled back, pleased his former and perhaps current prospect was still listening and interested. Perhaps he had worried for nothing. "Your arm is one of the best and if you were running the bases, well, you were usually trotting," continued the scout. "But, besides all that, your true value is your understanding of the game—I guess I'd call it your baseball I.Q. Yours is high, very high. You are what the Pirates need, and quite frankly, you are exactly who Ray Laws needs."

"Frank," began Gene, "I know I was pretty good—better than good. Great, even. But I feel like such a failure, and I can't seem to get over that feeling. It swamps my every waking hour."

Frank shook his head. "Don't say 'was' Gene, say 'am.' You are only twenty-four. Many men are just beginning their careers in the big leagues at your age. You still have plenty of time."

Heavy made another appearance to take their order, but both men waved him away. When he left, Frank finally took a sip of his coffee. "Gene, I'm not here to compliment you, pad your ego, or make you feel good. I'm here on business, period. I'm here to sign you to an agreement and send you to Greenville. Once you're there, you have to live or die by your abilities. Like I said last night, I can help start—or in your case, restart—your dream. But only you can live it."

Gene's back was to Heavy's screen door, so he didn't notice the people gathering outside the door looking in. A throng was growing by the minute. Frank had noticed the onlookers the moment they had moved from the counter to the table.

Gene nodded, exhaled loudly, and placed both palms flat on the table. "Frank. I would love to help Ray. You know I want to play."

Frank raised his voice so those outside the door could hear and said, "Then, play Gene! Why not? What do you have to lose? I have the power to sign you right now. We can make this happen. The Pirates want you."

The scout's words were exactly what the curious of Sesser wanted to hear. When the cheers erupted outside, Gene spun around to see what all the excitement was about. When he realized what was going on he turned back to the scout with a sheepish grin on his face. Frank only laughed, pleased to see an almost boyish look on Gene's face.

"These people love you, Gene. These people need you. They're never going to leave this town. But with you in baseball, they can live their dreams through you. Gene, play ball. Do it for the people of Sesser."

"What if I let them down again?" Gene asked.

"You only let them down if you say no. You go to Greenville and give it your best shot. Whether you make it or not, the people of this town will have had their time in professional baseball. You say no, well, everyone loses." Frank finished his coffee and stood. He looked down at Gene and then out the screen door at the gathering crowd. "Let's walk outside and see what they have to say." Without waiting for a response, the scout walked to the screen door, pushed it open, and stepped outside. Gene was still sitting at the table.

The sun was shining brightly, the storm of the previous evening now a distant memory. Jack Cockrum, the mailman, and Eugene Basso were at the head of the crowd. "Well, Mr. Boudreau, is he gonna play ball or not?" Jack demanded.

"I don't know," Frank shrugged, looking back over his shoulder at the screen door. "Why don't you call him out and we'll ask him."

Jack and Eugene looked at each other and nodded. "Gene!" they both yelled. No response. Jack waited a few seconds and shouted a second time. "Gene!"

Without any prompting, one person at a time joined in the chant. "Gene! Gene! Gene! Gene!"

The chant stunned Gene. It sounded as if the whole town was outside yelling his name. Heavy looked over the counter and smiled. "Hey, Gene, this is bad for business," he said. "No one could get in here to eat if they wanted to. Are you ready yet to play ball, or is becoming the town drunk more appealing to you?" Heavy always had a way with words.

Gene slowly stood. "I don't know, Heavy. That's a tough call to make on the spot. I'll think about it and get back to you." Heavy started laughing, and Gene joined him. He started moving to the door but stopped before he reached it. "A career as a drunk probably doesn't pay that much, does it?"

"No, Gene, I suppose it doesn't," Heavy replied.

"Thanks, Heavy." Gene took a deep breath and walked through the screen to find a crowd of almost 100 people gathered to encourage him to take full advantage of his second opportunity.

Frank held up his hand, and the crowd fell silent. "What will it be, son? Can the good people of Sesser count on you to be the best you can be, regardless of the outcome?"

Gene dug his hands into his pants pockets, pulled them out again, and then awkwardly stuck them in again. He looked shy, but happy. He looked more like the 15-year-old Frank had first seen eight years earlier at The Lumberyard hitting the ball a country mile.

"Where is Greenville, Mississippi, anyway, Frank?"

"Yes!" screamed Jack as everyone erupted in thunderous applause. People crowded in to hug Gene and show their appreciation. Each in his own way wanted to make some connection to the ballplayer. It was at that moment Frank realized he was witnessing a resurrection. Heavy's little restaurant had been like a tomb, Frank's offer from the Pirates had rolled away the stone, and the townspeople had called Gene out.

Sesser, Illinois, had been brought back to life.

Chapter 32

Reporting to Greenville

Gene spent the next two weeks working out. He stayed away from Bruno's, got off the alcohol, and slept normal hours. Most of each day was spent throwing a baseball again, and lightly swinging a bat. When he tried squatting behind the plate, however, his ankle refused to cooperate.

Gene massaged it every hour and did his best to stretch his muscles, but getting into a traditional catcher's stance just wasn't going to happen. He tried to convince himself that a few more days of training, a few more stretches, and a few more attempts would make it better. His inability to throw as hard as he once had saddened him, but he remained hopeful he could carry his own, the pain would diminish, and some of his mobility would return.

When the day arrived, Gene packed a bag, said his goodbyes, kissed his mom and sisters, and caught a ride to the Carbondale train station. As he was standing on the ramp waiting for the train, he remembered how, seven years earlier, a younger and much more innocent Gene Moore had left the same station to begin his hitch in the United States Navy. He was just a kid then—a kid who loved to play baseball more than drink beer from a bottle. He had been almost unaware of the war that deposited him in the Navy, seventeen, and in the best shape of his life. Now the man standing on the same platform was smoking a cigarette and walking with a slight limp. The changes were more than just physical.

The last time he caught the train from Carbondale, Gene was convinced no one in the world could play the game like he could. It was not his skill alone that gave him that confidence. It was his absolute and unconditional love of baseball. But he was a different man now. The game had broken first his ankle, then his heart, before tossing him aside for someone younger and faster. The game had almost forgotten about him, but he never forgot about the game.

Gene now had a second chance, but he was skeptical and apprehensive. His confidence was gone—or nearly so. He knew his sprint to first base was far from what it needed to be, and he knew again firsthand that getting in and out of his catcher's stance was painful. Once quick and agile, Gene was now slow and clumsy. Several times over the last half hour he had nearly convinced himself to leave the train platform and walk across to the Station Street Bar. Somehow he resisted the urge, but he knew if the train did not arrive soon, the bar would be a place of comfort. It was calling out his name.

Gene knew he liked to drink too much, but he denied in his mind what he knew in his heart. "I am not an alcoholic," he thought. I don't have to have a drink. I drink because I like it, not because I need it. I can quit anytime. "Heck," he thought, "I have only had three beers in the past two weeks." Gene decided to walk across the street and have just one beer, but as he turned and started to walk down the ramp someone yelled out, "Here she comes!" The train to Greenville was rounding the bend, slowing down as it prepared to stop in Carbondale.

Gene boarded and found his seat. It only took him a few minutes to discover that the train had a bar, so he headed for it. The pressure to succeed was immense. Frank, the whole town—everyone was pulling for him. He knew the last thing he needed was a drink, but he also knew the alcohol helped deaden the pain.

"Oh, what the heck," he mumbled to himself. "It's a long ride, and I'll just have a few to make the trip go faster. I won't drink again till the season ends."

Gene Moore headed for the bar, leaving the 15-year-old catcher behind.

"Next stop, Greenville, Mississippi!" the conductor bellowed as he walked through Gene's car.

Gene sat up. His head was throbbing. He was about to reach for his cigarettes when he realized he had smoked his last one a few hours earlier. How had he gotten back to his seat from the bar?

The train rocked back and forth and gradually slowed as it entered the Greenville station. Gene said a quick and silent prayer that he would not have to play ball that afternoon. The irony of the situation did not escape him. It was the first time in his life he actually hoped he would not have to play the game he loved so much.

When the train creaked its way to a complete stop, Gene tossed his old Navy seabag off the train and jumped down beside it. He cringed when he hit the ground. His ankle was killing him.

The station looked like it was a century old, small, and more in need of a paint job than The Lumberyard or Pop's barn. It appeared deserted.

"Gene Moore?" asked an older man as he stepped from the shadows. Gene nodded and smiled. The man looked at him more closely and called out his name again.

"I'm Gene Moore!"

"You're Gene Moore?" asked the man with surprise.

"Yes, I'm Gene Moore!"

The man stood with his hands on his hips. "You're Gene Moore, huh?" He looked Gene up and down, and said, "Hmm. You don't look like a ballplayer to me, but if you say you're Gene Moore, you must be." The man's accent was so heavy that at times Gene could barely make out some of his words.

"What do you mean I don't look like a ballplayer?" asked Gene, surprised by the stranger's arrogance.

"I work for the team part-time," he answered. "I'm retired from the brick factory. You know, we made the bricks our old stadium is made of. I do the running for the team now, picking up new players, taking those who are moving up or washing out to the train, just general runnin' round stuff."

Gene shook his head. "Well, that doesn't answer my question. Why do you say I don't look like a ballplayer?"

The man frowned. "Well, look at you. You look older than most of those who are here. You don't look like you're in shape. And if you don't mind me saying so, most people are ending their careers when they look like you, not startin one!" He smiled. "But what do I know, right? My name is Robert, but you can call me Bob. Nice to meet you."

Bob stuck out his hand, but it remained alone, hanging between them. "I'm not feeling like it has been that damn nice, Bob," Gene shot back.

"Moore, I call 'em as I see 'em. Don't like what I have to say, you can walk to the field. But if you do walk, you'll be late to the game, and they tell me you're startin' today. You're here to try out as catcher, right?"

Gene calmed down a few notches. Everything the man said was true, and he knew it. Could he smell the booze, too? "Yeah, I'm the catcher," he replied. "I used to be, anyway," Gene mumbled.

"Now see what I mean?" asked Bob. "Talk that way, I'll be taking you back to the train tonight." Bob stuck his hand out again, and this time Gene reached out and shook it. The Mississippi stranger who had retired from the brick factory loaded Gene's seabag into the back of his pickup truck and Gene climbed in the passenger side.

"You know, there was a Gene Moore used to play for the Pirates," Bob announced as he pulled out of the gravel lot next to the station. "Did you know that?"

"Yes, I do know that," Gene answered. "He came up through the Reds organization, then was traded to the Dodgers. I'm not sure how he ended up with Pittsburgh, but I know he was there. He was pretty good, I hear."

"Are you?" Bob asked.

"Am I what?"

"Don't play games with me, son. Are you any good?"

"Bob, I was raised not to brag. I guess you'll just have to see for yourself," Gene replied honestly, looking out the window as the truck bounced along the unpaved road to the field.

"Can I give you some advice?" asked Bob.

"I don't think I could stop you if I said no, could I?" Gene laughed. Bob didn't.

"Son, you got beer on your breath. Don't think I would show up my first day on the job with beer on my breath. But, I'm from the old school, I guess. You say you weren't raised to brag. Well, I was raised that you show up on the job ready to do your best everyday—especially your first day. But that's just me. You don't brag, I don't show up with beer on my breath, guess that makes us different."

Gene was caught off-guard by Bob's frankness. It was obvious he was right, and it was equally clear he couldn't show up to meet his new manager and teammates smelling like a brewery.

"Bob, you're right," conceded Gene. "I guess I had a couple too many on the train last night. I was bored, excited, and couldn't sleep." Gene paused and cleared his throat. "I'm sorry, Bob. I know I have made a terrible first impression. What would you suggest I do?"

Bob nodded but kept his eyes on the road. "Now, that's more like it, son. It smells like more than just a couple too many, and more recent than last night. But I have an idea." He pulled his old truck in front of the Greenville Produce Market, a ramshackle affair with large boxes of fruit, vegetables, and old junk littering the front on both sides of the door. "Wait here," he told Gene. He jumped back in the truck two minutes later holding a big white onion.

"Take a bite, slugger." Bob said, handing it to Gene.

"An onion?" Gene replied with a look of shock on his face. "A raw onion?"

"Yeah," Bob responded with a nod. "I know the guy who runs this team, Moore. You show up with beer on your breath, and you will be standing back on the platform six hours from now waiting for the ride home!"

Gene stared at the onion he was holding. "Okay, okay. I'll eat the onion," Gene said. He swallowed once and took a big bite. He grimaced as he chewed a few times before turning his head to spit a mouthful of white mash out the window.

"Shit, Bob! This is awful!" Gene gagged.

"No one will smell the beer now. If you are gonna keep drinking, you better get used to the taste of Mississippi white onions." Bob replied with a smile. "They's strong, huh?"

Gene nodded in agreement, and nibbled a few more times at the onion. Things had to change. By the time Bob pulled his pickup back onto the highway, Gene had made up his mind that his drinking days were done. Bob was right. He had to be ready to do his best. If he didn't make it with the Pirates, it would be because of his ankle, not his drinking.

Bob Allen, the man who picked up Gene at the station and handed him an onion ten minutes later, was a Greenville Pirates fan. He loved his team, and he loved doing small jobs to help out whenever and wherever he could. It provided a few extra bucks in his retirement, and gave him an excuse to hang out at the field.

"Bob, you said I'm starting today? Do you know that for a fact?"

"Ray Laws is pitching today and, from what I'm told, none of the other catchers want to be near the plate when he's on the mound. That forkball of his is something else. No one can catch it consistently. It doesn't matter if they can't hit it if our own guys can't catch it. Laws pitched a no-hitter three weeks ago, and we lost 1-0."

"Dropped third strikes and passed balls, huh?" Gene guessed.

Bob looked him over for a few seconds before putting his eyes back on the road. "You do know the game." He shook his head. "That poor guy's been crying for a catcher since the season started. Can you really catch that thing?"

"Yeah, I think so," Gene replied. "I used to be able to catch anything Ray could throw."

"There you go again, Moore. Talk that way and I'll be takin' you back to the train before you get unpacked. Either you can catch it or you can't. If you think you can or think you can't, either way you're right. So which is it?"

"Are you the manager, Bob?"

He laughed. "No, but I should be!"

The pickup rolled to a stop and Bob jumped out to grab the seaba Gene followed him and the two stood next to each other. Bob looke ' t ɔ player straight in the eye. "Every American kid would give his eycieeth to stand where you're standing right now, Moore." Gene nodded as Boo handed him the bag. "You're up now, son. And I don't smell anything but Mississippi white onion."

Veteran's Field was an older stadium, but Gene saw immediately that it was going to be the best-kept field he had ever played on. A red brick wall ran around the park, framing perfectly cut thick green grass. The infield was finely manicured, and a groundskeeper was laying down a chalk line between home and first base. Outside of Ebbets Field in Brooklyn, it was the prettiest ballpark he'd ever seen.

Bob tilted his head and motioned Gene aside. "Follow me, and I'll take you to the lockers."

Gene followed Bob into a freshly painted concrete-block locker room. Painted on the wall was the large Pirates logo. Gene stopped and stared at it for a few seconds. He wanted to pinch himself. Was he really standing there?

"Gene! Gene Moore!" A clatter of cleats on concrete filled the room as Gene turned to see Ray Laws trotting toward him.

"Ray!" Gene shouted back, moving to meet him.

The pitcher wrapped his arms around his favorite catcher and lifted him off the ground. "Am I glad to see you, buddy. I can't believe how long it's been."

"I'll leave you two to get reacquainted," said Bob. "Ray will show you around."

When Ray finally set him down, Gene pushed him back and said, "I hear the catchers down here are more afraid of you than the opposing team batters!"

Ray laughed. "That's one hell of a situation, isn't it? If I throw it so the batters can't hit it, my own catchers can't catch it, and I lose! If I throw it so my catcher can catch it, the batter sends it out of the park. Either way, I lose!" Both men laughed.

"Let me see if I can help you there," Gene offered. "Unless you're throwing something new since Camp Ruston, I think I can at least stop it before it reaches the backstop."

"I thought you were coming down in March? What happened?" asked Ray.

Gene sighed, then shrugged. "I don't know, long story I guess. But I'm here now."

"Thank God!" Ray exclaimed. "But the bad news is you get to room with me."

"I'd reserve judgment before you give thanks, Ray," smiled the catcher. "I've roomed with you before. Do you still snore?"

"Yes, and still as loud," he chuckled. "I'll tell you, Gene, I'm not sure if any of these kids could have made the grade over there. I don't know, maybe I'm just getting older and feel like I'm running out of time, but these young guys, I don't know if they could play the game with Nazi artillery shells dancing in the distance. I never thought I'd ever say it, but I kind of miss those days in the Navy. At least I had a catcher then."

"Well, you're stuck with the same one again, so let's see if we can show these kids how a battery operates." Gene briefly looked away and continued in a lower voice even though they were alone in the locker room. His voice was less confident and shaky. "Ray, last time I was behind the plate was the game where I broke my ankle. Except for the last two weeks, I haven't caught a ball or swung a bat in more than four years."

Ray took a step backward. "What? What the hell have you been doing?"

Gene licked his lips, which were dry. His mouth tasted heavily of onion. The thought of a cold beer was suddenly overwhelming. "Plowing, feeding hogs, and feeling sorry for myself."

Ray pushed his cap back on his head. "Now that doesn't sound like the Gene Moore I know."

A grumpy voice, old but loud and strong, boomed forth from the office next to the locker room. "Do you understand what I am telling you?" he was yelling at someone. "Yeah? Well then do it. Otherwise, get the hell off my team!" A young player, tall and handsome, walked out of the office and out the door leading to the field. He looked as though he was ready to cry.

Gene gulped. Ray laughed. "Go meet the old man. He's a piece of work."

Gene nodded and was about to walk away when Ray stuck out his arm and stopped him. "Do you have any toothpaste or gum, Gene? Your breath really stinks."

Gene knocked softly on the door and cracked it open a few inches. "Sir, I'm Gene Moore."

The man behind the desk didn't even look up. "Your gear's right there, in the corner," he pointed with a pencil. Two more were at the ready, one behind each ear. "You'll be number twenty-six. Your locker is marked with your uniform number on it. Go get dressed and start warming up Laws. If you're good, you can stay, if not, Bob will take you back to the train after the game. Any questions?"

The manager spit out his machine gun bullet points without even a glance in his direction. "No, I guess not," answered Gene. "I got that speech from Bob on the way over." He hesitated, but decided to ask anyway. "Can I ask your name, sir?"

"Middleton. Jim Middleton." The man behind the desk finally raised his eyes to look at Gene. The stub of a well-chewed cigar was hanging from his lips. It wasn't hard to read the surprise that crossed his face, if only for an instant. "Call me Skip. Everyone else does. Now, get out of my office and get dressed."

Gene walked back into the locker room. Ray had heard the whole thing. He laughed. "Turn around."

"Why?"

"I want to see if your butt's still attached, or if he chewed it clean off." The pitcher grabbed Gene around the shoulders and squeezed him hard. "Man, am I glad you're here!"

Gene found locker number 26, dressed quickly in the uniform of the Greenville Pirates, and stood for a few moments in front of a full-length mirror. It was the first time he had ever seen how he looked from head to toe in a professional uniform. The feeling was almost overwhelming. It felt good to be back.

"You ready to warm me up?" Ray asked.

"Well, you may have to warm me up first."

"No problem, boss," Ray responded. It had been years since he had heard that. Gene just smiled in reply. "Let's go see if you can still catch a ball."

Gene and Ray walked through the door out of the locker room leading to the dugout, then up the stairs to the field. Besides being nervous, the beer and onion were working hard inside Gene. After five minutes in the sun, he started to get dizzy.

The friends were playing catch, and Ray spotted it right away. "Hey, Gene. You okay?"

Gene nodded, then shook his head and fell down on his knees, vomiting into the grass.

Ray trotted to him and knelt on one knee. "Holy shit, Gene. Are you sick? You got a fever or something?"

"Yeah, I think I do," he replied, wiping his mouth on his sleeve. "And I'm nervous as all get out." Gene climbed back to his feet, and the two resumed playing catch. Another player had seen him vomiting and took a large cup of water out to him. The gesture did a lot to steady Gene's nerves and settle his stomach.

"Hey, Gene, let's make for the plate," suggested Ray. "And no offense, but you smell really bad. For the rest of the day, I want you to stay at least sixty feet, six inches away from me!"

Gene waved him off with his hand and walked toward the plate. He strapped on his gear and pulled his mask over his face. His ankle was already stiff and sore. When he tried to squat down, the stiffness only increased. He tried again, slowly. This time there was stiffness and pain. He stood back up again.

"Ray, I can't squat down," he admitted, jerking his mask off. "My ankle won't bend that way." Gene looked scared. He had only caught a handful of pitches in the past four years, all of them within the last two weeks. Each squat had been painful. Today, of all days, was the worst.

Ray nibbled his lower lip, as he always did when he was thinking about something. "Well, Gene, you can't stand up, because the batter's gonna take your head off," Ray replied. "How are you gonna squat if you can't bend your ankle?"

"I have an idea," the catcher answered. Gene squatted down on his right leg and extended his left leg straight out to his left side for balance. "I've tried this a few times. I think it might actually work."

Rays looked unconvinced. "Can your right leg take all that pressure? Nine innings of that?"

Gene shrugged. "We'll see. If not, Bob can take me back to the train this afternoon. Let me take a few pitches, and we'll see how it goes."

Ray turned around and climbed the mound, shaking his head all the way to the rubber. When he got there he turned around. When he saw his old friend behind the plate he could not help but smile.

Gene lifted the mask and smiled back. "Ray, no matter what happens, I want you to know that seeing you again from behind the plate is something I never expected to see again. It feels really good."

"Likewise, boss," answered the pitcher. "Here's something easy to begin with." Ray wound up and sent a smooth medium speed pitch across the plate. The ball popped into the mitt. It felt good—really good. Gene took it out and looked at it, rolling it around slowly in his fingers as though he had never seen a baseball before.

It was June 30, 1949. Ray Laws' pitch was the first ball he had caught behind a plate since August of 1945.

Chapter 33

The Second Shot

"I've never let balls past me before like this," Gene grumbled to himself after the game. "Nothing for the record books, that's for sure."

Gene's greatest source of pride as a catcher was that almost nothing got past him. But today, in the first inning, two pitches slipped through. Unfortunately, the second one scored a run. A big run. The Pirates ended up losing 4-3 against a team from Birmingham, Alabama.

Gene batted three times. He struck out the first two attempts, but connected well on his third. The ball sailed into deep left field, and for a moment Gene was sure he had tagged a home run. The ball, however, dropped twenty feet shy of the wall, where the outfielder pinched it into his glove for the out. Although discouraged by his inability to hit the ball, he was most disappointed in his two errors—his passed balls. One was outside and sailed over his glove. It wasn't that high or wide, but Gene completely missed it. The second was in the dirt between his legs.

As Gene walked off the field he recalled the first time he met Ray Laws. Ray was worried then because he pitched so well that no one could catch him. In the Navy, Ray had relied on Gene, and Gene had made Ray look great. "Ray needed me today, and I let him down," was all Gene could think about as he did the best he could to hide his throbbing lower leg from onlookers as he walked toward the dugout.

Gene was standing at his locker after showering when Ray walked over to him. Only a few players were still in the room. "Well, boss. Tomorrow's another day, and another game."

"Maybe for you, but if I was Skip, I'd send me home," Gene said with disgust as he threw his mitt to the bottom of his locker.

"You didn't have your best day—so what? You haven't played a game in almost four years, and you really connected with that last ball. There are guys who start who wish they could hit it that deep. Besides, it's the first bad day you've had in almost four years! No one else here can say that." Ray laughed, but Gene didn't see the humor in his performance.

"I'll tell you what happened today, Ray. It's never happened before, and if Skip keeps me for another day, it will never happen again." Gene looked around and moved closer to Ray. "I was just not ready to play."

Ray shrugged. "Yeah, well, it's not like you haven't been through a lot, you know? Tim Milner used to call you 'Mr. I Wake Up Thinking About The Game,' do you remember?"

The long-forgotten nickname finally brought a small smile to his face. "Where is Tim, do you know?"

Ray shook his head. "We lost touch after the Dodgers' traded him."

"I had no idea I would start as soon as I got off the train," Gene continued, needing to discuss his poor performance. "I figured last night was my last night to have a few drinks. I really don't know why. I've had enough over the last few years to last a lifetime, but I did. When Bob picked me up from the train and told me I was starting, I almost jumped out of his truck!"

"Yeah, well Skip is like that."

"Moore! Come see me!" Skip bellowed from his office.

Gene sighed and looked at Ray, who didn't acknowledge hearing Skip. No one else in the locker room did, either. Everyone knew, or thought they knew, what it meant. Gene put his hand on Ray's shoulder. "I stunk, but you know what? It was a good day anyway. I got to play baseball again."

"Yes, Skip?" Gene said quietly when he stepped into the manager's office.

This time Skip looked up when Gene arrived. "You played in the Navy with Ray, right?"

"I did."

"Baseball?" Skip asked sarcastically.

Gene's heart skipped a beat. "Yes, Skip. Baseball."

"You were a catcher?"

Gene hung his head. "I know I didn't play well today, and I'm sorry."

"When was the last time you caught a game?" Skip asked.

"You don't want to know," Gene responded.

"Damn it, Moore! Don't you tell me what I want to know. I asked you a direct question!"

Gene raised his head and looked at the manager. "About four years ago, give or take."

"Give or take, you say?" mumbled Skip as he rummaged through a drawer, found a cigar, and stuck it into his mouth. "That explains why you forgot how to squat behind a plate," he said, speaking out of the side of his mouth, throwing up his arms at the same time.

"No, I didn't forget anything. I have two steel bolts attaching my ankle to my leg. That explains the stance." Gene replied, a bit more boldly and proudly than he felt. "It's the only way I can get down, Skip. My ankle doesn't bend any more. I was injured playing in the Navy."

The manager removed his cigar, studied it a few seconds, and threw it against the wall. The pencil behind his left ear clattered onto the desk.

"Damn it, Steve! Get in here!" he yelled. "Are you listening to this? We released another catcher for this guy?" Steve Burgner was Skip's third base coach. He was outside speaking to one of the players when the manager demanded his presence.

"What's wrong, Skip?" Steve asked, poking his head into the office. When he saw Gene, he looked away.

"What's wrong?" answered the manager. "I'll tell you what's wrong! Frank Boudreau's prize catch hasn't caught a ball in almost four years! Count 'em, one-two-three-FOUR!" As he ticked off each year, Skip unfurled a finger on his right hand. When he hit four, he turned his hand palm out and stuck it in Steve's face.

Steve looked at Gene. "Is that right? Four years?" Gene nodded.

"Where the hell's my cigar?" asked the manager. When he spotted it in the corner, Skip walked over, picked it up, and stuck it back in his mouth. He had removed his jersey, and the muscle T-shirt he had on beneath it was soaked in sweat. "He can't squat behind a plate. He's out of shape, and while we are on the subject, he smells like he has beer and onions sweating out of his pores!"

"I'm sorry I wasted your time," said Gene, finally breaking his silence. "I didn't really wanna come here, anyway." He turned and walked out of Skip's door and back to his locker.

Burgner followed him out. "Moore, hold up!"

"Listen, coach. I don't need this crap," Gene said. "I broke my ankle in the last game I played, in 1945. I have two bolts holding it together. I was great once—maybe the best. That's what others told me. I'm not anymore. It's about as simple as that." He grabbed a towel and wiped the sweat from his face. "I didn't ask to come here. I got a letter saying you needed me. Frank Boudreau came and got me!" Gene turned and threw his towel into his locker.

"Forget Skip!" Ray interjected. "He's just a grouchy old man. I do need you, Gene. If you can get yourself back together, who cares about your stance? We can win some games. Maybe have some fun, and who knows, I think we can be playing in Pittsburgh before we know it."

Burgner nodded and offered a half smile. "Moore, shake it off. The old man is just trying to get your goat and motivate you. I think he sees something in you, kid."

"Well, tell him thanks. I feel all warm and fuzzy inside," Gene shot back. There was a long uncomfortable silence. Gene broke it by asking the obvious question. "So what now? Am I staying, or should I head back to the train station?"

Burgner laughed. "Where do you think you are? The train only stops in Greenville twice a week, so you're stuck here until day after tomorrow, which gives you two more shots at keeping your job. Come on guys, let's go grab a beer and a sandwich."

A wave of relief swept over Gene. "No beer for me, but I'd love that sandwich."

Gene, Ray, and Steve were walking toward the door when Skip stepped out of his office. "Moore, hold on a minute. Gene, right?"

"Yeah, it's Gene."

Ray looked over at Steve and asked under his breath, "More motivation?"

"You're a veteran. I respect that," Skip began. His voice was much kinder than it had been a couple minutes earlier. "I just got Frank Boudreau on the phone. He said I would be a damned old fool not to give you more than a single game's chance. I told him I thought he was a damned old fool for sending you here, but you served your country, and I'm grateful to you for that. If the Pirates can't give a veteran a fighting chance to make this team, well, we shouldn't be in this game. The Pittsburgh Pirates may not be the most successful organization in baseball lately, but by God we are grateful to our veterans. You deserve a chance. So let's see how you do tomorrow. You'll be catching an easier pitcher."

Gene sighed with relief. "Thanks, Skip. I'm grateful. I won't let you down."

"I have no tolerance for ballplayers who show up not ready to play. You show up again smelling like alcohol, and you are gone. Is that fair enough?"

Gene shook his head, looking down at the floor, obviously embarrassed that Skip had to say it. "Yes, Skip, that's more than fair."

The manager yanked the unlighted cigar from his mouth and picked a piece of tobacco off his tongue. "And I know all about that damn onion trick Bob tries to pull on me once in a while," he continued, pointing a calloused finger out the door toward the diamond. "You can tell that brick-making bastard I'm wise to him."

"Yes, sir," was all Gene could think to say.

Skip extended his hand to Gene. "I might have been born at night," he said with a smile, "just not last night. The onion didn't cover a thing. Are we agreed, then?" Skip looked around at Steve and Ray as if seeking agreement. He wasn't. It would be as he demanded, or it would not be at all. He stuck the cigar back in his mouth. "That smells like an agreement," he spat from the side of his mouth. "Now get the hell out of my locker room."

Once the door was slammed shut Ray turned to Gene and Steve, and began laughing. "Well, I'm certainly motivated! Let's eat!"

Chapter 34

Back in the Game

Gene, Ray, and Steve headed for Burger & Stein, the local hangout that all the ballplayers frequented. The place served up hamburgers—or gut bombs, as the guys called them—cooked on an open grill, and served ice-cold beer in tall frosted mugs, which was exactly what a ballplayer wanted after a hot day under the Mississippi sun. Unless your name was Gene Moore, in which case you settled for a bottle of RC Cola.

Burger & Stein was a surprisingly cozy neighborhood bar on a quiet residential corner a few blocks from the field. "It's not Bruno's," Gene thought as they walked in, but it looked good to him anyway. Most of the other players were already there.

"So tell me about this team," Gene said, as he, Ray, and Steve sat down in a corner booth.

"Well, other than the coaches, we're the oldest men on the team," Ray laughed. "It seems strange, but most, if not all of the others, they're not even old enough to have served at the end of the war. Can you believe that?"

"There's a load of talent here, though" Steve said, "but yes, they're very young. They look at Ray as the old-timer, and he's only twenty-six!"

"Tell me a little about yourself, Gene," Steve said. "Ray's been telling us you're the greatest catcher he has ever played with."

Gene smiled into his bottle of soda. "Well, Ray is a loyal friend, but maybe a bad judge of talent. We spent the war together, playing ball overseas, North Africa, the Azores, even Louisiana. I used to be pretty good, I guess."

"Used to be pretty good, he says," Ray said. "This guy was the glue that held the Navy team together. He's the best defensive catcher I've ever seen. He has an arm like a bazooka. I'm not so sure he doesn't throw harder than me. At the plate, he's Babe Ruth reincarnated," continued Ray, "you know, a regular Baby Ruth! Don't let him give you that 'pretty good' crap. Gene Moore is the best there is, period."

Steve looked over at Gene, who was actually turning red from the compliments. All three men knew the use of the present-tense description was no longer accurate. "And he's modest too," added Steve, tilting his head at the catcher.

"No, not modest. Not really," Gene paused, looking down at the table. "I just know it's not all true anymore. I haven't played for almost four years, and my ankle and foot are so swollen after today's game, I could barely get my shoe on. I struck out today, twice. I just don't want to get anyone's expectations too far out of whack."

"Well, let's see, Baby Ruth, arm like a bazooka, glue that held the team together," Steve said, "We don't expect too much! Besides, everyone strikes out, right?"

Steve glanced back and forth between Ray and Gene. The smile vanished from his face. "What? What did I say?" Steve asked.

"He's never struck out twice in a row, so this day was especially hard to take," Ray answered for his friend.

Gene shrugged and added, "That's no big deal, I guess, given everything else."

"What? That's not possible," Steve protested.

"No, Steve, it's a fact," Ray insisted.

"Well, it doesn't matter. It will never happen again," Gene declared.

"Hey, Martha," Ray hollered. "Can we get some service over here?"

"Hold your horses, Ray," the short squat woman in the apron said as she placed an order at the bar. "The way you guys played today, you'll be lucky if I come to your table at all!"

"Hey! Be nice!" Ray laughed. "Martha is our biggest fan—and our harshest critic."

"What will it be, boys?" the waitress asked as she walked up to their table.

"Martha?" Ray began the introduction. "This is Gene Moore. Gene and I played together during the war in the Navy."

She studied him closely. "You're that new catcher. What's that thing you were doing with your left leg? I ain't never seen a catcher do that before."

"Hi, Martha," smiled Gene sweetly. "It's nice to meet you, too."

"Gene's a trendsetter, Martha. I bet within the year, all the catchers will be doing it," Ray said with a serious look on his face.

Martha looked at Steve, who nodded in support of Ray's statement. She squinted her eyes at Ray. "You pull my leg all the time, so I don't believe half of what comes out of your mouth, Ray Laws." She pretended to pout for a few seconds before asking, "Really?"

Gene shook his head as Ray and Steve burst out laughing. "Martha, I broke my ankle in a game in 1945. Bolts hold everything together. My ankle doesn't bend in a way that allows me to squat on both legs, so I have to stick my left leg out to the side."

"Oh, sorry to hear that," the waitress replied. "You related to that other Gene Moore?"

"No, not that I know of, but everyone asks."

Martha looked at Steve and asked, "What can I get you boys?"

"We'll have three beers," Steve ordered, "and three burgers."

"Make that two beers," Gene chimed in. "I'll have an RC Cola with my burger."

"Ray?" Martha asked.

"I'll take the beer, and have Gene's, too!"

Gene, Ray, and Steve spent the next few hours eating, drinking cola and beer, and talking baseball. Before thirty minutes had expired the whole team had gathered around their booth. Ray began by telling stories about their time in the Navy, but soon enough it was clear that Gene was the life of the party. He told several hilarious jokes, shared Navy baseball stories with the guys, and laughed like he had not laughed in years. Ray couldn't help but notice how captivated the players were: Gene held them in the palm of his hand. He had seen it before in Africa and Louisiana.

As the evening wore on, and the alcohol continued to flow, Steve suggested to Ray that they call it a night. "We have a game tomorrow. You're not pitching, but Gene and these kids are playing, and I'm afraid they've all had a little too much to drink—except Gene, here," said Steve as he patted the catcher on the shoulder. "If Skip walked in here right now, he'd have all of our heads."

"Good idea," Gene said. "Ray, I'm staying with you. I need to soak this ankle and get some sleep. Ready to call it a night?"

"What?" Ray asked. "Have you forgotten how to have a good time, Gene? What have you been doing in that little hick town back in Illinois, anyway? We're just getting started!"

"Ray, I can't afford to show up not ready to play. I've already tried that. I don't have your magic pitch and Skip isn't going to cut me any more slack. I have to be ready to play."

Ray nodded in agreement. "Alright, okay," he replied, reaching over to hug Gene and spilling the last inch of beer in Steve's mug. "I'm just so happy to see you, Gene. A little celebration was in order. I'm ready to go now. Besides, you're starting to sound like a cross between my mother and Skip—and that's one ugly combination!"

As the players slowly made their way out the front door, Steve pulled Ray to one side. "Gene's only been here twelve hours, and these kids love him. Man, he knows every subtlety of this game, that's for sure."

"The guy has it, Steve. Ballplayers are drawn to him because they know he knows everything about baseball. It was that way in the Navy. But it's not just kids. In North Africa, many of the officers took their lead from Gene and even looked to him for approval. It was weird, frankly. Age didn't matter then and it doesn't now, either. Anyone who spends time with Gene loves him. What do they call it?"

"Charisma?" answered Steve. "What we need is a catcher who can catch your pitch and show up to the field each day ready to play. I like Gene a lot, but I'm not sure he is up to it any longer. I guess we will know tomorrow."

Ray's face suddenly grew serious. "Gene will show up ready to play. He didn't have a drink tonight—did you notice that?"

"Ray, you knew him four years ago. Things change. Skip was right. I don't know if he was drunk when he showed up today, but he sure smelled like it."

Ray remained quiet for a moment, picking his next words carefully. "I know, Steve. He talked to me about it. He wasn't expecting to play today. He's embarrassed and he's sorry. You give Gene Moore two weeks to find his game—just two weeks, regardless of what he does tomorrow or the day after that—and you're gonna see what this guy's made of."

"I'll talk with Skip."

Ray smiled and slapped Steve on the back. "Boy, are you in for a show. Together, Gene and I are unstoppable."

Gene was leaning against the lamp post on the corner when Ray caught up with him. "Ready to go, boss?" he asked.

"I heard what Steve had to say, Ray."

"I wouldn't worry about it," Ray answered.

"I'm not, which is sort of surprising to me, but I don't want you to worry, Ray. I want you to know you can count on me to give you whatever it is I have left. In truth, Steve's right. I wasn't ready to play today. You asked what I've been doing in that hick town for the last few years. I think you have a pretty good idea now."

"Gene, forget it," Ray said, slapping the air with his hand as if trying to wave away the truth.

"I've been drowning the pain of being out of baseball by drinking," Gene continued. "Last night on the train, the thought of failing scared me near to death. I was so afraid I could hardly tie my shoes. So I had a few drinks. Then I had a few more."

The conversation made Ray uncomfortable. "You're here now, boss, and we're gonna win some games together, just like old times."

"I hope so, Ray—you have no idea how much I want that. But I need to finish telling you. I decided in Bob's pickup, on the way from the train station to the stadium, not to have another drink until I'm back on track, and maybe not even then. I'm not gonna have another drink until we truly have something to celebrate. Please don't ask me to drink with you, Ray. I never really liked it that much. I did it to deaden the pain. I need you to help keep me in check. Can you do that for me?"

Ray nodded and swallowed. "Gene, I would do anything for you, and you know it."

"I do know it," he answered. "I've got a second chance here. I know it is a ridiculous long shot, and I wouldn't be here if you hadn't pulled for me—you and Frank. I won't let either of you down. And I can't let my friends back home down. Everyone's counting on me."

"Sounds fair to me, boss. If 'true confessions' are over, can we go get some sleep?"

Chapter 35

I Heard You Was a Hitter

Three weeks had passed since Gene arrived in Mississippi. He was finally getting his game back. His team loved and respected him, both for his skill and his personality. Gene made them laugh, but most importantly, he inspired them to play harder and better than they thought possible. He had become the unofficial captain of the team—on and off the field. Gene still suffered intense pain in his ankle, but his focus was once again on the game of baseball. True to his word, he did not have a drop of alcohol in Mississippi.

Gene and the team celebrated hard, in victory and sometimes in defeat. Everyone enjoyed being with him after the game, having fun and talking baseball. Even his hard, crusty manager began to ease up on him. To everyone's surprise, Skip began taking a real interest in each of his players, both professionally and personally. For the first time in a long time, he demonstrated a genuine concern for them as human beings, and not just ball players. Even more shocking was the discovery that Skip had a sense of humor. Sometimes, during practice or on the bus, he would tell a joke or two. He even stopped by Burger & Stein once in a while to enjoy a celebratory beer with his team. As the relationship between the players and their manager improved, so did the team's performance on the field.

And every Greenville Pirate knew who to thank. There was no doubt Gene's influence had brought about this welcome change in Skip and the Greenville Pirates.

"Too damn bad about that ankle," Skip said to Steve one afternoon as the coaches watched Gene practice behind the plate. "He plays so damn hard, but he can barely walk off the field after a game. His arm is still a rocket, though, and his bat is outstanding—what's he batting? .378?" Skip shook his head. "This kid could have been one of the all time greats, but he wanted to teach the Krauts how to play ball. Can you believe that? Now that's irony for you."

Steve nodded in agreement. "That's true, Skip, but the players love him and his coaching ability is invaluable. He has such a positive influence on them. He's still got something."

"Charisma," Skip replied. "Moore's got charisma. One of those infectious personalities that are as important in the locker room as they are on the field." Skip sighed and looked up at the clouds gathering in the western sky. "I love this game, Steve, but there are parts of it I really hate."

"I know."

"I don't think he's got much of a future left in baseball. That . . . damn . . . ankle."

"Maybe he'll end up with your job," Steve said while doing nothing to try and hide his wide grin.

"I sure hope he ends up with something," Skip replied. "It's hard not to love this guy. He plays with such passion. Some of these kids whine about a sore finger or sore muscle or sore this or that. This guy plays every play in pain—and loves it! Go figure."

Skip pulled his wet cigar from his mouth and turned to face Steve. "I've seen ballplayers who enjoy this game, but this guy, he's different. I think you come across a ballplayer like Gene Moore maybe once in a decade, maybe not that often. Thirty years in this game and I can count 'em on one hand. One!" And then he proceeded to do just that.

The next day, the Greenville Pirates took their rickety fifteen-year-old bus up to Tuscaloosa for a three-game series with the Tuscaloosa

Braves. Tuscaloosa was the best team in the league, and had a comfortable four-game lead over their nearest rival. Leo "The Mouth" Gambini managed the Tuscaloosa organization. Leo and Skip were arch rivals. The Pirates' manager could think of nothing sweeter than to sweep Leo off his home field with three wins in a row. Skip liked his chances. Roger "Frog" Roussell was pitching that afternoon, and Ray was starting the next day.

The door to the locker room was slightly ajar, and Skip smiled when he heard laughter pouring out of it. Inside was a team whose players were beginning to believe they could win, often and big. He was about to enter when he heard a familiar voice behind him. "The Mouth" was approaching. Skip reached out and closed the door. The sound of his enthusiastic team was replaced by the voice of a man he disliked more than anyone he had ever known.

"Well, if it's not Jim Middleton," Leo said, extending one hand in the air while the other held a smoking cigar. "The Mouth" refused to use Skip's nickname.

"Hello, Leo," Skip responded with a fake smile, returning the handshake.

"How's the team, Jim? I hear you've got a peg-leg catcher and a bunch of kids!" Leo laughed, continuing to hold onto Skip's hand.

"Yeah, that about sums it up, I guess," replied the Pirates' manager out of the corner of his mouth. He shifted his own cigar to the right side of his mouth with his tongue. "We aren't much to look at, Leo, but we hold our own." Skip looked Leo right in the eye, tightened his grip slightly, and pulled the opposing manager in close. "I don't think we'll embarrass ourselves today." Skip let go of the hand like it had the plague.

Leo stuck his cigar in his mouth and began puffing up a storm. "No, I'm sure you won't. You take your teams to respectability, even if you can't win the games that matter."

Skip folded his arms and leaned against the locker room door. He could still hear the laughter of his team from within. "Leo, do you need something? If not, I think I'll just head into the locker room and get ready for the game."

"Hey, Jim. No offense. I didn't mean you weren't a good manager. You just haven't had the talent on your team to put together a run at a pennant."

"No offense taken, Leo," the manager lied as he opened the door and moved to step inside. He hesitated and then turned around. "We're different, you and me. See, I save my energy for the game. You waste yours talking about it before it even happens. I guess that's where you get your nickname." Skip slammed the door hard in the face of "The Mouth."

"Alright, guys, gather round and sit down!" Skip hollered. The players did as he asked.

"You know, I've been around this game for a long time," he began, his voice soft and almost gentle." I've seen it all, and done most of it myself. Some of it, I shouldn't have done. But believe it or not, I've mellowed with age." The room filled with laughter as elbows dug into rib cages. "But one thing I'll never get used to is listening to that fat son-of-a-bitch"—Skip pulled out his cigar and pointed it behind him, over his shoulder—"sit on his butt on the other side of the field and run his mouth off!"

Shouts and jeers filled the room. Skip let it continue for a few seconds before waving them into silence. "My mother always taught me to not speak ill of others, and so I won't tell you exactly what I think of him," Skip continued, his words prompting laughter once again. He lifted his palms to ask for quiet. "You know I don't like to lose," he began again. His voice was almost soothing. "Sometimes you do, and that's that. You play hard, ball takes a bad hop now and again, some two-bit umpire makes a bad call because his eyes were closed—and that's that." Skip looked at each of his players in turn as he spoke. "But losing to that lousy son-of-a-bitch is intolerable to me!" he yelled out, kicking a trash can across the room with his foot. "I don't care if you like me, but I do demand that you play hard for me. I want to sweep that rotund mouthy bum and his team out of here over the next three days. If we do that, we will gain three full games on them and put ourselves right back in this race. That is exactly what a championship team—I said a championship team!—does. Can you do that for me?" Every player jumped to his feet and shouted with enthusiasm.

The manager waited until they had nearly shouted themselves hoarse. "You should also do it for yourselves," Skip added. "Can anyone tell me why?"

"Because that's what champions do?" asked one of the younger players.

"Now this boy has something upstairs." Skip sighed, removed his cap, and rubbed his head. "Let's face it. The Pittsburgh Pirates are the worst team in the National League. Hell, they have not won a pennant in years. They're looking hard at their farm teams to see who they can find to bolster their line up. They're looking for winners . . . for champions. They're trying to build a pennant winner, but are missing a few pieces of the puzzle. I would like to think those pieces are right here in this room." Skip took a long look around before adding, "Let's go get 'em."

Gene grabbed his gear and looked around for "The Frog." He was standing in the back, tucking in his jersey. "Hey, Frog, you heard the man. We gonna win today?"

Frog smiled and nodded. "You keep me calm and focused, and I'll take care of the first win."

"That's fair enough. We'll call that a deal," smiled the catcher. "Just keep 'em low and away from these guys. Make them reach for the ball. Keep them off balance. You got a great team behind you that will play good defense, so don't get too troubled if they hit you. Follow my mitt, and we'll deliver a win for Skip."

"You got it, Gene."

By the time Gene and Frog walked out, the rest of the team was throwing balls. Gene squatted with his left leg extended, and Frog began warming up. After about a dozen pitches he began to throw harder. The problem was he was all over the place. "This should be interesting," Gene thought. He took a few more pitches, stood, and winked at Frog. "Calm down, Frog. We'll be fine. Low and away, low . . . and . . . away."

Gene and Frog were sitting in the dugout when Skip stepped in. "How you feeling, Frog?" he asked.

"Feeling good, Skip."

"Okay, we need you at your best. Can't let that son-of-a . . ."

"I know, Skip. I know," Frog cut in.

"I mean . . . can you hear him?" Skip asked as he got up and began pacing up and down the dugout. He turned to face the team. "Are you listening to him?" Skip yelled, pointing his unlighted cigar toward the opposing dugout. "He runs his mouth all day, all night, never stops. You know what he said to me outside in the hallway? Huh? Do you know?" No one said a word. "He said this team had a peg-legged catcher and was nothing but a bunch of snot-nosed kids and geriatrics." He turned to Gene, and asked, "What do you think of that Gene?"

Gene's jaw tightened as he stood and faced the rest of the team. He cleared his throat as though he was about to give a speech. Then he broke out in a toothy grin. "Sounds like a pretty good description of our team to me, Skip." The entire dugout hooted and hollered at the unexpected answer. Two of the players were laughing so hard they fell off the bench. Gene looked over at Skip. He was nodding without smiling. The catcher sat down.

"Fine," Skip replied, doing his best to hide a smile. "He's about to get his ass beat by a peg-legged catcher and a bunch of know-nothing yahoos. Damn it, now. Don't let me down!"

Greenville shortstop Mike Kick opened the game at the plate. He swung on the first pitch of the game and hit a looping fly ball over the second baseman's head for a base hit. "Now that's how I like to start my games!" thundered Skip, who had threatened to light his cigar if they didn't win the game. The second batter, Bernie Thompson, took four straight balls and trotted down to first base.

Gene was up next, with a man on first and second and no outs. As he started for the plate, Steve Burgner hollered down from the third-base coaching box, "Is this the peg-legged catcher I've heard about? I heard he was a hitter in the Navy. Show us how it's done, Gene!"

The Sesser native took a couple practice swings and stepped into the batter's box. The Braves pitcher, Robby Helling, wound up and sent a fastball high and inside. Gene swung and missed. The next two were low and away for balls. The count was now 2-1. Helling shook his head twice at the catcher, checked his runners, and delivered another fastball high and inside—the exact pitch he had first given Gene. With lightening speed, Gene turned on the ball and swung hard.

"Crack!"

Everyone knew it was gone from the sound alone. The centerfield fence was four hundred ten feet, and the scoreboard was easily another forty feet beyond and above the fence. Gene's ball hit the scoreboard—hard. No one had ever hit the scoreboard in Tuscaloosa before. Gene laughed out loud and raised his fists in the air when he spotted Leo throw his cigar into the dirt and stamp on it with his foot.

It took awhile and it hurt a lot, but when he rounded third Steve was there to slap him on the butt. "Way to go, slugger!" When he crossed the plate, the two men he had knocked in were waiting to shake his hands and congratulate him. Ray ran all the way over from the bullpen and lifted him off the ground with a bear hug. "Holy shit, Gene. Way to go!"

Gene limped his way toward the dugout. The old feeling of elation mixed with total excitement had grabbed his soul again. Skip met him before he could sit down. "Gene, in my entire career, I have never coached a player who hit a ball that hard, and that far. If it weren't for that damned scoreboard, I think it would still be going!" Skip walked back to his seat. "Peg-legged catcher! Is that what you called him?" he yelled toward Leo's Tuscaloosa Braves. "Let's see you run your mouth off about that!"

The Pirates held on to win 3-0.

Chapter 36

The Perfect Day

Game two of the three-game series against the Braves was played on a hot and sunny afternoon—a day made for baseball. The Braves always drew a crowd. The local buzz about Gene's home run the day before had made the rounds, so the crowd for the second game was larger than normal.

Ray Laws was on fire beginning with the first pitch. He retired the Braves in order through the first four innings. Other than a few foul balls, no one was able to connect. By the bottom of the fifth inning, Gene knew he was watching history in the making. He had never seen Ray this focused, this perfect. He wasn't speaking, he wasn't even smiling. He just stared off the mound at Gene, got his sign, concentrated on Gene's glove, and sent the ball sailing. Even though he was used to guiding and even controlling the game, Gene was not about to interrupt Ray's rhythm. Three up, three down. Ray walked off the field, cold as ice and simply unhittable.

There was one problem, however, and it was beginning to tick Ray off. It was now the top of the sixth, and the Pirates had yet to score a run. Ray was pitching a no-hitter, but the game was still tied at 0. Gene knew Ray had pitched several nearly-flawless games in his career, and had lost most of them because of poor defense and quiet bats. Not today, Gene decided. He wasn't going to let that happen to Ray again.

The bottom of the sixth closed like the first five: three strike outs in a row. Leo "The Mouth" had puffed on, thrown down, and stamped out half a dozen cigars, and looked to be at his wit's end. He was nearly thrown from the game when a low pitch was called as the third strike against his best batter. Even Gene thought it was a ball. "The Mouth" ran onto the field and nearly mugged the plate umpire. If he was in any other park, Leo would have been sent to the showers. Turnabout was fair play, however, and the Braves quickly retired the Pirates in the top of the seventh.

Two strikeouts into the bottom of the seventh, Ray's heart skipped a beat when the third batter, shortstop Don Warren, hit a long fly ball into deep left. It looked to be gone, but the outfielder caught it on the warning track and somehow managed to hang on when he slammed into the wall. Ray glanced at Gene, wiped the sweat from his brow, and walked off the mound. The score was still 0-0.

As the eighth inning began, Gene decided it was about time to break his silence. "Alright guys," Gene said, clapping his hands together and moving through the dugout. "Ray's been doing all the work. It's time we joined him!"

"This one's for you, Ray," Big Jerome Kuntz announced as he headed for the batter's box. "Big Jerome" was the first baseman. He stood two inches taller than six feet, weighed twenty pounds more than two hundred, and was as strong as an ox. But that wasn't the only reason his teammates called the farm boy from Missouri "Big." He could usually be counted on to smack the long ball, and his bat was desperately needed today. "Big Jerome" had fouled out twice, both times deep along the left field line. This time he connected with the first pitch and sent it over the left field fence. Although the next three batters went down in succession, the Pirates took the field for the bottom of the eighth up by one.

Ray Laws continued to pitch as though it was the first inning. His arm was loose, his shoulder still felt good, and his fastball had not lost a thing. His forkball was dropping down so well that not a single batter had touched it—even to foul it away. Like the previous innings, the bottom of the eighth was another exercise in flawless pitching. Big Jerome's home run had motivated the team and given Ray enough of a second wind to continue his success. Three up, three down.

The same was not true for Gene. His ankle throbbed as he limped to the dugout. It had been bothering him since the fourth inning. By the eighth, the pain had become excruciating. No matter how he held his leg, the sharp stabbing agony was affecting his game play. Gene gritted his teeth and sat down on the bench to catch his breath. He willed himself to stay focused and hang in there for Ray. He had to finish what they had begun together. Ray had put down twenty-four batters. All he had to do was retire the next three, and his perfect game would be one for the books.

Gene led off the top of the ninth. He shuffled near the plate and took a practice swing. The pain from the easy twist soared up his leg and into his brain. He dropped his bat top down into the dirt and leaned on it to keep from falling over.

Skip saw what was going on and took a few steps toward his catcher. "Moore, you alright?"

Gene waved him off with a nod of his head and stepped into the batter's box. So far he had struck out, flied out, and walked. Ray was having the career-best game Skip had demanded from each of them, but Gene was not, at least not with his bat. To make matters worse, his ankle was so swollen he could barely walk on it. He knew he would have to send the ball deep into the outfield just to get on base.

The pitch came in across the letters. Gene swung hard and missed. The pain was making it difficult to concentrate. He took the second pitch low and away for a ball.

"Damn!" Gene muttered under his breath when he fouled away the third pitch.

Steve, coaching as usual behind third base, clapped his hands and shouted, "Gene, that scoreboard is a bit too close! Can you move it back a bit?" Gene did not even step out to check Steve's signal or acknowledge his joke.

The next pitch was high and away. Ball two. The count was now 2-2.

"Ball three," the umpire yelled when the next pitch came in high and inside. The count was now full: three balls and two strikes.

Gene stepped out of the box and took a breath. He was rarely nervous at the plate, but this time was different. Ray had a perfect game going, and there was no room for error. All he could think about was giving him another run before going into the bottom of the ninth—and last—inning. He stepped back in and focused his eyes on the pitcher, worried that if he took a practice swing he might hurt something.

The Braves' lefthander wound up and threw hard. The final pitch came in high and away and Gene should not have swung at it, but he did. The crisp crack of the bat hitting the ball brought every player on both sides to his feet. Every eye in the stadium watched the ball sail high over the first baseman's head into right field. The ball dropped about ten feet short of right-fielder Paul Milano. It should have been an easy base hit, and for anyone else it would have been. Milano knew Gene was hurting, and when he saw him limping up the first base line, he scooped up the ball and fired it to the first baseman.

"You're out!" the umpire yelled, pumping his fist to the side. It wasn't even close.

Gene limped back to the dugout, humiliated and ashamed. Never in all his years as a ballplayer had he ever seen someone thrown out at first base by a right fielder with a ball hit that deep. Ray met him at the entrance to the dugout with a big smile and a pat on the back. "Thanks, Gene. I'm grateful."

"Grateful for what?" groaned Gene as he moved inside and sat down hard on the bench. "I just made an ass of myself! What makes you grateful?"

"If I don't blow it, in about ten minutes I will have pitched my first no-hitter."

Gene had no idea what he was referring to. "Ray, what the hell are you jabbering on about?"

Ray motioned for one of the players to scoot down, and took a seat next to Gene. "Yesterday, when you almost knocked over the scoreboard, you gave these people something to talk about for years." The smile suddenly left Ray's face. "I'm grateful you didn't do it again! I want them talking about me tonight, not you!"

Gene was still mystified when the entire dugout erupted into laughter. A split second later Gene caught on and joined them. A few players threw their gloves at Gene, joking it up and trying to lighten the mood. "Yes," thought Gene, "this should be Ray's day." They were still up 1-0, and the odds were they would win the game. The next Pirates' batters struck out to end the inning.

Gene was strapping on his gear for the bottom of the ninth when Skip walked over. "Have you looked at your ankle, Gene?"

"Nope," answered the catcher without looking up. "Don't have to, Skip. I can feel it."

"The damn thing is blowing up like a balloon, Gene" Skip said. "Can you finish this inning? I don't think you can—or should."

"What? You think I'm gonna miss this? We're watching a future Hall-of-Famer at work here, Skip! He'll be in Pittsburgh soon, and we both know it."

"Well, I think you should watch him from here. I can throw Larry behind the plate for the final inning."

"No way, Skip. Behind that plate I have the best seat in the house. I'm watching history being made, and I am the history-maker's catcher!" Gene smiled, winked at Skip, and hobbled out to the plate.

"Damn shame," Skip said to no one in particular as he walked back to take his seat on the bench.

"What do you think, Skip?" Steve asked as he sat down next to the manager.

"What do I think?" he repeated as he pulled his cigar out of his mouth. "I think that if it wasn't for Gene's ankle, we would be watching two future Hall-of-Famers today instead of one."

Gene crouched behind the plate into his unorthodox squat and waited for Ray to toss a few warm-up pitches. Instead, the pitcher just stood there, shaking his head. Gene lifted his mask. "You want to throw a couple, Ray?" he asked.

"Nope." He turned away from the plate and began rubbing the shine off the new ball.

"Let's go, gentlemen!" shouted the umpire. "We have one heck of a game to finish up here."

Ray struck out the first two batters with eight pitches. The next batter was Paul Milano, the right-fielder who had thrown Gene out at first base.

Ray motioned for Gene to come to the mound, but met him before he had taken more than ten steps. Gene spoke first. "Ready to finish this one off, big guy? I'd consider it a personal favor if you would strike him out."

"How's your ankle, Gene?"

"Focus on this guy, and we'll talk about my ankle after the game."

"You nearly missed the last two pitches, Gene. Can you hang on for three more?"

"I can hang on, Ray. Take care of business."

Ray looked up into the afternoon sky and smiled. "I'm actually going to miss playing here in the minors."

The catcher from Sesser nodded slowly. "I'm gonna miss it too, Ray. But I hear they have even better fields where we're heading."

Gene returned to the plate and crouched down. For a reason he couldn't explain then, and never could for the rest of his life, the throbbing in his ankle had subsided. The pain was once again manageable.

Ray's first two pitches were perfect: low and away, and low and inside. Milano swung at both and missed. The next three, however, missed the plate. The count was three balls and two strikes, and the crowd was on its feet. The entire game had come down to this, a single final pitch.

Ray looked at Gene for the signal, and the catcher called for his money pitch—the forkball. Ray nodded and smiled for the first time on the mound the entire game.

Milano took a practice swing, stepped into the box, and geared back, wobbling his bat back and forth as if anxious to swing it. He was a good and dangerous hitter, and was long overdue for one of his trademark standup triples. Ray wound up and let it fly. The ball came in fast and dropped, hitting the dirt right behind the plate. Milano thought the pitch was coming in just above the knees and swung hard, but missed. Gene tried to scoop it up, but knocked the ball out in front of him beyond the plate. It was a dropped third strike, and Milano took off running for first base.

Gene leaped up and forward as best he could, grabbed the ball, and was moving his arm back to throw it when his ankle gave out. He released the ball toward first base as he fell to the ground.

It was as if time slowed to a crawl. Gene watched the ball and the batter, moving in slow motion, both racing toward first base. Gene hit the dirt before he could see which got there first.

The reaction of the hometown crowd answered that question when the spectators erupted in loud cheers. Gene was on his back, pounding the dirt with his left fist, in time with the throbbing of his painful ankle. He had blown Ray's perfect game by dropping a ball he had caught hundreds of times—and on a third strike! Before he could look up, Ray joined him in the dirt, screaming as loud as he could. Gene didn't blame him for being angry. How could he not be?

"You're amazing! Damn, boss, how did you do that?"

Gene lifted his head and shook it as if he was not hearing Ray correctly. Within seconds the entire team was leaping on Ray and Gene, rolling around in the dirt but being careful to leave Gene's legs exposed and untouched.

"I got him?" Gene asked incredulously. "I GOT HIM?"

Ray pushed his face next to his friend's and hollered, "I knew it! I just knew it! I just threw a perfect game, and at the very last moment you figured out how to upstage me!"

It was not only the players who ran onto the field. Skip was there with the rest of his team, pulling the guys off Gene and Ray, chomping down on his cigar and barking out orders. The manager looked over toward the Braves' bench and smiled when he saw Leo "The Mouth" glaring in his direction, his hands on his hips and his head shaking side to side.

"A peg-legged catcher?" he shouted out, pulling his cigar from his mouth and throwing it at the opposing manager. "Did you see what this peg-legged catcher and bunch of kids did to your ball club?" Leo lifted his middle finger, turned, and left the field. Skip turned back to the pile, which had fallen away to reveal a very happy pitcher and catcher. "Let's get some ice on that thing, Gene. Not a bad throw. Put a little more of at least one leg into it next time!" Skip laughed at his own joke.

"Sure thing, coach," Gene replied with a smile as "Big" Jerome Kuntz slowly helped him to his feet.

Skip turned his attention to Ray. "Ray Laws!" he yelled, reaching out to shake his hand. "Congratulations, son. That was the best-pitched game I've ever seen. It's certainly one I will never forget."

The team carried Ray and Gene off the field on their shoulders. Ray would not have had it any other way.

Chapter 37

The Day After Perfection

"Gene! Where have you been?" Ray was beside himself.

"I overslept a bit, but I'm on time. What's the big deal? Where's the fire, chief?"

Ray shook his head. "Skip's on the warpath. I've been waiting out here so I could warn you before you went in."

"Warn me about what, Ray?"

"Skip is fit to be tied," replied the pitcher. "A couple of the guys are sprawled out on the floor in the locker room, and a few others are sitting next to the toilet. We kept them out too late last night, and he is madder than a hornet. And this one's stinging today."

They were entering the locker room when Skip yelled out, "Someone go over and get Moore's ass out of bed and into my office!"

"I'm here, Skip," Gene replied calmly.

Skip spun around and stared at Gene, narrowing his eyes as he looked him over from head to toe. He pulled his cigar out and pointed it at the catcher. "I told you how much I hate that fat son-of-a-bitch Gambini! I told you I wanted to sweep him this weekend, didn't I?"

"Yeah, Skip," Gene said, "And we've played twice, and won both."

"Those games are over with! History! All I care about is today, and you went out with these kids and kept them out all damn night! I'll be damn lucky if I can find nine healthy ballplayers to take the field! Mike Kick's in the shitter right now turning himself inside out! Bernie Thompson can't stand for thirty seconds without getting dizzy!"

Gene frowned. "Skip, with all due respect, those kids have minds of their own. I didn't keep 'em out, and I'm certainly not their keeper." Skip just glared at him. "And in case you are wondering, I had four RC colas last night, and that's it."

Skip stuck his cigar back into place and spit a piece of it out the side of his mouth. "No, you're not their keeper, but they don't seem to see it that way. They try to talk like you, act like you, hell, sometimes if I didn't know better, I think I see them limping like you!"

Gene glared back at the manager. "Well, I'm here and I'm ready to play ball. If they want to act like me, tell them to get their candy asses up off the floor and get ready for the game! They already know I don't drink, so this has nothing to do with them wanting to be me."

"Gene, let me tell you something," the manager continued, lowering his voice a few notches. "You're a natural leader, whether you like it or not. If you go out at night, drinking or not, they are going to go out. Hell, some of these kids aren't even old enough to go into a bar." Skip started to walk away, but changed his mind and stepped up in Gene's face. "Gene. Listen to me. You take these kids out, I don't care if you're not drinking. If they drink all night, I will release you. And damn it, I mean it!"

Gene could not believe what he was hearing. He threw down his mitt and turned his hands up as if to plead his case. "Wait a minute! Let me get this straight. I'm not hung over and I'm ready to play, but if they're out drinking, you'll release me? Did I get that right, Skip?"

"Listen, I don't have time to baby-sit a bunch of hung-over wannabes who are out trying to keep up with you. Do you understand me, mister?"

"No, Skip, I really don't understand you," the catcher shot back. "But you're the manager, so whatever you say, goes."

"That's right, and don't forget it!" Skip turned toward the rest of the team, or at least those players not still hugging toilets. "Get suited up and get out on that field before I say something else I don't mean and doesn't make sense!"

Gene shook his head and sought out his locker. He was surprised by Skip's attitude, and even thought it humorous in a way, but by the time he was ready to tie his cleats the whole conversation was starting to eat away at him. Steve was walking by when Gene slammed his locker door shut.

"You okay, Gene?"

"Did you hear the crap I got from Skip, Steve?"

The third base coach shrugged. "Yeah, I heard it. You still don't get it, do you?"

"No, I guess I don't, coach," Gene replied. "Explain it to me."

"You're the leader and these kids will listen to you. You're older, you've been to war, you've been part of the Dodgers organization. This team was not going anywhere until you arrived. Skip can smell a shot at the league championship. So can I."

Gene took a deep breath and sighed. Steve was right. "Coach," he began before being cut off.

"Gene, listen. It's not just you and Ray who are trying to make it. Skip and me, well, we would love a shot at managing in Pittsburgh, or anywhere else for that matter. We all want to move up, Gene. You think you aren't a young man any more? Skip knows his time's running out fast. He needs this team to win and he needs you to get these kids under control. That's all he's really asking for. He's not mad at you. The old guy just wants to win. Will you help him, Gene?"

A few lockers away, Mike Kick was suffering from the dry heaves. "Sure, coach," Gene sighed. Everyone has dreams and goals. Gene of all people knew and appreciated that.

"Look out, Gene. Skip's about to give his pre-game speech," warned Steve. "He has his stool with him. Be ready to duck!"

"Alright everyone, hear this! Take a knee!" Skip announced while standing on a stool at the other end of the locker room. The Pirates gathered around him. "I'm madder than hell. I don't give a rat's ass how sick or hung over you are. You will play today, you will play well today, and you will win today. We're gonna sweep that fat son-of-a-bitch, and leave here with all the marbles. Am I making myself clear?"

Skip stepped down without waiting for a reply or a question. He grabbed his stool, threw it against the wall, and stormed out the door and onto the field.

"Told you to duck," Steve said to Gene.

It was well above one hundred degrees on the field that day. Not exactly the perfect weather for a hang over. Gene sat the game out, his ankle wrapped in ice. For a couple innings the game remained tied at zero. It busted wide open in the third, and the Greenville Pirates were shut out by the Tuscaloosa Braves 7-0. Skip's sweep of Leo "The Mouth" Gambini was not to be.

The players loaded their gear on the bus for the long ride home. Gene found a seat near the front.

"Gene, you got a minute?" Skip asked. He was remarkably calm after the game, almost eerily so.

"Sure, Skip, grab a seat."

"First of all, let me tell you something," he began. "I don't apologize well, Gene. I hate it, but it's the truth. I'm sorry."

"No need, Skip. I'm fine," Gene responded.

"I wanna tell you what was on my mind this morning and why I acted like I did. Hell, I know what I said didn't make sense, and I knew it when I was yelling it. You wait until you have kids. You'll find yourself yelling stupid things at them all the time." He shook his head.

"Skip, you don't have to tell me anything."

"Yes, I do. So hear me out."

It was then that Gene realized something besides that day's loss was bothering the manager. "Okay, you're the boss."

"When you first got here, I didn't think you had a snowball's chance in hell of making it," Skip admitted. "I was mad as hell with Frank for sending you to me. Your ankle, it's a mess, and you have to admit," Skip continued, trying to keep his voice as low as he could, which took some effort, "you didn't exactly make a stellar first impression."

Gene smiled, remembering how he arrived smelling of beer and onions. "No, I suppose I didn't."

Skip pulled out his cigar and studied it. "But you've made a believer out of me. If you had two good ankles, you'd be catching in Pittsburgh right now and we'd all be reading about you in the papers." He sighed. "But that's not how it is, son. You're here, on this old bus, playing in the minors with a has-been old manager on the wrong side of sixty, and your ankle is what it is. You know what I mean?"

"I know it, Skip, and it eats at me every day. I have no illusions about my future. My goal is to get Ray to Pittsburgh. If I can do that, I've done my job."

"I want you to make it to the majors, Gene. More than I've wanted any other player to get there. Your ankle is what it is because you served your country. But you have the bat, and you still have the arm— everyone knows you have the heart. It seems only right for you to make it all the way." Skip pulled at his nose as if the compliments made him uncomfortable.

Gene shrugged. "I try not to think about it, Skip. Being here in Greenville, I've come to terms with reality."

"I sense that, I do" answered the manager as he eyed his catcher closely. "You're protecting your feelings. But Gene, if you are going to make it, it will be only because you believe you can and play as if there is no tomorrow. I was angry this morning—not really at you, but about you. I'm going to bat for you, son. I will make sure the Pirates take notice. I want you playing at Forbes Field. I want you to own that damn old stadium. Do you understand what I'm telling you?"

Gene didn't know what to say. He thought for a few moments before replying, "I appreciate it, coach. Let's get Ray there and we'll see what happens with me. Fair enough?"

"No, damn it!" Skipped barked, "that's not fair enough and that's what I'm getting at. If you don't believe in yourself, it will not happen, period. You believe more in Ray Laws right now than you do in Gene Moore."

Gene tightened his ankle, felt the ache, and bit his lip into silence. "There is a good reason for that," he thought.

The player and manager sat quietly for a few moments. Skip broke the silence by slapping Gene's thigh and standing up. "We should be leaving soon. Try to get some sleep."

Gene nodded and limped to the back of the bus. Skip looked out the window, and when he saw Ray and Steve talking, decided to join them. "What are you two yapping about without me?" he asked as he stepped off the bus.

Steve answered, "Nothing important, Skip."

"Well, let me give you something to talk about, and it's damn important," Skip said. "I think we've got a problem. I don't think Gene believes he can make it. He's playing great, but I see it in his every move. He's doing this for you, Ray. If you weren't here, the pain he's in he'd quit tomorrow. His goal is to get you to the majors, and that's admirable, but he's cutting himself short."

"How can you say that, Skip?" Ray protested. "The guy almost knocked over the scoreboard two days ago, and saved my perfect game yesterday. That's what you call giving up?"

Skip dug into his pocket to find another cigar. "Laws, I know you got something upstairs, so try and focus on what I am telling you." When he found his fresh cigar, Skip bit off one end, spat it to one side, and stuck the stogie into his mouth. "I didn't say he's given up. I just don't think he's got that edge that comes with realizing your dream is within your reach. He's still a great ballplayer, and how the hell he catches like that is a real head scratcher. I'm just saying that with his ankle, he has to be better than great, or the Pirates won't take a chance on him. They know his story, and they want to. But they're a business that depends on winning."

"Let me talk to him," Ray answered. "I'll get him motivated."

"That's not it, Ray," the manager continued. "The guy is already the most motivated player on this team, but he's motivated to move *you* up and I think he'll be satisfied when that happens. Unless he's flawless and down right dazzling, when you move up Ray, they'll move him out." No one said a word. They all knew it was true.

"If Gene will listen to anyone about this, it's Frank Boudreau."

"I thought of that already," replied the manager. "But I doubt the head office will look kindly on me if I call in a scout from halfway across the country to help me convince a ballplayer he can make it." Skip sighed heavily and looked at Steve. "I wonder where Frank is."

"I can find out in the morning," replied Steve.

"Alright, do it. But don't make a request to have him here. Not yet, anyway. If he's in the area, great. If not, well, let me think on it a while." Skip glanced over at the bus. "We've got one of the greatest ballplayers I've ever seen sitting on that old bus. He's only missing a healthy ankle. Damn it all to hell, I'd give him my leg if I could. I surely would."

Skip, Steve, and Ray boarded last. The door closed behind them and the lights went dark. The rickety mode of transportation supplied by the Pirates slowly headed back to Greenville, leaving behind it a trail of dirty gray diesel smoke.

Chapter 38

Frank Boudreau

Gene walked into the locker room a few days later and heard Skip calling out his name. "Gene, come in to my office."

Gene entered to find a familiar face waiting for him inside. "Mr. Boudreau!" Gene exclaimed, offering his hand to the smiling scout. "What are you doing here?"

"Well, if it's not the pride of the Egyptians, Gene Moore!" laughed the scout. "After all these years, though, would you please call me Frank?" He reached out and clasped Gene's hand in both of his own. "To tell you the truth, I was close by, scouting some kids, and thought I'd drop in and see how you're doing."

"It's so good to see you, Frank. I've been wondering how you are and what you've been up to," Gene replied.

"I'm getting older, I guess, and up to no good. I hear you almost knocked down the scoreboard in Tuscaloosa! Really connected, huh?"

"Yeah, I still get lucky now and then."

Skip got up from his chair and walked to the door. "Frank, I'm going to leave you and Gene alone to talk up old times. My favorite cigars are in the top left drawer, and I have them counted, so keep your hands out of them!" The manager left, closing the door behind him.

Gene stopped smiling, and felt a small wave of anxiety course through him. "This is the first time all season I've seen the door of this office closed. I guess this isn't exactly a social visit, is it?"

"Not entirely, Gene," Frank admitted. "Skip asked me to come by and speak with you."

Gene sighed and nodded. "Do I take the train home today?"

For a moment Frank looked confused, but he replied quickly, "Oh, no. Not at all. Your numbers look good, considering your ankle, and Skip tells me you have moments of greatness that are becoming more and more frequent." Frank pushed aside a few items and sat down on the edge of Skip's desk. "He tells me he thinks you don't believe you can make it to the majors. Is that true?"

Gene's eyes narrowed as he considered the question. "Frank, are the Pirates, or any other team for that matter, looking for a crippled catcher?"

"Nope," Frank answered honestly, "I'm sure they're not. Is that what you think you are?"

Gene rubbed his eyes and slumped into a chair. "I don't know Frank. At times, I feel as if there isn't anything I can't do. No pitcher I can't hit, no play I can't make. Then, after a few innings, the pain—it gets so intense . . . I guess it brings me back to reality."

"How's your Greek mythology?"

"Come again?"

"How's your Greek mythology?"

"Frank, you're talking to a kid from Sesser who dropped out of school in the eighth grade to help his family on a small pig farm."

Frank smiled and said, "Well, I thought you might have had a pig named Homer." Frank lifted his eyebrows and waited for a response.

"A pig named Homer," repeated a completely bewildered Gene. "No, can't say I remember that one. Why?"

Gene didn't understand his humor. "I'm sorry. Bad joke," Frank explained. "Achilles, he was the greatest warrior in the entire ancient world. He inspired his fellow Greeks to feats of combat and bravery even they thought impossible, and he struck fear in the hearts of the Trojan enemy." Frank paused. "You have heard of Achilles and the Trojan War, haven't you? The subject of Homer's *Illiad*?"

Gene nodded and shook his head at the same time. "Sort of."

Frank continued. "Well, when Achilles was on the field of battle, victory for the Greeks was assured. I was driving here today and I thought of you . . . and Achilles. It was then it struck me how similar you two are, one in the same, really. You inspire your team and strike fear in the hearts of your opponents. When Gene Moore is on the field, the outcome is rarely in doubt. When I see you, Gene, I always call you what?"

"The pride of the Egyptians," he laughed. "What are you getting at, Frank?"

"Well, Achilles was the pride of the Greeks. When he was born, his mother dipped him into the river Styx, which protected him against any mortal injury. But he remained vulnerable in one place."

"His heel, the Achilles Heel," offered Gene quietly.

"That's right," Frank replied with a nod. "His mother had held him by the heel to dunk him, and so the water never touched that part of his body. During the siege of Troy, a God told Paris where to send his poison arrow, which struck Achilles in the only place that could hurt him. It took him down in the end, but not before he made history and inspired nations not yet in existence—millions of people not yet born. More than two thousand years later, Gene, in this dirty old locker room in Greenville, Mississippi, we're sitting here talking about Achilles." Frank paused and cleared his throat. "Gene, your ankle is your only weakness. And it will be your demise . . . someday . . . in baseball. We already know that. But you can make history along the way. Someday, somewhere, sometime, I want someone . . . like me, maybe, or your kids . . . to tell the story of Gene Moore to a few kids who will be inspired to overcome the odds and accomplish something special in their lives."

Gene swallowed hard and looked at the floor. "I don't know what to say, Frank."

Frank leaned across the desk toward the catcher. "Then let me tell you what to say, son. Look me in the eye and tell me you believe you can make it to the big show. Tell me you believe you are the best who has ever played the game of baseball behind the plate. Tell me that even with your bum ankle, you're going to give it everything you have, to achieve your dream of baseball greatness. Tell me that regardless of what happens, you will play in a way that will inspire others, and make people remember you for years to come."

Gene lifted his eyes and looked at the scout. "I don't think I can say that and mean it, Frank. You take a peek at my ankle about the fifth inning of any game. Do that, and then tell me what you think."

"I know, Gene. Skip told me. But Gene Moore can do more in five innings than most major leaguers can do in an entire game." Frank looked into Gene's eyes and could tell his words were making Gene think. For the first time since the day way back when on the dusty old ball diamond in Sesser, Illinois, Frank could see the sparkle in Gene's eyes. "You think about what I've said, Gene. Think about whether you can tell me what I want to hear—and mean it. Go out there tonight and play like you are Achilles. Inspire your team, as you always do. Strike fear in the hearts of your opponent. Then, after the game, look me in the eye and tell me what I want to hear." Frank waited for a reply, but Gene merely nodded and looked away.

Frank stood up. "I'm going to go watch this game. I hear Greenville has a hot catcher with a strange squat." Frank hoped the words would trigger a smile, but they didn't. "Go win this one, and I'll buy you dinner."

"Okay, Frank." Gene finally answered. He even managed a weak smile. "It's a deal."

Frank shook Gene's hand. "It's always good to see you, Gene. I'm only here tonight because I care about you, and want nothing for you but the success you so richly deserve."

"Frank, I owe you everything. I won't let you down. I'm grateful for your concern. I know you're right . . . I know Skip's right."

"I'll be up in the bleachers. Let's see what you can do." He turned to leave.

"Frank."

"Yes?" The scout turned around and looked at Gene.

"Thank you for coming back to Sesser to get me."

Frank lifted his head proudly and offered his favorite player a deep, warm smile. "You were worth the trip." The scout turned and opened the door.

"Frank, wait."

When Frank turned back around a second time, he saw Gene standing next to Skip's desk. He had pulled the top drawer open. "Here, catch," Gene ordered as he reached inside and tossed something at the scout. Frank reached up and caught one of Skip's cigars. He smiled as he ran it under his nose, inhaled deeply, and tucked it inside his pocket.

"See you after the game, Achilles."

Ray was already warming up when Gene arrived on the field. He thought about the giant strides Ray had made this season. There was not another pitcher in the Major Leagues throwing any better than Ray Laws. The chatter was dead on. Ray was bound to be called up very soon.

The game began and Gene was hot from the start. Batting cleanup, he stepped up in the bottom of the first inning and hit the second pitch into the stands. Two players stepped on the plate before he did. Just like that the Pirates were up 3-0.

In the top of the second, the lead-off hitter for the Memphis team hit a single. Gene threw him out trying to steal second. Knowing Frank was watching was a great motivator, just as it had been when he was 15 playing in The Lumberyard in Sesser a lifetime ago. In the top of the fourth inning, Gene hit another deep shot into left centerfield. The ball cleared the wall by twenty feet. The Pirates were now up 6-0.

The bottom of the seventh was coming up. Gene was putting his gear back on when Ray walked up. "Let's pitch this next guy inside," Gene began. "He can't hit anything tight . . ."

Ray cut him off with a laugh and a light shove. "Show off! What are you gonna do next, pitch a few innings?"

"I'm feeling good tonight," Gene admitted. His ankle was sore, but not overly so.

"Feeling good?"

"I'm feeling better than good," chuckled the catcher.

"Everything go okay with Frank?" Ray asked.

"Yeah," he nodded. "It's good seeing him again." Gene paused, buckled his left shin guard, and looked up at his friend. "I guess I didn't realize I wasn't doing my best, Ray."

"I don't want to go to Pittsburgh without you, boss. I won't go unless you're with me. Skip, Steve, Frank, we just want you to believe you can do it, because we know you can."

"You guys want to play ball, or shall we call it a night?" growled the umpire. The Memphis batter was glaring at them. He was already standing next to the plate.

"Let's put this guy away," Ray said. "I'm hungry."

Gene was walking to the plate when he noticed some commotion a few rows behind the Pirates' dugout. "What's going on up there, ump?"

Both men could see people running to and from the area. "Look's like a fight to me," he replied. "Let's play ball!"

The game continued and the Pirates won 7-0. Gene turned in another stellar performance. Ray pitched a three-hit shut out.

After the game, Gene and Ray were standing in front of their lockers dissecting the game when Coach Burgner walked up. His face was red, and he did not look well. "Gene, can I see you in Skip's office?"

Gene looked the third base coach over. "Sure," he replied. "You look flushed, Steve. You feel okay?"

"No, I don't, now that you ask. Ray, it might be better if you joined us," suggested Steve as he led the way into the manager's office.

Gene and Ray swapped glances, shrugged, and followed him into Skip's office. Skip was sitting at his desk, his head resting in one of his hands. "Shut the door, Steve," he said without looking up. "Gene, Ray, have a seat."

"What's going on, Skip?" asked Ray. Both players looked at Steve, but he refused to catch their eye. Gene and Ray exchanged confused glances.

Skip used his free hand to rub the side of his face before straightening up and facing them. "There is no way to tell you boys this easy, so I will just tell it to you straight up. I got some bad news."

Gene knew what was coming, and leaned over and whispered, "Congratulations, Ray. You're going to Pittsburgh. I'm heading back to Sesser." Ray grimaced and shook his head.

The manager heard Gene's guess and sighed. "Frank Boudreau had a heart attack tonight up in the bleachers during the game."

Gene felt as though someone had just punched him in the gut. He leaped to his feet. "Where is he, Skip?"

"He didn't make it."

"What do you mean, he didn't make it?" Gene asked, even though he knew what those four terrible words meant.

"Frank's dead, Gene."

Ray gasped, hung his head, and covered his eyes with one hand. Steve chewed on his lower lip and looked away. Gene just stood there, frozen and unable to fully comprehend the news he was being told. "He's what?"

"I'm sorry, Gene. Frank's dead."

"Oh my God, no . . . Oh dear God, no," he whispered, turning around to lean his forehead against the concrete block wall. He didn't want anyone to see the tears. "Frank would not have been here if I hadn't been screwing up."

At that, the old Skip surfaced for a breath. "Well, that has nothing to do with nothing!" he said firmly. "Frank had a heart attack. It had nothing to do with you, and it had nothing to do with him being here. You weren't screwing up. It's a damn shame what happened tonight, but Frank died doing what he loved to do. We should all be so damn lucky. When it's my time, I want to die in that dugout over there," he pointed, this time without a cigar in his hands. "Or the one in Pittsburgh, come to think about it. So get that thought out of your head. This has nothing to do with you, Gene."

Gene nodded and turned back around. "I loved Frank as much as my own father," he said softly, wiping tears from his cheeks. "More in some ways. He was the most important person in my life. That wasn't totally clear to me before tonight. He was always there for me. He cared about me, not just as a player. . . " Unable to continue speaking, Gene stopped and sat back down next to Ray, whose own tears were also flowing. Frank had found him, too, pulled him up from a dead end town and pointed him toward the big leagues. He had given them both life.

"That cigar-stealing SOB told me just today you two were the best players he ever scouted. No offense, Ray," continued Skip as he nodded toward his pitcher, "but he told me over and over these past few weeks that Gene was 'the best damn overall ballplayer' he ever laid eyes on—so you're in good company." Skip rubbed his eyes and sat quietly for a few moments before quietly adding, "We all owe a great deal to that man."

The room fell silent. Gene closed his eyes and pictured the scout's face on that hot day so long ago when the tall stranger paid a visit to Sesser. He remembered the first words he ever heard come out of his mouth: "You catch one heck of a game, son." The words echoed over and over in his mind.

"I need to see him, Skip," Gene informed the manager. "How do I do that? Where is he?"

Skip looked at Steve. "Well, I don't know if you can. And if you can, are you sure you want to?" he asked. "I don't know what good it's gonna do."

Gene stood again. "I need to tell him something. I told him that after the game tonight I would tell him something. I need to do that."

Skip, Steve, and Ray accompanied Gene to the Greenville hospital to view Frank's remains. The facility was holding his body pending the arrangements necessary to send him home to his family in Circleville, Ohio. It took some doing to get in because none of the men were next of kin. Luckily, the fellow who ran the hospital morgue was a fan of the local Pirates and authorized the visitation.

Gene went in to see Frank alone, and spent a full twenty minutes with him. No one ever knew what it was Gene said to Frank, and no one ever asked.

Chapter 39

Sacrifice Play

"Gene!"

The catcher rolled over in bed and tried to open his eyes. By the look of things, it was barely dawn. Someone was knocking loudly on the door. "What is it?" Gene replied as he pulled back the covers and sat up. "Ray, is that you?"

"Gene! We're being called up!"

The catcher leaped to his feet and threw open the door. Ray was standing outside hopping up and down, excited and out of breath. Once he made the team, Gene took a small room in a boarding house. Now Ray was standing in the hall, looking like he was going to bust wide open.

"What? What did you say?" He could not believe his ears.

"Coach Burgner . . . he told me . . . in confidence, of course," gasped the pitcher. "We got the call! We're headed for Pittsburgh! Did you hear me? I said 'we' are going, boss!"

Wide awake now, Gene was unsure how to respond because he didn't believe it. "Are you pulling my leg, Ray? I don't think this is very funny."

"Gene!" Ray screamed, grabbing him by the shoulders and shoving his face in next to Gene's. "Coach Steve told me. He heard Skip on the phone. Boss . . . we got the call!"

The friends hugged one another for several seconds, separated, and then hugged again. Gene broke away and turned to look for his clothes. "Where are my pants?" he asked. "I can't find my pants!" He turned back to face Ray. "Damn it, are you *sure*?" He found his pants and started putting them on.

"Steve overheard Skip on the phone last night," continued a breathless Ray. "He was talking to Pittsburgh. He heard them say I was starting this weekend against the Cardinals. Gene, we are moving up!"

Gene froze, with one leg buried deep into his pants. He could feel the blood pounding in his temples. "Ray, that doesn't mean I am moving up with you."

"Of course it does!" he exclaimed. "We are a team. We are a battery. Hell, we are THE battery! Steve heard Skip ask for a new pitcher and catcher to be sent to Greenville from Mobile. Why would they need a new catcher if you weren't going up? Huh? Answer me that one!" When Gene had no response, Ray continued. "They both should arrive tomorrow. Today is our last start in the minors, Gene."

Gene finally exhaled and broke a slow, tentative smile. He had been waiting for more than ten years to hear this news—something he wanted more than anything in his whole life. "I guess that must be right then," he said slowly. "Well, let's give them a game today they'll never forget."

"Gene, the coach told me this in confidence. You can't let anyone know that you know, or I'll be in hot water."

"Got it," Gene responded.

"I have to get back," said Ray. "Remember, act surprised!"

Ray ran back to his apartment, which was only three blocks away, gathered his gear, and headed for the field. He was starting today against Tuscaloosa—his last day in the minors. He could barely stop himself from screaming as the energy and excitement built within him. He was equally as excited for Gene. He knew he had played a big part in pulling Gene's baseball career back together, but he also knew and appreciated that no minor league catcher could handle his forkball. They were a team. They were equally indebted to each other. And today, it had all paid off. They were going to be playing with the Pittsburgh Pirates!

When Ray arrived at the field Gene was already there, blocking the door to the locker room. They exchanged glances, and knowing smiles, but somehow kept from yelling like wild men at their good fortune.

It was like any other August day in Greenville, hot and humid with a clear blue sky. Something else was in the air that day: excitement. Every player on the team could feel it. By the time batting practice began, everyone knew something was up, and that Gene and Ray were somehow involved.

Gene was first in line, and sent the first pitch over the leftfield fence. On the second pitch he slammed the ball against the centerfield wall. The third went screaming above the same wall into the scoreboard—450 feet away. Gene took a few more practice swings before heading for the dugout. His ankle was barely aching today. He was ready to play ball.

"Gene!" Skip called out to the catcher as he walked back to the dugout. "I need to see you for a minute."

"Sure, Skip. Right now?"

"Yeah, in my office."

Gene followed the manager into his small office. Steve stepped in behind them. "You want me to stay, Skip?" he asked.

"I'd appreciate it, yes," Skip answered quietly. "Close the door."

"What's going on?" Gene asked as he sat down and glanced from Skip to Steve, and then back at the manager. Skip leaned forward on his elbows. He looked as though he had not shaved or slept in three days. His eyes, large and bloodshot, had puffy bags beneath them. "Skip, if you keep showing up juiced, I might see you catch a train home tonight," joked Gene. "Bob's got an onion outside you can chew on." When neither coach said a word or cracked a smile, Gene realized something was seriously wrong. "You don't look too happy."

"We're not happy, Gene," admitted Skip. "Not too damn happy at all. That's because we have bad news." On his desk was a cigar. It hadn't been touched.

Gene knew what was coming. "I'm being released. That's why you called for a new catcher."

Skip leaned back and shot a look at Steve. "What the hell did you tell him?" he barked.

"Nothing!" replied the coach. "Not a thing."

"How'd you know about that?" Skip asked, turning back to Gene.

Gene shrugged. "Just a hunch." He remembered his promise to Ray and there was no way he was going to break it.

Skip stood and began pacing behind his small desk. "I don't know what to say, Gene. The Pirates, they know that with a good ankle—."

"Forget it, Skip. I already know this story . . . and how it ends," replied Gene. He was trying hard not to show any emotion, but his voice was quivering and his hands were shaking. His eyes began filling with tears. He took a deep breath, held it for a few seconds, and then exhaled. "Should I pack up my things now?"

"I'd sure like to see you play one more game, son. And I need to ask you for a favor I know I have no right to ask."

Gene wiped his eyes on his sleeve. "Ask anything you like, Skip."

"Ray was called up two weeks ago, Gene."

The news was almost as stunning as the news that he was being released. "Called up? What are you talking about?"

"When he found out Pittsburgh wasn't taking you, he told the Pirates, well, basically he told them to take their offer and shove it. He told them he wasn't moving up without you. They didn't take him until they gave you one long last look. Their head scout has been shadowing the team for a while now."

A sudden realization struck Gene. "That's why Frank was here."

"Yeah. That's why Frank was here." Gene nodded, the threads of the story finally coming together and making sense. Skip spoke again. "Gene, the scout Frank was sitting with told the Pirates that you're an amazing ballplayer, but in his opinion your ankle would never hold up."

Gene sighed and nodded slowly. "You said you needed to ask me something."

"I need you to convince Ray to go to Pittsburg without you. They told me flat out they will not call him again. If he refuses after today, they plan to trade him and pass the problem on to someone else. Quite frankly, I'm worried he may just walk out of here with you. I can't imagine—oh hell, what am I talking about? I've been around baseball all my life! I know how painful this must be for you, but we can't let Ray do that."

Unable to speak, Gene nodded and turned to walk out of the office. Skip reached over and grabbed his arm. Gene turned back and Skip looked him in the eye. "Everything Frank Boudreau said about you . . . and more . . . was true. You did yourself proud here in Greenville, son."

Gene wiped his face a second time with his sleeve, but this time managed a small smile when he heard Frank's name.

"Can you get yourself together and play today?" Steve asked.

"Today's my last game. I can do it. Is that scout still here?" Gene asked.

Skip looked over at Steve. "Yeah, he's still here," answered the coach. "You want to meet him?"

"No," Gene shook his head. "I just want him to see me play one more time. That's all."

"Will you speak with Ray for me?" asked Skip.

"Skip, Ray will go to Pittsburgh if I have to carry him there on my back. I'll see to it. For now, just let him think I was called up with him. Okay? Just don't tell him about me yet. I'll take care of the rest."

"Thanks, Gene."

Gene wiped his eyes again, took a deep breath, and walked out of Skip's office into the locker room. He spent a few minutes at his locker composing himself before grabbing his equipment and heading for the field to warm up. Ray was standing outside the door waiting for him.

"You ready to pitch today, Ray?" Gene asked with as big a grin as he could muster.

"You ready to catch what I'm throwing today, boss?"

"Depends on whether you can throw what I'm calling for!"

"You've brought me this far. You call for it, and you'll get it," smiled Ray. "But Gene, if I were you, I'd put a little extra padding in that glove today. That ball will be blazing. Can you handle the heat?"

"I think I can handle the heat, Ray," Gene said slapping his friend on the back and stepping outside to face the diamond. When Gene stopped walking, Ray turned around and gave him a quizzical look.

"What's wrong, boss. You forget something?"

The sight of the freshly cut diamond had brought Gene up short. As his eyes soaked it in, a deep sense of sadness washed over the catcher from Sesser. He pictured his Pop sitting in the stands, with Ward on one side and Frank on the other. All three were eating peanuts, drinking sodas, and cheering him on to knock the ball out of the park. Only a few hundred people had arrived and taken their seats in the stands, but Gene could hear the roar of the crowd; it was intoxicating—overwhelming. The lines had yet to be chalked, but he could already feel the dust on his fingers. Not a ball had been thrown, not a bat had been swung, but the sweat of athletes lingered in the air.

"Gene?"

He blinked a couple times, took a deep breath, and reached out for Ray's shoulder. "God I love this game, Ray," he said as he put his arm

Gene and Ray

around his friend and squeezed tightly. "And I love walking out onto the field with you. I just wanted you to know that."

Ray smiled. "I love it too, boss."

Only one of them knew they would never do it again.

After Ray's final warm-up pitches, Gene walked out to the mound. "I want this to be a special day."

Ray smiled. "It is a special day! The next time we talk on the mound, it will be as Pittsburgh Pirates!"

Gene nodded. "Yeah, you're right. But let's make this our best game together—ever."

"Sure, boss. Think we're leaving tonight or tomorrow?"

"Don't know, but it's my job to keep you focused on the here and now. Let's close out this place with a great game today, Ray."

"You know it, boss. My arm feels great."

Gene turned to walk back to the plate, but Ray stopped him. "Gene? I want to say thank you. You're a big part of the reason I'm moving up today."

Gene frowned. "What do you mean? You're a great pitcher. You deserve to be brought up."

"Every great pitcher needs a great . . ."

"You don't need me," he cut his friend short. "You don't need anyone, Ray. You'll knock' em dead with or without me. Focus on this guy and let's play ball. Forget about me, Ray. Got it?"

Gene returned to the plate knowing it would be the last time he would ever begin a game. Getting into position, he looked over the field, pulled the mask down over his face. He held his breath and waited for the two words he loved the most.

"PLAY BALL!" yelled the umpire.

"God, I love this game," he said aloud. "I love to catch!"

"If you love to catch so much, quit yapping and call for a pitch!" said the umpire. Gene smiled and punched his fist into his glove as the lead batter stepped into the box. Ray was just beaming. "Might as well call for his best pitch first," Gene thought. He flashed two fingers: forkball. Ray nodded, wound up, and let it fly.

Ray was right. The ball sizzled through the air and popped into Gene's mitt. Ray was also right about the extra padding. That one hurt. "The first pitch of the last game," Gene said softly to himself.

The game progressed well and Ray was solid all night. Gene hit two homers, ground out to second, and popped out deep in centerfield. He also threw a man out attempting to steal third. By the bottom of the eighth inning Greenville was winning handily 7-2. Gene stepped up to bat with two outs. He took a couple of practice swings and stepped into the box.

"This is it," he said under his breath. "This is how it all ends."

The first three pitches were all low and away for balls. Gene stepped out, took a practice swing, and looked at Coach Steve down the third base line. He signaled no swing. With three balls and no strikes, players ordinarily keep their bat still and make the pitcher throw a strike or take a walk.

"The heck with this," thought Gene, as he stepped back to the plate. He leveled his bat across the plate and looked at the pitcher. "Right here!" he yelled. "Come on! Here!" The Tuscaloosa pitcher glared at Gene, spit a shot of tobacco to one side, and went into his wind up.

To the end of his life, Gene thought the pitcher intended to come in high and walk him. Instead, the ball dropped several inches and crossed the plate at his shoulders—or would have if Gene had not come around on it and given it a deep ride into left-center. The ball sailed all the way to the fence. He ran as hard as he could, but by this time in the game his ankle was so swollen and sore he was nearly hopping on one foot. "Come on, come on, come on!" he puffed as he rounded first and headed for second, the first base coach waving him on. The ball had gotten past the center-fielder, so a double looked easily accomplished. The fielder picked it up and fired it to the shortstop, who was acting as the cutoff man. Coach Steve put up his palms and signaled to Gene to stay put. Instead, Gene rounded second and kept running—or limping fast—toward third base.

"What's he doing?" Ray yelled, jumping up from the bench. "Hold him up! Hold him up!" he yelled at the coach.

The third baseman was in position and waiting for the throw. Gene laid back and hit the dirt with his good leg down and slid toward third, but was easily tagged out.

"You're out!" yelled the umpire, flashing the familiar pumping fist signal. But Gene didn't get up. Instead, he rolled over in the dirt holding his bad ankle and screaming in agony. The umpire waved for Skip to come onto the field. Skip and Steve both ran out to third, but Ray beat them there.

"What in the hell were you thinking Gene?" Ray yelled at him. "You take a slide, are you nuts or something?" Gene didn't answer. With his eyes screwed shut he rolled over, bared his teeth, and continued holding his ankle. Ray noticed the tears in Gene's eyes and knew it had to be bad if he was crying—especially if Gene was not cracking some sort of joke about it. Ray and Steve helped him to his feet and carried Gene into the locker room.

"The doc's on his way," Skip said as Ray and Steve helped Gene stretch out on the bench. "Ray and Steve, what the hell are you clowns doing in here? Get back to the dugout!" Ordered the manager. "There's a game still being played! You think I trust that bastard Gambini to not try and buy off an umpire or pull some sort of underhanded shenanigans while we're in here!"

"I'm not going anywhere," Ray protested. "I'm staying right here until the doc arrives."

Skip put his beefy hands on his hips and glared at his pitcher. "Ray, this is your last game with us, and you need to finish it. Don't make me have someone come in here and carry you out!" he shouted. "I am still your manager, and I am telling you to get your prima donna butt back into that dugout!"

Gene grimaced and nodded his agreement. "Go, Ray," he uttered through clenched teeth. "I'll be here when you come back."

"Sure, boss, whatever you say, but no dancing, okay? We're headed for Pittsburgh."

"Yeah, no dancing. Now get back to the game."

Once Ray was gone, Gene sat up and looked at Skip. "He'll go. We just have to tell him my ankle is now completely shot. Then he'll have no choice."

Skip pulled out his cigar and threw it across the room, where it hit the far wall and disintegrated into several pieces. "Ah, damn it! That was one of the expensive ones!" Skip turned his eyes back to Gene. "Are you telling me you're not hurt and this was all a stunt?"

"Does it matter, Skip?" asked Gene, a small smile forming around the corners of his mouth. "I'm gonna pack my seabag and get out of here before Ray comes back. As luck would have it, there's a train heading north in just over one hour. I can still catch it. You just tell him . . . tell him I went to the hospital and I'll catch up to him later in Pittsburgh. Okay?"

For once in his life, Jim "Skip" Middleton could not think of a single word to say. He just stood there and nodded, overcome with emotion.

Gene quickly changed into his street clothes and closed his locker with a slow push until it clicked shut. He stood there for a few seconds, transfixed. While one hand lightly caressed locker #26, the other wiped the corner of an eye. He sighed softly and patted the outside twice and limped out the door to go back to his boarding room, pack up his few belongings, and catch the train out of Greenville. He didn't try to tell anyone else goodbye because he knew he would not be able to get the words out.

Skip, Steve, and Ray never saw Gene Moore again.

Chapter 40

Is That the Story
You Expected to Hear?

A long silence settled across our table when my dad stopped speaking. I wiped my eyes for the umpteenth time that evening as I stared past my father into the bustling restaurant beyond, completely lost in his past. It took me several moments to regain my focus and remember it was May 12, 1983, and I was inside the George Diamond Steak House with my dad. It was dark outside. He had been speaking for hours.

"Gary," my father whispered. I lifted my eyes to meet his. They were wet, too. My dad let out a long, slow sigh. "I guess that was the long answer to your question of whether I reported to Greenville."

All I could do was nod. After all these years, I finally understood my father.

"Baseball broke my heart, and I was afraid you would follow in my footsteps. I didn't want you to run the risk of being hurt, so I did everything I could to steer you away from baseball. The Pirates," he shrugged his shoulders, "they gave me a fair shot. I could have, I *would* have, made it. But life is so strange. It's shaped by brief and unexpected moments that spin you in a different direction. An instant," he snapped his fingers, "can change everything. The Friendship Game with the German sailors . . . what would have happened if I just had stopped at third and not slid at home to score in a game that was meaningless?"

Dad stared down at the table, lost in his own thoughts for several seconds. "But had I done so we would have lost the game. If I had a chance to score and win, and didn't take it—well, I just could not have done that. It isn't in me. So instead, my life was forever altered. It was one of those brief moments that changed everything, forever."

I nodded again, but did not say a word. I wanted to hear more, and I sensed he still had more to explain to me. Maybe more to explain to himself.

"I served my purpose, though," dad continued. "I got Ray Laws to the majors." Those seven words brought a wide smile to Gene's face. "They had no choice but to let me go. I know it today. I knew it then. But that didn't make it any easier when it happened, and it didn't get any easier as the years passed." His eyes filled with tears that finally, after all these years, began to run down his cheeks. He looked up and smiled. "So yes, I reported to Greenville. And now you know."

I exhaled and leaned back in my chair. It felt as though I had been holding my breath for hours. My head was spinning.

What shocked me was that my dad, the once-great Gene Moore, was embarrassed by his past. At the same time I was struck by both the integrity of the man, and the burden he had been carrying for all these decades.

"Does mom know all of this?" I finally managed to ask.

"Of course she does," he replied. "She knows everything about me."

"How did you meet her?" It was only at that instant, when the words slipped from my mouth, that I realized I didn't even know how my parents had met.

He pursed his lips for a second or two and said, "Well, again, it was one of those brief moments that change your life." He looked up and caught the waitress' attention. "May we get one more cup of coffee, please? Gary?"

"Yes, please."

"I didn't return to Sesser," my father continued, picking up the story where he had left off. "I walked out of the locker room in Greenville and wandered around the South for a bit, doing odd jobs, mostly bartending and such. It took me more than a year to slowly work my way back home. At that time I felt like I had no purpose for my life. Really, I didn't care if I lived or died. I started drinking again—a lot. By the time I got as far as Salem, Illinois, I was in terrible, terrible shape." He paused and thought for a few seconds, as if wondering whether or not to share some slice of his past with me.

Judy (Jenkins) Moore in 1945. She spent the war years as a welder at the naval shipyard in Oakland, California.

"Your mom—or the woman who would one day be your mom—found me lying on a barroom floor. I think I was closer to being dead than alive, and why in the world she did what she did, well, she has never fully explained to me. She nursed me back to health and got me back on my feet. Your mom saved my life. I don't know what would have happened to me and where I would be now without her."

"Tell me more," I urged him. "Tell me more about you and mom."

As it turned out, Judy Jenkins and Gene Moore had a lot in common. Both had come of age during the Great Depression, and both had endured their share of heartaches and setbacks. Judy had been married to a man who beat her. She left him and took their three boys, Kenneth, Carl Ray, and David, and got a job waiting tables in the bar and grill where she found dad one night passed out on the floor. Judy had a friend named Ed who owned the local hardware store. She convinced him to hire Gene as a deliveryman. Judy and Gene began relying on each other in many ways.

Mom suffered the loss of her middle son, my brother Carl Ray, to polio in 1952. It was Dad who helped her through her grief. Dad never got over the loss of his baseball career, and mom never got over the loss of Carl Ray to polio. Early in 1953, Gene moved to Kankakee, Illinois, to try and find a better paying job. When he was hired at the ammunition plant in Joliet, he sent for Judy and her kids. Their mutual dependency grew into a strong relationship. Late in November 1953, Judy broke the news to Gene that she was pregnant.

Warren Eugene "Gene" Moore and Elnora "Judy" Jenkins married on November 27, 1953, at the Kankakee County Courthouse in Kankakee, Illinois. Gene's sister Erma and her husband Francis served as witnesses. Gene and Judy were now set to begin building their life together. Gene switched jobs shortly thereafter and began delivering bread. Gary Warren Moore was born on July 21, 1954.

As we left the restaurant, I could not shake a question that had been nagging at me for a while. If Dad had not broken his ankle, he never would have met mom, and the family I loved so much would never have come into existence.

Gene Moore, holding his infant son Gary, complete with a baseball cap, in 1955.

We climbed into the car, where we looked at one another without speaking. I finally turned the key and slowly pulled out of the parking lot. Dad noticed how quiet I was. For a while he did not say anything. After a long bout of silence, he said, "Something else is bothering you, Gary. Is there anything else you want to know?"

"Yes, there is," I replied with some hesitation. Was I afraid of the answer? I think I was. "Do you wish your life had been different?" He knew what I meant and pondered my question for a while.

"Let me finish the story."

Chapter 41

Old Friends

Bradley, Illinois, June 13, 1959

Gene hadn't bothered changing out of the blue shirt and dark blue trousers, which was the uniform of a bakery delivery driver, before heading over to Skinny's Tap in Bradley, Illinois. He always worked until 2:00 p.m. on Saturday, completing his rounds early. Tired, he sank into his barstool and sipped from his glass of RC Cola.

"Hear this song, Skinny?" Gene asked.

"Yeah. It's 'Gotta Travel On' by Billy Grammer," Skinny answered. "It's a big hit. They play it on the radio all the time. What about it?"

"I grew up with Billy. He was my best friend when I was a kid, up until the war broke out. Then we lost contact."

Skinny dropped his mouth open. "You don't say! Are you kidding with me?"

Gene nodded. "He used to sit in the bleachers and play his guitar, and watch us play ball back at The Lumberyard in Sesser. He was great then, but now—he's the best in country and western music. I always knew he'd make it big. And he did." Gene paused and sighed. "Billy's living his dream."

Skinny still wasn't convinced. "Come on, Gene. You know Billy Grammer?" he asked. "I've never met anyone who was famous."

"Yeah. I knew Billy real well. We were good friends. And I've met someone famous," continued Gene.

Skinny's eyebrows shot up. "Who?"

"I used to play ball with Ray Laws."

Skinny raised his hand and waved away what he believed to be an obvious lie, and then began to chuckle. "Ok, you had me going there for a second. Now you're going to tell me you grew up with Ray Laws, and he married your sister? Ray's one of the best relievers in baseball today. That forkball pitch of his!"

Gene studied his glass of soda. When he answered, his voice was soft and low, but his eyes were raised and staring directly into Skinny's. "No, I didn't grow up with him. I was his catcher for almost four years in the Navy, and then for a season in the minors in Greenville, Mississippi. I helped him move from the minors to the Pirates. I caught his perfect game in Greenville."

Skinny's eyes narrowed as he listened to Gene's answer. "Yeah, I heard from someone a while back you played some ball in the minors, but you never talk about it. I didn't know you played with Ray, though," replied the bartender and he shook his head and began washing a glass behind the bar. "That's really something, Gene. Boy, there's a story for your kids someday."

Gene nodded without speaking. He was watching the Cubs play on the small black and white TV above the bar when another customer walked in and approached Skinny at the other end of the bar.

"Excuse me. I am looking for a Gene Moore. Do you know him?"

Skinny looked up from his work at the sink and eyed the man warily. His accent was heavy—foreign. And he was dressed in clothes that did not look local. Skinny slowly nodded in Gene's direction. The familiar voice had already caught Gene's ear, and he slowly turned to see a face he never thought he would see again.

"Heinrich? Heinrich Mueller?" Gene jumped from his stool and knocked it to the floor in his hurry to get up and greet the German. Both men stood for several awkward seconds, unsure of how they should greet one another. They shook hands, leaned this way and then that way, and finally embraced in a heartfelt hug.

"What in the world are you doing in Bradley, Illinois?" asked Gene as he stepped back and looked at a man he had not seen in fourteen years, and never thought he would see again. "How did you get here? How did you find me?"

Heinrich sighed and used his hands when he talked, as he always had. "Well, you see, there are many reasons for my visit. I wanted to come back to America, only this time as a friend and not a prisoner," he laughed. "I also wanted to see my old friend, Gene Moore."

Gene motioned for Heinrich to sit down "Let me buy you a drink. Judy won't believe this. You have to meet her." Gene looked at the German and shook his head. He was as dumbfounded by the man's sudden appearance as he had been when Frank Boudreau stepped into Bruno's ten years earlier.

"What are you drinking?" asked Heinrich as he sat down next to Gene.

"I'm watching baseball, so I'm drinking RC," Gene laughed. "Old habit, I guess. I never drink when watching baseball. Would you like a beer?"

Heinrich shook his head. "No, I find American beer, well, I'll have what you're having."

Skinny had not missed a word of the conversation, so when Heinrich finished speaking he left and returned with an RC Cola, which he deposited on the bar in front of Heinrich, along with a glass of ice. Skinny eyed the stranger suspiciously. He had never seen anyone who had fought for the Germans in World War II.

Heinrich nodded his thanks to Skinny and turned back to Gene. "It is a day for surprises. Judy and I have already met. I left Julia, my wife, and our son at your house with Judy. We have been visiting there for two hours now, waiting for you to finish working. Judy dropped me off here, but said I should come inside alone."

Gene chuckled and shook his head. "You're kidding! You've been at my house with Judy?"

"And Gary Warren and Debra Jean," Heinrich said. "You have a fine family, my friend. We both have much to be thankful for." Heinrich raised his glass of soda and Gene did likewise.

"How did you get to my house?" Gene asked.

"We have time, yes?" Heinrich asked. Gene nodded. "My old boat, the 505, is now on display at your Museum of Science and Industry in Chicago. You can't imagine our surprise—or our embarrassment—when we learned after the war you Americans actually captured it! We were sure it had sunk. Now we understand why we were kept away from everyone else and were not allowed to send letters home."

"We didn't know much, either," Gene replied.

Heinrich nodded and continued. "When we received news the boat was saved and put on display, we made plans and traveled from Germany to see it. It was hard decision—harder than I thought it might be. She looks good. But the memories, the pain of that day—ah, well, it is the past," Heinrich said, clapping his hands once in front of him and wiping his palms against one another several times as if washing them.

"But how did you find me?" asked Gene.

"The world is a much small place today," he continued. "You told me where you lived several times—Sesser, Illinois—and that it was 'close to Chicago.' I never forgot that. I explained to the staff at the museum about you, and they helped me find your telephone number. I called and spoke with Judy. She invited us to your home. She thought it would be a good surprise."

Gene just shook his head in amazement. "It is a wonderful surprise," he replied. "I think of you often, of course, but when I read they were moving your boat to Chicago—what was it, four or five years ago now?—I began to hope somehow we would meet again. Last year, I met another old friend. His name is Buck Nelson. He was my coach in the Navy. He was on one of the destroyers that captured *U-505*. He visited the sub and called me when he was in town. He's doing great, owns an insurance agency in Indianapolis." Gene lifted his glass, drained what was left, and asked Skinny to bring another bottle of cola. He turned back to his friend. "I'm sure glad they saved that old U-boat!"

Heinrich lifted his glass. "I will drink to that!" Gene lifted his glass of ice, and together they clinked glasses.

"Are you still playing football?" Gene asked.

Heinrich shook his head. "Football is over for me. As you can imagine, my country was in shambles, and there was no organized league when I returned. And no time to play games. The British would not let me, a German, play. I got a position teaching English at what you would call high school here, and I coach football there. But I no longer play, and that is fine. I have Julia and our new son. Many times aboard U-boats I was sure I was dead, but I managed to jump off the devil's shovel over and over again. Life is good for old lucky Heinrich!" Both men laughed. Gene stopped first and became suddenly pensive.

"Heinrich, I'm sorry. I know football was your life—at least that's what you told me in Louisiana."

Heinrich shot Gene a puzzled glance. "No, football was not my life," he said slowly as he shook his head. "It was something I did. I enjoyed playing football, very much. I was good at it. But it was never who I was. I did not define myself by a game. Now, my life is Julia and my son. They are all that is important to me now. Football," he shrugged, "it is a game. So I kick the ball into the net. What does it prove? What does it mean? Does it put food on my plate? Does it raise my son? Does it rebuild the country I love and erase the terrible mistakes we made? Now, I teach Gene to kick the ball into the net."

Now it was Gene's turn to shoot Heinrich a look of bewilderment. "Thank you, but I can't play baseball anymore because of my ankle. So I'm sure I can't kick a ball."

Heinrich laughed. "I don't mean you, Gene. I mean my son, my little Gene! I named my son after you. I name him after the great Gene Moore! His name is Warren Eugene Mueller and we call him Gene."

Gene was nearly speechless. "I don't know what to say, Heinrich, other than how honored that makes me feel. I can't wait to meet your family."

"May we leave soon, then, and go to your home?" Heinrich said. "There we will all meet."

Gene nodded. "Yes, but tell me first how can you can say football was not important to you? From our long conversations on the ball diamond, I got the impression it was all you cared about—all you wanted to do."

Heinrich paused and thought carefully before answering. "Let me say it this way, Gene. Today, I miss football but care more about my family and the present. I told your wife, Judy, that I was there when you broke your ankle. She told me how sad you are about not playing baseball, that you think about it every day, all day and that it is eating you up inside. I understand this feeling, Gene. But think for a moment," he continued, placing a forefinger against his temple and tapping it several times. "If you were playing baseball on the radio or television right now, you would not have met Judy. You would not have your three children and a fourth on the way. You cannot know what else might have happened to you—maybe something worse than what did happen, yes? This makes sense to you?"

Gene listened to each word before tilting his head back to look at the ceiling. He sighed and faced his friend. "I know. I know what you are saying is logical and true. But Heinrich, you don't fully understand. Baseball was my destiny. It is what I was supposed to do. It was the only thing I could do."

Heinrich lifted his shoulders and held them in a high shrug for several seconds. "So now, be a good father and a good husband. Judy loves you because of who you are, not because of what you once could do. Baseball used you for your talent, and once it was used up, it did not need you anymore. Your family will always need you, Gene. I learned from you while I was your prisoner. You think you taught me how to play American baseball. But you—and even Ray Laws—taught me much more. Now, maybe I can teach you something. Baseball was not your life and it never was. I don't believe a game was ever your destiny or you would be playing it today. Your game was only a path that led you to your destiny, which is your life with your family."

Gene listened and knew every word was true, but accepting reality had always been difficult. "Heinrich, you don't fully understand what I had in the palm of my hand."

"Gene, hear me," Heinrich said putting out a hand gently holding his friend's upper arm. "After all that happens on this earth, our lives are only about who we love, who loves us, and what we build together. You have confused baseball with life and love it too much, and so you are only a bitter man, sitting alone in a bar. Love your family, and you build something for the ages."

Heinrich drained the last swallow of RC from his glass and continued. "Gene, you have something priceless. You have a wife who picked you up when you were down. She told me the whole story. She gave you strength to stand up again. She loves you and does not care if you catch or hit a ball. You have adopted Judy's youngest son. You are going to give him a wonderful life."

"Yes, I love him as if he were my own," Gene said. He could feel his eyes tearing up.

"Yes, of course a man like you would. You are their provider, their teacher, and the living example they have of how a man should live his life. That is more important than any game or any team. Your family is now your team, yes?"

Gene nodded his head. "Yes, I guess so."

"Good," replied Heinrich. "Then you must teach and lead your family the same way you taught and led your baseball team."

To Gene, the realization of what Heinrich told him felt like a punch in the gut. He didn't know how to respond, and did not trust himself to make eye contact with Heinrich.

"Let me ask you a question, Gene," Heinrich asked. "Do you love Judy?"

Gene slowly turned his head and looked at Heinrich. "Of course I do."

"Do you love David, Gary, and Debra Jean?"

"Yes, of course."

"If you had not broken your ankle, where would you be today?"

Gene thought for a moment. "I would probably be catching for the Dodgers, or with some other professional team in the majors."

"Yes," Heinrich said. "I suppose you would be, given how good you were." Heinrich was beginning to wonder if Gene would ever fully understand what he was trying to tell him.

"Gene Moore, if you had to make a choice right now, a choice between playing baseball or having your family—this very family that you have—which would you choose?"

The question caught Gene off guard. "I don't have to make that choice," he slowly replied. "If I did, my choice would be to have both my baseball career and my family."

"But that is not an option, Gene. The loss of your career led you to this wife and family. Yes, you could have your career without your broken ankle and you may have had a family, but not this family. Judy told me how you met. Do you not see the hand of God at work here, bringing you together? It sounds like Judy may have saved your life. You were brought together at a time when you needed her. But she also needed you at the very same time. Do you believe that it was chance?" Heinrich leaned closer and looked Gene firmly in the eye. "It was not an accidental meeting. It was meant to be. So I ask you again, which would you choose?"

Gene's eyes slowly filled with tears, but this time he did not turn away. "I wouldn't trade this family for anything. Not for money, not for fame and . . . and not for baseball."

Heinrich smiled and patted his arm. "You now have exactly what you want in life, and know it is more important than any game."

"Thank you," Gene whispered.

"There is nothing for you to thank. I still owe you more than you can ever know." Heinrich looked at his watch. "Ah, it is getting late. Come and meet my son and wife."

Gene nodded and pushed back from the bar. "I can't think of a better idea."

The Cubs game had ended and Skinny clicked on the radio as they were walking out. Billy Grammer's hit song was playing: ". . . wanna see my baby . . . want to see her bad . . . she's the best girl, this poor boy ever had . . ."

A few minutes later, Gene and Heinrich pulled up in front of a small little yellow house on the corner of Crestwood and Longwood Drive. Judy met them at the door holding their baby girl in her arms. She was six months pregnant with their next child. Gene put his arms around her and pulled her close. It was as if he had not seen her in months.

She pushed him back and laughed, "What's gotten into you?"

Gene just smiled at Heinrich and replied, "This is a great day."

My dad stopped talking and looked at me. He didn't have to say anything else. I knew exactly what he meant.

Chapter 42

Death of the Boy
Who Loved to Catch

Gene Moore spent the rest of his life devoted to his friends and family. He drove a bread delivery truck from 1954 through 1973. He had no love or passion for such mundane work. It was just a job, something he did to make a living to support all of us. And then, in 1973, his life changed again.

Exactly how it happened I am not sure, but Gene took a job selling vacuum cleaners with Filter Queen, a direct-selling company. He loved it. For the first time since being cut from the game of baseball, Gene was passionate about his work. He loved to sell, and he was very good at it. After less than a year he was the number one Filter Queen salesperson in the nation.

In 1974, Gene and Judy Moore started their own Filter Queen distributorship. They worked hard and well together, night and day, to make their little venture succeed. And it did. The whole family helped in the business. When I graduated from college in 1976, I began working with my mom and father full-time. Together, we built a successful selling operation with more than 50 employees.

Gene Moore had found a renewed sense of purpose and direction in his life. To him, conducting business was a game—a challenge. It was something to go to bed thinking about, and something to look forward to doing again the next morning.

Gene and Judy Moore at their 25th wedding anniversary in 1978. Gene is holding his grandson, Toby, while Judy is cradling grandson Brandon Scott.

Friday, May 13, 1983, started like any other day. Gene climbed out of bed about 7:00 a.m., took a shower, and enjoyed a cup of coffee with Judy while watching Good Morning America. He arrived at work about 9:00 a.m., placed a few phone calls, joked with and motivated some of his employees, and then drove to Chicago Heights for a luncheon meeting with me. During lunch, dad made an uncharacteristic statement. "Well, today is Friday the thirteenth," he told me. "This is the first of three Friday the thirteenths this year. If I make it through this day, I think I'll be okay." His observation struck me as odd because Gene was not a superstitious guy. Maybe he was just joking around, but it did not sound like it. To this day, I don't know why he said it.

After lunch, Gene drove to another appointment in the western suburbs of Chicago and had dinner with Chuck Smith, a business associate. Dad left for home about 6:30 p.m. and arrived two hours later after fighting his way through rush hour traffic. He was pale and exhausted when Judy met him at the door. Dad had already removed his sport coat and loosened his tie. When Judy saw him, he was holding his left arm. His watch, which he wore on his left wrist, was later found on the floor of his car.

Judy hugged him and helped him into the house, where he collapsed on the floor. He died there, with Judy by his side. Gene Moore left Judy's life while lying on the floor—the same place he had entered it.

He was just 57 years old.

Judy was the only person who knew the intimate details about Gene's remarkable life story until my dad opened up and bared his soul to me just twenty-four short hours before he died. It was Judy who had shared his secret, his burden, his inner turmoil. She provided the strength Gene needed to carry on.

My mom never remarried. She lived in Indianapolis, Indiana, until her death on January 3, 2004. She told everyone until the end of her life that the only man she ever really loved was Gene, and that was enough for her.

Looking back now, decades later, I realize just how little I really knew about my parents when I was growing up. A few memorable incidents from the shadowy past of my youth only make sense now. The passage of time has a way of clarifying what was once confusing.

When I was about twelve years old, I was shopping with mom and dad at Montgomery Wards. Dad wandered off and I followed him into the sporting goods department. He stopped in front of a rack of baseball bats on an aisle end cap. I had no idea what was going on in his head, but I could tell his mind was somewhere else. He slowly reached for a bat and slid it carefully out of the rack. He took it in his hands lovingly, as if he was holding something he adored. I stood next to him and heard him say slowly and softly, "You know, there are no two of these in the world that are exactly alike." I didn't say anything because it was obvious he was not talking to me. "Every one is different," he continued, "slightly different in weight." As he held the bat in his left hand, he began running the index finger of his right hand carefully and deliberately along the grain. "The balance and feel, the grain patterns from different cuts of the same tree or a different tree altogether, make each bat unique. The bat has to match the personality of the batter or they are unequally yoked. But when you find the perfect match, it is as if magic happens. Every bat has its own personality and temperament." He sighed. "No, there are no two bats alike anywhere."

I was just a young kid, and so had no idea what he was talking about. What I do remember is how much it bothered me because it did not sound anything like the dad I knew. I had never heard him talk that way before about anything—especially baseball.

As we both stood there, staring at the same object but seeing two entirely different things, my mom walked up behind us, put her hand on Gene's shoulder, and slowly turned him to face her. The bat he was holding slowly dropped to my dad's side, where it hung loosely gripped in his left hand. He took a deep breath, sighed deeply, reached out his right arm, and pulled her close. They embraced for what seemed to me an eternity. Looking back, I understand now he was transferring the emotion that holding the bat churned inside him into his wife—the only person in the world who could truly understand what he was thinking and feeling at that moment.

Another incident about this time has also remained forever with me. One day my dad came home from work and looked more excited than I had ever seen him. "Gary, the Pittsburgh Pirates are in town to play the Cubs," he told me. "How would you like to go see the game?"

A big league game at Wrigley Field? Was he kidding? I couldn't believe it. He had never taken me to a game. In fact, he rarely mentioned the word "baseball" and would not even play catch with me.

"Dad, are you serious? Really?"

"Yeah" he answered with a big smile.

"Yes!" I answered with an explosion of youthful enthusiasm.

We reached Wrigley Field early. We guided our way down to where the players were taking batting practice. We stood there for several minutes, my eyes glued on the first Major League ball players I had ever seen in my life. My dad looked around, stiffened, narrowed his eyes, and called out a single name: "Roy!"

Elroy "Roy" Face, a pitcher for the Pittsburgh Pirates and one of the country's best, turned to see who was calling his name. When he saw my dad, the pitcher's jaw dropped. "Gene!" he shouted before trotting over to where we were standing.

Roy was one of the finest relievers in the game. I remember he greeted my dad warmly, and they talked for some time. Unfortunately, I have no recollection of exactly what they talked about. I just remember standing there in awe as my dad chatted away with one of my idols.

A few minutes later they said their goodbyes and we walked back up into the stands and found our seats. I could not believe what I had just witnessed.

"Dad," I began, "how do you know a pitcher like Roy Face?"

My dad just shrugged. "Roy is an old friend. I knew him a long time ago."

"How did you meet him?" I asked, hoping to continue the conversation.

"It's not important, Gary. Let's watch the game." He refused to say anything more about it.

Today, Roy Face is a candidate for the Baseball Hall of Fame. He played his final game in August of 1969. Like Ray, Roy is also best remembered for throwing a pitch called the forkball.

The love of baseball was something that never left dad. He suppressed, even hid, his past, revealing it now and again only to my mom. I really don't know why. If he could have shared it with others, I think his life would have been much richer. Perhaps he could have reconciled the events that led him to the deep grief he suffered through the loss of his baseball career. He chose instead to hold his pain deep inside and only show his children the face of a loving father who worked hard and supported his family. Inside he was fighting an entirely different war, battling demons that denied him the life he felt destined to live.

My dad was hospitalized four times in my life because of bleeding ulcers. Once, while the rest of our family was away for the weekend, we returned to find him in bed, barely conscious. He had lost a tremendous amount of blood which, according to his doctor, should have killed him. The stomach ulcer had eaten through the wall of his stomach and into his aorta, a major artery. Doctor Burnett, who became a lifelong family friend, said to me at my father's funeral, "I always thought it would be his ulcers that took him, not a heart attack."

Knowing full well that health problems are hereditary, I asked the doctor if I should be more careful about what I ate. He looked at me, smiled, and shook his head. "It is not what your father ate, Gary," he replied, "but what was eating him that caused the ulcers."

After Dad's death, I found his Purple Heart in one of his dresser drawers. "I understand now about dad's wound," I said to my mom. She smiled and looked at me, her eyes filling with tears. She didn't respond aloud, but her eyes held within them the story of their life together.

The truth is that my father was wounded, and he carried the results of that injury with him for the rest of his life. His wound was not of the flesh, but of the spirit. Although his physical injury largely healed, the experience left an indelible scar on his heart no one around him could ever fully remove.

Postscript

Except to his family and a few close friends, Gene Moore was lost to history—or so it seemed.

He never played Major League baseball. There are a few letters here and there, my father's conversations with me, and of course my mother and the many other people around the country I have since interviewed who remember him and his life in and out of baseball. All in all, however, there is precious little published detail about Gene's life in general, and in particular, his time in Louisiana. The German sailors of *U-505* were held there under special terms that bypassed the rules of the Geneva Convention. This denied them not only Red Cross access, but contact with the outside world. There is no record of playing baseball with the enemy.

Or is there?

While conducting research for this book, I discussed life at Camp Ruston with Keith Gill, curator of *U-505* at the Chicago Museum of Science and Industry. When I brought up baseball he shook his head. "There is no mention of baseball. Some of the sailors remembered working in farm fields outside the camp. A few claimed to have worked in the timber industry. The odd thing about that," he continued, "is it's not timber country. I don't think there is a sawmill close to Camp Ruston."

"Then why would they say that?" I asked.

"I don't know," he continued. "Some of the *U-505* sailors claim they left the camp to work at a place they called The Lumberyard."

Fifteen . . . forever

Afterword

Since the first edition hardcover of *Playing with the Enemy* was published, new information has surfaced. In an effort to write the most accurate story of Gene's life, his town, and the times they shared together, I made a few adjustments to dates and other minor facts to correct mistakes or fill in information I did not know when the first edition went to press.

Joe "Vino" Caveglia was a mainstay of Sesser baseball and served as an umpire for many of the Egyptians' home games. Joe's granddaughter, Allison Caveglia Barash, read my book and shared his name with me. I later met Allison and her husband Mark during a visit to Pittsburgh. Allison and I seem to be kindred spirits in our love for Sesser, even though neither of us ever lived there.

I have only been able to find one photograph of Gene playing with the Egyptians (see page 9). Try as I might, when the first edition went to press in 2006, the only player I could identify was my dad. Thankfully, several people have come forward to name a father, a brother, or an uncle, and their names appear in this edition. Let me be the first to extend a hearty welcome to umpire Joe Caveglia and Gene's Egyptian teammates Barney Daniels, Harry Boyd, Walter Klein, and Hobart Sammons. They were always there, but now history knows their names.

A woman approached my table at a book signing in Herrin, Illinois, clutching an old black-and-white photograph of her relatives, Heavy and Ezra Turner. As readers of *Playing with the Enemy* know, Gene refers to Heavy as the "town philosopher." The chapter "Resurrection" takes place inside Heavy Turner's café. The photo appears in this new edition on page 217. I also learned a funny little story about Heavy and my dad. Heavy used to keep a bowl of hard candy on the counter. When my dad was young, he and his friends would sit at Heavy's counter, where one of them would distract Heavy by asking a question or dropping something, while another reached up and snatched a piece of candy. The boys thought they were pulling something over on Heavy, but he knew it all the time. He put the candy out there and played their game so the boys could have fun thinking they were fooling ole Heavy Turner.

We now know that locals from around Ruston, Louisiana, watched Gene and his teammates play ball with the German prisoners from *U-505*. This is documented in Wesley Harris's book about Camp Ruston, *Fish out of Water*.

Sonny, a reader from Florida, called to fill in a small piece of my father's life during his tenure with the Sesser Egyptians. As a young boy, Sonny often helped out with the team. One day, the team was loading into three pickup trucks to drive to the championship game in Litchfield, Illinois. Because Sonny was too young to play, the older guys made the decision to leave him behind. As the trucks pulled away, Gene spotted Sonny standing alone, visibly heartbroken at being left behind. Gene jumped out of the truck and refused to make the trip unless the team made room for Sonny. The Egyptians were not about to leave their star catcher behind, so the guys squeezed together to make room. "That's just the kind of man your dad was," explained Sonny.

Beyond the new information there is another story playing out in Sesser, Illinois, which verifies the old adage that truth really is stranger than fiction.

No one expected this. Mayor Mitchell certainly didn't. So when people from across the country began showing up unannounced in little Sesser, Illinois, heads turned and eyebrows rose. The visitors walked or drove slowly down the streets, stood on street corners, and asked for directions to the Lumberyard or the little house on the corner of Matthew and Mulberry. The locals often spot visitors sitting quietly on curbs or in their cars with no particular destination in mind. Just being there was what was important. Most of the visitors, all readers of *Playing with the Enemy*, can't explain why they made the trip. They just *knew* it was something they had to do.

Sesser, the wonderful small Midwestern town featured in *Playing with the Enemy*, has never been a magnet for visitors or national attention. Since the first release of my book in 2006, Sesser and its "country boy who could hit the ball a country mile" have attracted attention from across the country and even around the world. No one expected that my father's story would generate such a deep passion in the hearts, minds, and souls of readers, or that it would be such a success. No one had ever heard of my dad, and as a first time author, no one had ever heard of me. Who would buy such a book, and after reading it, why would they take hours or days out of their busy lives to travel to Sesser? It took a while, but I think I understand now.

An outpouring of thanks and emotion reaches me daily. Each letter, phone call, or e-mail touches me deeply, and I am grateful for each and every one. Everyone has a dream, a goal, and a desire for his or her life. Reality has a way of interrupting those dreams. Some people have a very hard time coming to terms with setbacks and failure. As Gene's remarkable life in and out of baseball makes plain, it is not whether we reach our dream that is important in life, but who we become along the way.

I am so thankful that *Playing with the Enemy* inspires people to talk about their own family stories and connect with their parents, children, and long-lost friends. Most of the correspondence or phone calls I receive are very similar. Each begins with kind words about the book, but go on to relate a very personal story. Sometimes it is about a missed opportunity in life and the pain in learning to deal with it. Readers often share stories about their fathers, or mothers, brothers, sisters, or friends, and how fate dealt them a difficult, haunting blow. The "healing" aspect of Gene's life story (scores of people have used that adjective to describe it) connects with people from all walks of life and inspires them to connect and reconnect with their own families and loved ones. With their permission, I would like to share a few letters with you.

The first letter I received was from a man who has since become a good family friend. "We are baseball people," Jim L. began. "My grandson had his Bar Mitzvah at Dodger Stadium three years ago. I have had season tickets at Dodger Stadium for more than 45 years. However, this was not a baseball story. It truly was a story of love, warmth, character, and belief." Jim explained that *Playing with the Enemy* is the only book he, his son, and his grandson could enjoy and discuss together.

Steve R., a lawyer from the Chicago suburbs, shared his love for my dad's story in a way, I suspect, quite unlike his normal lawyerlike personality. Steve has recommended the book to numerous people and even organized a private reading and signing in his home that was attended by more than fifty of his colleagues. Gene's inspirational story moved these tough Chicago lawyers in an unexpected and profound way. Steve's passion has touched my family and me deeply.

One particularly moving phone call was from a judge. Someone left a copy of my book in his courtroom, and he read it. "Your dad's story has helped me see how fortunate I am, and how successful and meaningful my life has been." It also helped him understand and appreciate his brother's unsuccessful baseball career with a major league team.

The connections with readers across the country are as varied as they are heartfelt. A Vietnam veteran told me how a war injury ended his football career and how Gene Moore's quiet struggle moved him to tears and helped him deal with his loss. A twelve-year-old boy explained that *Playing with the Enemy* so inspired him that he was dedicating his baseball season to my dad. The book inspired a pair of songs—"Field of Broken Dreams" by Pat Hegewald, Mary Cairo, and Matt Meyer and "I May Be Down but I'm Not Out" by Mike Puleo. "The pride of the Egyptians" lives on in the hearts and minds of readers around the corner and across the globe.

Gene Moore's story doesn't end with the hometown boy hitting a home run and winning the game. It is not amenable to tying up in a neat little package with a bow on top. Life is not perfect, and neither was Gene. Bad things do happen to good people, and our dreams do not always become our reality. But in the end, Gene learned that his life was worth living even without his dream, and that the skills the one-time baseball prodigy used so well on a ball diamond were just as valuable raising a strong family, building a successful business, and making a legion of friends. His is a shining example of a life well lived.